Incorporating F

Outcome Asse

Incorporating Progress Monitoring and Outcome Assessment into Counseling and Psychotherapy

A Primer

SCOTT T. MEIER

Oxford University Press is a department of the University of Oxford.
It furthers the University's objective of excellence in research, scholarship,
and education by publishing worldwide.

Oxford   New York
Auckland   Cape Town   Dar es Salaam   Hong Kong   Karachi
Kuala Lumpur   Madrid   Melbourne   Mexico City   Nairobi
New Delhi   Shanghai   Taipei   Toronto

With offices in
Argentina   Austria   Brazil Chile   Czech Republic   France   Greece
Guatemala   Hungary   Italy   Japan   Poland   Portugal   Singapore
South Korea   Switzerland   Thailand   Turkey   Ukraine   Vietnam

Oxford is a registered trademark of Oxford University Press
in the UK and certain other countries.

Published in the United States of America by
Oxford University Press
198 Madison Avenue, New York, NY 10016

Library of Congress Cataloging-in-Publication Data
Meier, Scott T., 1955–
Incorporating progress monitoring and outcome assessment into counseling and
psychotherapy : a primer / Scott T. Meier.
pages cm
ISBN 978–0–19–935667–6 (hardback)
1. Counseling.   2. Psychotherapy.   I. Title.
BF636.6.M4556 2014
158.3028'7—dc23
2014022209

9   8   7   6   5   4   3   2   1
Printed in the United States of America
on acid-free paper

CONTENTS

How do therapists know they are making a difference with their clients? Even when employing empirically supported treatments, considerable uncertainty surrounds a high percentage of difficult and complex cases. How willing is the client to talk about her or his problems? Is the client motivated to continue the process, or will she or he drop out? How severe are the client's problems, and does insurance reimburse for a sufficient enough number of sessions? Although therapists may have once had the opportunity to explore complex client issues over many sessions, increased accountability and decreased funding have made therapeutic work more stressful for both the clinician and client.

Progress monitoring and outcome assessment (PMOA) measures are powerful tools for therapists dealing with a large, difficult caseload. Progress monitoring refers to the use of test scores for providing feedback during the ongoing process of counseling and psychotherapy, and outcome assessment provides information relevant to the overall amount of progress made by a client. The noteworthy feature about therapeutic approaches that employ PMOA measures is the close connection between assessment data and intervention. In traditional therapy, assessment typically takes the form of an initial interview that provides information about the presenting problem(s) and important contexts such as family history and social supports. Based on this information, the clinician may assign a diagnosis and develop a plan that focuses on an evidence-based treatment. But the majority of clients respond to interventions in diverse ways, often presenting the clinician with difficult decisions about whether to continue, alter, or discontinue particular treatment approaches. With PMOA measures and their clinically relevant data, the therapist receives feedback about effectiveness as treatment progresses. When employed in the context of psychotherapy theory and research, such data can inform the clinician about how to proceed more effectively, particularly in terms of how to decrease treatment failure.

Psychotherapy researchers, on the other hand, sometimes complain that clinicians do not pay enough attention to empirical results in academic journals. Concerned with discovering general laws, researchers write reports of psychotherapy outcome studies that focus on data demonstrating the overall effectiveness of psychotherapy and associated factors. These reports emphasize sophisticated statistical analyses and methodological approaches that decrease their communicability to nonacademics. And by necessity, such global reports typically do not address the complexities of change in therapy, particularly what can go wrong.

Clinicians appear to prefer different types of information than what researchers consider significant. Clinicians know that in general, psychotherapy is effective. From my experience, many prefer to read case studies because such descriptions provide more elaborate procedural knowledge. That is, the details of the case include descriptions of the client (such as history and current functioning in terms of cognitions, affect, and behavior), the interventions (both techniques and therapeutic strategies), and how the two mix (which usually includes significant obstacles that could lead to failure). Good case studies present the reader with problematic real-world situations that require action while coping with incomplete information and uncertainty (Nilson, 2010). These cases appear *plausible* to practicing clinicians.

Consequently, a major goal of this book is to present information that is relevant and actionable to graduate students and practicing clinicians. The book's structure is modeled on manuals for psychological tests, which typically present test procedures and results that can be quickly and efficiently understood, employed, and interpreted. Thus, early chapters focus on (a) case studies of PMOA with measures designed for repeated use with children/adolescents and adults who vary in their treatment progress (but the details of which have been altered to protect confidentiality; cf. Clifft, 1986); (b) the clinical, theoretical, and research literature that forms the basis for use of PMOA measures and clinical feedback; (c) how to use interpretative reports associated with PMOA measures; and (d) how to properly administer PMOA measures, with an emphasis on problems that can arise in the process of repeated assessment. The research focus is not neglected: Later chapters describe how test construction procedures influence the ability of PMOA measures to detect change, how to interpret reliability and validity estimates in the context of PMOA measurement, and how to understand the statistical tools used in interpreting data. Two final chapters focus on rater training needed for use of some PMOA measures and use of PMOA data as feedback in supervision.

Two other aspects of the book are noteworthy. First, the book emphasizes visual displays such as tables and time series. Well-constructed time series, for example, enable the viewer to gain a sense of the direction and amount of a client's progress. The variation evident in a time series provides deeper information than a yes/no clinical feedback system; when used in conjunction with other information (such as progress notes), visual displays stimulate the viewer to consider the causes of the displayed data patterns. Test interpretation of PMOA data should include visual displays, and their frequent use in this book helps the reader become familiar with them as a way to reason about clinical progress and consider contributing influences.

This book also attempts to bridge the traditional textbook with the increasing availability of web-based materials. Many of the learning activities and exercises in the book are online activities that include content such as videos and assessment-related exercises. The videos are publicly available on http://www.youtube.com and provide excerpts of psychotherapy that are employed in conjunction with PMOA learning exercises. Online psychotherapy videos provide realistic simulations of actual therapy as well as ease of access; students can perform the video-related exercises as homework and as in-class assignments. Other learning exercises include practice ratings of PMOA measures using transcripts of psychotherapy sessions, and creation and analysis of data in visual displays. The exercises and activities have been designed to be basic so that the learner can focus on the progress monitoring aspects of the task. The book also includes a glossary, which describes the boldfaced terms throughout the text.

Teaching about PMOA measurement and feedback during clinical training is a natural integration of science and practice. Educators of psychotherapists need to improve on the proportion of students who have both the skills and attitudes to practice using scientific knowledge and methods. Many training programs appear to assume that all graduate students have the capacity to integrate the information taught in separate courses in research design, testing and assessment, and counseling theory and practice; however, many students cannot make this integrative leap (Meier, 2003). The content in this book can be taught in practicums and assessment classes for graduate students as well as workshops and seminars for practicing mental health professionals.

Although the field has demonstrated initial positive results, the science and practice of PMOA use are relatively young. Reviews of frequently employed measures typically show overlap among only a few; a consensus has yet to be reached about the most useful tests. In this book, I reference about 20 different measures but primarily employ four to illustrate important concepts, procedures, and results. Thus, instructors may wish to supplement presentations with measures relevant to their particular clinical audiences. And despite its youth, PMOA research and practice has a history that is worth knowing. Consequently, I include older references to give readers (a) a sense of how important problems have been previously addressed and (b) a perspective on the fact that many measurement issues were not resolved but simply dropped, only to resurface again in later work.

Thanks to Bianca Jones, Shannon McClain, and Michael Savage at the University of Texas and University at Buffalo for permission to use their case materials in the book. Thanks to Michael Infranco, the latest graduate assistant who has helped with this project. Finally, I wish to express my thanks to Sarah Harrington and Andrea Zekus for shepherding this book from start to finish.

Scott T. Meier
Buffalo, NY
August 2014

Incorporating Progress Monitoring and Outcome Assessment into Counseling and Psychotherapy

Introduction and Rationale

INTRODUCTION

Progress monitoring (PM) refers to the use of measures that produce clinical data for **feedback** about client progress during counseling and psychotherapy. Similarly, **outcome assessment** (OA) refers to the use of measures that produce clinical data about the amount and type of change clients experience from the start to the end of therapy. The distinction between the two is important: PM provides feedback during the ongoing process of counseling and psychotherapy, whereas OA provides information relevant to the amount of progress made by a client in particular domain(s) at the conclusion of therapy. Routine or regular monitoring of client progress is a different procedure than examining client outcomes. When data from progress measures are used appropriately, the primary benefit is the timely feedback they provide about a client's improvement or lack thereof. Research has documented that PM measures can identify clients who are failing to improve or worsening, allowing clinicians to reconsider the provided interventions in the light of possible **treatment failure,** the ultimate outcome that clinicians would like to avoid.

With PM, data may be produced every session or on some other frequent schedule (such as every third or fifth session) to track client change over time. The schedule of assessment may depend on practical constraints inherent in the clinical setting, such as frequency (e.g., daily, weekly, bimonthly) or length (e.g., 50 minutes, 15 minutes) of sessions. The general rule of thumb is to produce data for PM as frequently as practically possible so that clinical feedback can be delivered in a timely manner. In contrast, OAs are typically intended to provide a summative answer to the question, Did the client improve? They are often administered as part of a pre/post design that includes an assessment at intake and termination.

The key question about the **validity** of measures intended for progress monitoring and outcome assessment is whether their items are sensitive to change, particularly the types of change produced by psychosocial interventions. Whereas traditional test development procedures aim at producing scores that reflect stable individual differences (e.g., intelligence; Meier, 2008), **change-sensitive** tests require a largely different set of test development procedures. Chief among these is that items on such tests should change in response to a psychosocial intervention and remain stable over time when no intervention is present.

FACTORS INCREASING THE USE OF PROGRESS MONITORING AND OUTCOME ASSESSMENT MEASURES

Although some impetus to perform OAs in counseling and psychotherapy has existed for decades, four current trends are increasing the use of progress monitoring and outcome assessment (PMOA) measures, as detailed in the following sections.

Implementation of Obamacare

The **Patient Protection and Affordable Care Act** (PPACA, often referred to as Obamacare) means that a significant proportion of the 40 million Americans who are currently uninsured will be seeking health insurance, including mental health insurance. This is likely to translate into an increase in the use of mental health services and in the need for mental health providers. However, the increased provision of services will be accompanied by a push for accountability (Botcheva, White, & Huffman, 2002; Gibbs, Napp, Jolly, Westover, & Uhl, 2002; Thayer & Fine, 2001). Botcheva et al. (2002), for example, observed that "in the service arena, practitioners recognize that they need to implement systems of data collection and performance measurement to prove their effectiveness to funding agencies" (p. 422). Data are needed to help inform decisions about whether to initiate, continue, modify, or end therapy. Whereas previous attempts to increase accountability, particularly by managed care companies, appear to have been designed to decrease costs by withholding payments to providers and services to clients (Davis & Meier, 2001), PMOA measures have the potential to provide essential information such as (a) estimates of progress over brief periods of time (e.g., since intake) and (b) feedback about when to alter treatment (Hatfield & Ogles, 2004).

High Failure Rates in Counseling and Psychotherapy

One of the reasons for increased accountability is accumulating research about treatment failure rates in counseling and psychotherapy. These estimates suggest that treatment failure occurs with 10% to 50% of all clients (Persons & Mikami, 2002). Lambert (2012; also see Streiner, 1998) noted that even with empirically supported treatments (ESTs) provided by well-supervised therapists, between 30% and 50% of clients do not improve. Moreover, Callahan, Almstrom, Swift,

Borja, and Heath (2009) reviewed research that indicates that premature termination can be as high as 75% in training clinics (compared to 40% to 60% in other outpatient settings) and that successful improvement with clients may happen more slowly with clients of trainees. In addition, some research indicates that many clinicians are unable to detect when their clients are failing (Hatfield, McCullough, Frantz, & Krieger, 2010). The combination of cost and high failure rates is likely to translate into further pressure for individual clinicians to adopt methods that decrease treatment failures and costs.

Success of Feedback-Enhanced Therapies

Feedback-enhanced therapies (FETs) are therapeutic approaches that employ PMOA data to provide feedback about the client's status during therapy. In these approaches, clinical data become an integral part of the decision-making process regarding whether to continue therapy or alter therapeutic procedures. Evidence has been accumulating for decades about the broad effectiveness of FETs (Beutler & Harwood, 2000; Meier, 2008; Paul, 1986; Paul, Mariotto, & Redfield, 1986). More recently, Lambert and his colleagues performed a series of studies that demonstrate that providing clinicians with regular feedback about client progress can significantly decrease treatment failures (Lambert & Hawkins, 2001; Reese et al., 2009). The addition of PM data to any therapeutic approach appears likely to decrease treatment failures, thus meeting the need for increased accountability.

Emerging Mobile Technologies and Electronic Medical Records

New mobile technologies will allow healthcare providers and mental health professionals to input and access PMOA data in real-time applications. Using smartphone and tablet technologies, mental health professionals and their supervisors can quickly track progress and outcomes with individual clients and groups of clients. These tasks can be done anywhere and any time, allowing the clinician to easily input data and generate reports. These technologies will facilitate the adoption of one of the major methods for increasing accountability, the use of electronic medical records by mental health professionals. Part of the mandate of Obamacare is creating an infrastructure for storing and accessing patients' medical records in an attempt to increase the efficiency of the US healthcare system.

In the United States, currently over 100 companies are engaged in creating database systems for **electronic medical records** (EMRs) that can be employed by hospitals, physicians, and healthcare providers. While information about EMRs related to mental health can be difficult to find, some estimates suggest that a $5 billion market exists for psychological testing and tracking of mental health data as part of EMR systems. It is likely that mental health clinicians will be required to complete qualitative progress notes and quantitative measures of progress and outcomes in EMR systems. The resulting data may be employed by the clinician for feedback about continuation or alteration of the counseling approach, as well as deciding whether to continue or terminate therapy. Supervisors and program evaluators may also examine these data to address such questions as how the particular clinician compares to others working with similar client populations and how clinicians can improve their outcomes.

A PUSH FOR ACCOUNTABILITY

For the past two decades, mental health professionals have been hearing about a need for greater accountability. In 2001, for example, Division 29 (Psychotherapy) of the American Psychological Association called for clinicians "to routinely monitor patients' responses to the therapy relationship and ongoing treatment" (Ackerman et al., 2001, p. 496, cited in Reese et al., 2009). That call, however, has seldom been accompanied by sustained, effective actions in PMOA. Utilization reviews, for example, have been scaled back by many insurers because of their minor effect on quality of care and efficiency. Incorporating PMOA measures into the therapy process, however, presents an opportunity for therapists to use clinical data, of both qualitative and quantitative types, to improve their practice. Although mental health professionals have been slow to develop or adopt PMOA procedures, other fields from medicine to finance have demonstrated how evidence-based analysis can contribute to the improvement of quality and performance.

The accountability focus is heightened by the fact that the need for mental health services is persistent and pervasive. About 60% of men and 50% of women report at least one traumatic event during their lifetime (Kessler, Sonnega, Bromet, Hughes, & Nelson, 1996). Rates of depression appear to be increasing over time in the United States (Castonguay, 2011). The US Surgeon General reported that mental illness is the second leading cause of disability and affects about 20% of all Americans; only about half of such individuals, however, receive treatment. Ringel and Sturm (2001) noted that only about 15% to 20% of children with mental health problems in the United States receive treatment. Given this enormous need, it follows that mental health services should be employed as efficiently as possible. The PPACA is just the latest in a series of policy and funding initiatives from government and private insurers that pairs the funding of mental health services with increased accountability from mental health professionals.

DATA FROM CLINICAL MEASURES PROVIDE FEEDBACK ABOUT PROGRESS AND OUTCOME

A noteworthy feature about any approach that emphasizes PMOA is the close connection between assessment data and intervention that results in structured clinical feedback (Meier, 2003). In traditional therapy, assessment takes the form of an initial interview that provides information about the presenting problem(s) and important contexts such as family history. Based on this information, the clinician may assign a diagnosis and develop a plan that focuses on an evidence-based treatment. But the majority of clients respond to interventions in diverse ways, often presenting the clinician with difficult decisions about whether to continue, alter, or discontinue particular treatment approaches. With PMOA measures and their resulting clinically relevant data, the therapist receives explicit feedback about treatment effectiveness. When employed in the context of a change-based theory, such data can greatly inform the clinician about how to proceed more effectively.

One of the important new approaches in school settings, for example, is called **Response To Intervention** (RTI). With RTI, assessors employ screening measure(s) to identify at-risk children and adolescents so that they can be provided with increasingly intense academic and/or behavioral health services (McDougal, Bardos, & Meier, 2012; Shinn, 2007). Beginning with a screening of the school population to identify at-risk students, school personnel provide targeted students with evidence-based interventions. Assessment continues via regular monitoring of student progress to gauge the interventions' effectiveness; if students are not responsive to the first tier of intervention, more intensive interventions are provided. RTI approaches have been found to reduce antisocial behavior (McCurdy, Mannella, & Eldridge, 2003) and improve academic performance (McCurdy et al., 2003; Nelson, Martella, & Marchand-Martella, 2002).

RTI is one of a variety of contemporary approaches that emphasize the potential for PMOA data to help clinicians improve their therapeutic practices. Lambert (2007), for example, has demonstrated that the use of the client self-report *Outcome Questionnaire-45* (*OQ45*) can decrease client deterioration rates through simple feedback about the rate of client progress. Lambert et al. (2001) recently demonstrated the positive effects of feedback with clients failing to make progress in therapy. Using the *Outcome Questionnaire* with 609 university counseling center clients, this study examined the effect of two factors: feedback versus no feedback to therapist, and clients making therapeutic progress versus those who were not (on *OQ* scores). Feedback consisted of graphs and progress markers, colored dots that indicated whether the client was (a) functioning in the normal range (of *OQ* scores), (b) showing an adequate rate of change, (c) evidencing an inadequate rate of change, or (d) failing to make progress. Lambert et al. found support for the major hypothesis of the study: *OQ* scores at termination were higher for clients who were initially not making progress but whose therapist was receiving feedback compared to clients who were not making progress and whose therapist received no feedback. In fact, the latter group worsened over time. Lambert et al. also noted that the effect size comparing the difference between the two groups' posttest scores was larger than that found in studies comparing different types of psychotherapy.

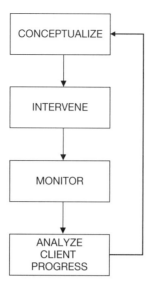

Figure 1.1 Sequential Relation Among Conceptualization, Intervention, Assessment, and Analysis of Intervention Effects in Progress Monitoring. *As a result of an intake interview and initial sessions with a client, clinicians develop a **case conceptualization** and treatment plan. One or more interventions follow from these activities, along with monitoring of the intervention's effects and effectiveness with the client. Analyses of the resulting data can be fed back into conceptualization and treatment planning to increase the likelihood that psychotherapy will ultimately be successful.*

As shown in Figure 1.1, the desired process in PM can be seen as a **feedback loop** (cf. Meier, 2003) that consists of the following:

1. Conceptualization, treatment planning, and selection of PMOA measure(s) for a specific client
2. Implementation of selected intervention(s)
3. Assessment of the intervention's effects on the client
4. Analysis and interpretation of those effects
5. Results provided to the clinician (and, perhaps, the client) so that the conceptualization and intervention(s) can be reconsidered and adapted if necessary

Figure 1.2 displays an OA loop. Here the assessment and analysis of treatment effects occur at the beginning of therapy and at a potentially natural ending point (e.g., the end of an academic semester in a college counseling center). Analysis of the intervention's effects and effectiveness provides feedback about whether the client benefited from therapy and whether therapy should be continued, altered, or ended. Whereas the PM loop provides more immediate feedback during therapy, OA data provide a summative or overall evaluation of treatment effects and effectiveness.

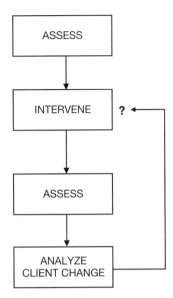

Figure 1.2 Sequential Relation Among Assessment, Intervention, and Analysis of Intervention Effects in Outcome Assessment. *In this approach, clinicians perform an assessment of the client's current status at the beginning of therapy and again following an intervention, often near a natural ending point such as completion of a therapeutic program. Analysis of the intervention's effects and effectiveness provides feedback about whether the client benefited from therapy and whether therapy should be continued, altered, or ended.*

These feedback loops can provide clinicians with useful information for creating treatment plans and adjusting therapy as circumstances change (Howard, Moras, Brill, Martinovich, & Lutz, 1996; Lambert et al., 2001). Gottman and Leiblum (1974) recommended that clinicians employ continuous PM and use the resulting feedback to decide whether to continue, adjust, or end the provided interventions.

WHAT SCALE(S) SHOULD BE EMPLOYED FOR PROGRESS MONITORING AND OUTCOME ASSESSMENT PURPOSES?

Modern standards of educational and psychological testing emphasize that test validity depends on empirical evidence supporting test use for particular purposes. Historically, tests have been employed for the purpose of **selection**, such as admission to college or screening for depression (Meier, 2008). Selection tests assume that the test is identifying a stable trait and that the test can subsequently predict some aspect of future behavior (e.g., success in college, future occurrences of suicidal feelings). To identify these traits, test developers seek test items or tasks that evidence maximum variability across individuals, stability over time, and high correlations with similar items (i.e., items that load on individual factors in a factor analysis). These criteria, however, do not necessarily lead to finding items sensitive to change from psychosocial interventions.

For psychological tests, the function of **screening** is comparable to selection, since the purpose is to identify individuals at risk for a psychological problem. Most psychological tests now in use for PMOA purposes, such as the Beck Depression Inventory (*BDI*; Beck & Steer, 1987), were originally developed for screening and subsequently employed for measuring progress and outcomes without modification. As a screening instrument, the *BDI* has the capacity to distinguish between individuals with little depression, moderate depression, or intense depression. That capacity, however, is different from the items' change sensitivity, the ability to detect change resulting from psychosocial interventions. *BDI* scores, for example, may partially reflect individual differences on items that reflect genetic or biological effects largely immune to short-term psychotherapeutic interventions.

As described further in Chapter 3, the methodology for identifying change-sensitive items involves (a) creating a group of test items thought likely to show change over time (preferably on the basis of psychotherapy theory or research) and (b) administering those items repeatedly (at least 2 times) to two groups, one consisting of individuals receiving a psychosocial intervention that has some reasonable expectation of being effective and the other of individuals who are not receiving an intervention (i.e., controls). Items that show change in the intervention group are treatment sensitive; that is, they show change in response to the intervention. The items that evidence change in the treatment condition but not the control condition are the items that should be scored in subsequent uses of the test.

Important methodological issues also remain to be resolved. Although most current PMOA measures are self-reports, for example, research findings suggest that for assessing negative affect (NA) states repeatedly, psychotherapist ratings may hold advantages over self-report (Persons & Fresco, 2008; Sloan & Kring, 2007). Persons and Fresco (2008) reported that researchers have found "that repeated administration of the *BDI* consistently resulted in a lower score, even when research participants were not depressed and were not receiving treatment" (p. 115). In essence, repeated administration of many psychotherapy-related self-report measures may result in client **self-monitoring**, a reactive method known to change the monitored behavior, typically in the same direction as an intervention (Craske & Tsao, 1999; Nelson, 1977). In addition, clinicians may have access to information sources, such as client nonverbals, that provide more unbiased information about client states (Shedler, Mayman, & Manis, 1993).

Also, many PMOA measures may be atheoretical, which can lead to difficulties when deciding what adjustments to make when PMOA suggests a client is failing to make progress. One key theoretical construct likely to be important across therapeutic approaches and client characteristics is **avoidance**. Related theoretical constructs such as defensiveness and resistance are key pieces of clinical data relevant to therapeutic progress and should be included (Hayes, Strosahl, & Wilson, 1999; Kashdan & Breen, 2007; Sloan & Kring, 2007). Avoidance of affect, cognitions, and behaviors may be both a cause of clinical problems and a major reason that clients have difficulty providing valid reports of their psychological functioning. And although knowledge of individuals' tendency toward avoidance may be helpful for assessing their ability to benefit from psychotherapy, asking clients in therapy to self-report avoidance is likely to produce invalid data.

USERS, USER QUALIFICATIONS, LIMITATIONS, AND CAUTIONS WITH PROGRESS MONITORING AND OUTCOME ASSESSMENT TESTS

Limitations and cautions relevant to all psychological tests generally apply to the use of measures for PMOA (McDougal et al., 2012). These include understanding how the test construction procedures affect the psychometric properties of the resulting scale, particularly the ability of the test to detect changes that occur in counseling and psychotherapy (discussed in detail in Chapter 3). Users should also understand potential errors (described in Chapter 5) related to the administration and scoring of such tests. Users typically obtain this knowledge through graduate courses and practicums in psychological assessment and psychotherapy.

More specific guidelines include the following:

1. The PMOA measure should be employed with clients of appropriate age. Tests are typically developed for at least one of two age groups: children and adolescents, or adults. Although these two categories can be divided further depending on the test purpose, in general, tests developed for one of these groups should not be employed with the other until empirically validated.
2. Measures created for detecting change should not also be employed as diagnostic or screening devices. Change-sensitive measures may not be stable enough to provide reliable information about the classification of individuals into specific diagnostic groups.
3. Decisions about the continuation and type of treatment should not be made solely on the basis of PMOA scores, but should also include clinical judgment and other sources of information. Use of data from other sources and methods increases the chances of a valid assessment and related clinical decisions, but ultimately, responsibility falls on the clinician and/or supervisor.
4. Users who interpret scores on PMOA measures should be familiar with the relevant test manual and with standards for educational and psychological association offered by appropriate professional organizations. Users who administer, score, and interpret these measures are ultimately responsible for the appropriate use of the test materials.

SUMMARY

A new generation of PMOA measures provides clinicians with actionable feedback about client progress and outcomes. Particularly for individuals who are failing to improve in psychotherapy, data from PMOA measures have the potential to indicate when a client is not making progress and when the mental health professional should alter the intervention. Yet despite their potential for providing clinical feedback, many mental health professionals have not systematically employed PMOA measures (Clement, 1999; Goodman, McKay, & DePhilippis, 2013; Zimmerman, 2008). Despite the call for PMOA use by professional organizations, many clinicians see such assessment as a burden on themselves or clients, and many do not receive training in graduate school about how to select, create, or employ such measures (Hatfield & Ogles, 2004). Outcome measures have also been associated with an accountability movement in psychotherapy that has focused on managing and limiting the provision of care rather improving quality (Davis & Meier, 2001).

Historically, creating valid measures of progress and outcome has been problematic. Traditional tests such as the *Minnesota Multiphasic Personality Inventory* and *BDI* are too long for repeated use in PM and were developed for screening and diagnostic purposes, not to be sensitive to the effects of psychosocial interventions. As Persons and Fresco (2008, p. 116) concluded in their review of measures of depression, "we were often unable to rate assessment tools for treatment sensitivity and clinical utility, as these qualities of assessment tools have not received much attention in the literature." Measures originally designed for screening and diagnostic purposes may also display puzzling or unexpected results: Scores on the *BDI*, for example, have been found to show sudden, unexpected change that does not correspond to events in psychotherapy (e.g., Kelly, Roberts, & Ciesla, 2005; Kendall, Hollon, Beck, Hammen, & Ingram, 1987).

New guidelines for creating and evaluating PMOA measures have appeared that offer improved methods for creating change-sensitive tests. These efforts are in their early stages, however, and much research remains to be done about such factors as the optimal frequency of administration of PMOA measures, the best methods for providing PMOA feedback to clinicians, and how much training for clinicians and/or clients is required to produce useful feedback. Repeated administration of self-reports, for example, may result in improved scores that have only a modest relation to changes in clients' actual thoughts, feelings, and behaviors. It is also unclear how often and what types of PMOA feedback should be provided (e.g., which data displays and analytic techniques are most understandable to clinicians and clients) and to what extent such feedback should be a component of clinical supervision. These topics are addressed in the remaining chapters of this book.

Case Studies

INTRODUCTION

This chapter describes psychotherapy cases to demonstrate how progress monitoring and outcome assessment (PMOA) data can be incorporated into the therapeutic process. PMOA data are frequently **quantitative** because this type of data can be efficiently collected and interpreted. However, cases in this chapter illustrate how both quantitative data from change-sensitive tests and **qualitative** data from sources such as **progress notes** can provide useful clinical feedback about children, adolescent, and adult clients receiving psychosocial interventions. Qualitative data can be particularly useful for providing hypotheses about the causes of client change evident in quantitative data. And given the early stage of the scientific work in PMOA measurement and clinical feedback, the case examples include important cautions and limitations about the use and interpretation of PMOA data.

QUANTITATIVE ANALYSIS OF NOMOTHETIC DATA FROM A CHANGE-SENSITIVE MEASURE: THE BEHAVIOR INTERVENTION MONITORING ASSESSMENT SYSTEM

McDougal, Bardos, and Meier (2012) described the case of a sixth-grade student, John, identified for behavioral treatment during the course of Response To Intervention (RTI) screening at his elementary school. This case provides an illustration of the application of RTI procedures in the context of screening and progress monitoring using the Behavior Intervention Monitoring Assessment System (BIMAS; McDougal et al., 2012).

RTI consists of two major components: (a) screening of all individuals in a school system to identify students with problems and (b) increasingly intense (as needed) psychosocial interventions accompanied by progress monitoring to determine the interventions' effectiveness with groups or specific individuals. The BIMAS assesses children and adolescents' problems with Conduct, Negative

Table 2.1. Interpreting the Direction of Behavior Intervention Monitoring Assessment System Scores

Scale	Typical Problems	Higher Scores Indicate
Conduct	Aggression, anger, defiance	Worsening
Negative Affect	Anxiety, depression, shame	Worsening
Cognitive/Attention	Attention, behavior control	Worsening
Academic Functioning	Follow directions, grades	Improvement
Social Skills	Disinterested, awkward	Improvement

Affect, and Cognitive/Attention tasks and strengths in Academic Functioning and Social Skills. See Table 2.1 for a brief description of scale meaning and how to interpret high scores on a scale. Intended for use with elementary and high school students, the BIMAS includes forms that can be completed by teachers, parents, clinicians, and students (self-report). In addition to the standard items that make up the major component of the test, the BIMAS also includes a bank of Flex items that more specifically describe individual problems.

On an initial screening, John evidenced difficulties on two BIMAS teacher-rated subscales, Negative Affect (NA) and Academic Functioning (AF). Additional information was available via school records, parent and teacher interviews, classroom observations, and the *BIMAS* parent and self-report forms. As shown in Figure 2.1, John's initial *t* score of 78 for the teacher-rated NA scale put him at *high risk* (category range, 70 to 85; over 2 standard deviations above the mean), a designation on the *BIMAS* indicating that mental health services are needed to prevent this student from experiencing further social, emotional, and academic difficulties. The NA scale assesses internalizing problems such as anxiety and

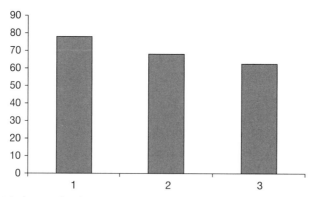

Figure 2.1 **John's Initial** *Behavior Intervention Monitoring Assessment System T* **Scores for Negative Affect (NA) as Rated by His Teacher, Mother, and Himself.** *Bar charts 1, 2, and 3 refer to John's NA t scores as rated by his teacher, mother, and self, respectively. Lower scores indicate less NA. With a mean score of 50 and a standard deviation of 10, the self-report score (63) falls nearest the mean and the teacher score (78) falls almost 3 standard deviations above the mean.*

depression. John's teacher had indicated that John was very often sad or with-drawn, often had thoughts of hurting himself, and sometimes was depressed. John's *t* score of 23 on the teacher-rated AF scale (Figure 2.2) indicated that John scored well below average compared to the normative sample on class prepara-tion, grades, and absences. John's responses on other scales indicated that John had difficulty staying on task, organizing, and planning; he also had some dif-ficulties with social interactions, although he could be friendly and work out problems with others.

Given this initial picture, what services should be considered for John?

To mental health professionals, the possibility of suicide rises to the top of any list of concerns. Interviews with John alone and with his mother, however, indicated he did not intend to act on his thoughts of self-harm. Nevertheless, predicting future client behaviors such as suicide (and homicide) is very difficult; consequently, it would be important to monitor the possibility of self-harm. For progress monitoring with John, individual items were selected from the bank of *BIMAS* Flex items. These Flex items were tracked weekly and the *BIMAS* stan-dard items (which have norms) were readministered 10 weeks after interventions began.

Figure 2.3 shows teacher ratings of one item that assessed John's thoughts about self-harm each week. Such **time series** graphs can help illustrate trends over time and lead to new hypotheses related to the causes of clients' behavior (Mattaini, 1993). Data indicate that John's thoughts decreased from often (3) at Week 1 to Never (0) at Week 6 and thereafter continued at this level. In addi-tion to elevated NA scores provided by a teacher, John's mother (***t* score** = 75) and John (*t* score = 68) reported higher scores for NA (see Figure 2.1). *T* scores for AF were uniformly low across raters (23 for teacher, 28 for parent, and 34 for self-report, as shown in Figure 2.2). Given these indicators, the assessor

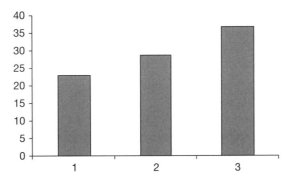

Figure 2.2 John's Initial *Behavior Intervention Monitoring Assessment System T* Scores for Academic Functioning (AF) Scales as Rated by His Teacher, Mother, and Himself. *Bar charts 1, 2, and 3 refer to John's AF t scores as rated by his teacher, mother, and self; low scores indicate poorer academic performance. With a mean score of 50 and a standard deviation of 10, the teacher score falls about 3 standard deviations below the average score of the normal distribution.*

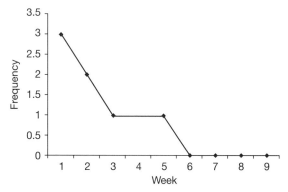

Figure 2.3 Time Series of John's Teacher-Rated Scores for Self-Harm Item. *This time series depicts John's self-harm thoughts decreasing over time.*

suggested a broad set of interventions that focused on group interactions; academic work around class preparation, homework, and attendance; and peer mentoring. John participated in a weekly support group, received daily academic services, and began working as a peer tutor to read books to younger children.

Readministration of the *BIMAS* Standard items approximately 2 and 4 months later produced indications of improvement for John on the NA and AF scales. Figures 2.4 display time series graphs for these two scales. In addition to time series graphs, the *BIMAS* software also calculates **Reliable Change Index** (RCI) and **effect size** (ES) statistics to provide feedback about the amount of change. These statistics produced slightly different results for the evaluation of the amount of John's change on NA: The 10-point change in *t* scores across the first and second administrations was a statistically significant change, whereas the ES change was small and considered no change by *BIMAS* guidelines.

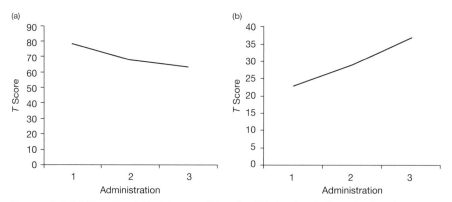

Figures 2.4 (a) Negative Affect Across 6 Months. (b) Academic Functioning Across 6 Months. John's scores on *Negative Affect and Academic Functioning* both show improvement over time, moving to about 1 standard deviation from the mean of the normative sample.

Taken as a whole, these PMOA scores suggest substantial decreases in John's thoughts about self-harm and modest improvements in NA and AF. If the school system has implemented an RTI screening program that readministers a PMOA measure at regular intervals, John's scores could be rechecked to determine his current status. It is important that John's scores do not stabilize at high levels or worsen, two commonly occurring outcomes in psychotherapy (Lambert, 2012). If John does not continue to improve, additional interventions and hypotheses about John should be considered. One possibility, for example, is that he is avoiding NA. That is, John's lower self-reported responses on the NA scale, in comparison to teacher and parent scores, suggest he may be underreporting or avoiding NA. Avoidance has been proposed as an important variable in the development of psychological problems and may interfere with therapeutic procedures designed to ameliorate those problems (Meier, in press). If John avoids the experiencing of NA, then he may not be experiencing the full benefits of any provided counseling. Most therapeutic approaches have methods for helping clients with avoidance, although some research indicates that therapists may differ substantially in their ability to detect client avoidance (Meier, 2014).

Finally, the task of interpreting score changes across time and sessions should be performed with caution. In the context of counseling and psychotherapy, examining change in a single individual over time usually occurs in what can be considered an **intensive single-case design** where data are collected repeatedly with a single individual over time (Heppner, Kivlighan, & Wampold, 1999). The dependent variable in such a design is the PMOA measure(s). Therapy is the independent variable of interest, but multiple other factors can potentially affect the PMOA measure, perhaps more powerfully than therapy.

Attributing client change to therapy will always be problematic without a control group or a **baseline** period of no change. Decisions on whether to continue or stop therapy should never be made only on the basis of test data, but by responsible decision makers who interpret the data with the best interests of the client at heart. With John, for example, a case can be made that he has made improvement and his interventions can be stopped since his *t* scores are approaching a normal or average range (in relation to the *BIMAS* norm groups). However, it is unclear what is causing those gains and whether the gains can be maintained over time; the client's therapist and his or her supervisor may be in the best position to make such a determination.

Other sources of information, such as school records, parent and teacher interviews, and classroom observations that were previously gathered about John, may provide information that can partially explain trends in John's PMOA scores over time and any need for further sustained or intermittent intervention. As described in Chapter 9, progress notes from John's therapist may be an especially important source of information because they are likely to contain descriptions of important events and situations that influenced John's NA and AF.

USING AFFECTIVE LEVELS OF INTENSITY TO GAUGE TREATMENT PROGRESS: THE DEPRESSION/ANXIETY NEGATIVE AFFECT SCALE

The literature review in Chapter 3 describes how problem resolution in psychotherapy is typically accompanied by decreasing reports of **negative affect**, particularly its intensity, "the strength of a particular affective state" (Diener, Larsen, Levine, & Emmons, 1985, p. 1263). The *Depression/Anxiety Negative Affect* (*DANA*; Meier, 2012) scale describes NA in five item clusters representing increasing intensities (Table 2.2). These include Transient NA (Level 1), Increasing NA (2), Moderate NA (3), Intense NA (4), and Extreme NA (5). Levels 1 and 5 represent the extremes of affective experiencing. The affective states in Level 1, Transient NA, such as *Bored* and *Deflated* may be considered part of normal human experiencing.

One of the *DANA*'s key scores is Highest Intensity Level (HIL). HIL refers to the most intense level of any NA descriptor endorsed per session. If a rater endorsed the *DANA* terms *Anxious, Fearful*, and *Actively suicidal*, the corresponding intensity levels would be 3, 4, and 5, respectively. Level 5 is the highest level of the endorsed terms, so HIL for this session would be 5. If therapy is successful, clients should receive decreasing intensity levels of NA over time. Test development studies (Meier, 2012) indicate that most clients start near *DANA* Level 4; on average, clients who demonstrated improvement in the test development studies evidenced about a one-level decrease over brief intervals of therapy (e.g., about five sessions on average). In general, change in *DANA* scores across sessions will provide information relevant for gauging therapy progress.

Figure 2.5 displays *DANA* HIL data for a 19-year-old Caucasian female who completed 10 sessions of therapy across one academic semester in a college counseling center. What can we say about this case on the basis of these PMOA scores?

All 10 HIL values equal 2 (*Increasing NA*) or 3 (*Moderate NA*); six of the 10 HIL scores equal 2. The client's HIL scores increase by one level from Session 1 to Session 2 and from Session 9 to Session 10, but decrease from Session 8 to Session 9. However, the overall picture is of stability over the first 10 sessions of therapy: This is likely to be a client in moderate discomfort who is failing to improve in therapy. Persons and Mikami (2002) observed that a substantial

Table 2.2. Depression/Anxiety Negative Affect Intensity Levels

Level	Description	Example Items
1	Transient negative affect (NA)	*Bored, Unrelaxed*
2	Increasing NA	*On edge, Irritable*
3	Moderate NA	*Embarrassed, Worried*
4	Intense NA	*Demoralized, Weeping*
5	Extreme NA	*Enraged, Traumatized*

Figure 2.5 Relative Stability in a Client's Highest Intensity Level (HIL) Scores for the First 10 Sessions. *An HIL score of 3 indicates that the therapist rated the client as evidencing a moderate negative affect (NA) intensity and an HIL score of 2 as increasing NA intensity. The dotted line indicates the typical starting point on HIL for outpatients; the median score for HIL at Session 1 equaled 4 and the mean 3.75 in a clinical sample (Meier, 2012).*

percentage of a typical therapist's caseload may consist of individuals who are failing to improve:

> Many patients who are not making progress are quite happy to meet weekly with a supportive therapist whom they like and respect. Therapists…find it easy to believe that because the process is so pleasant, something good must be happening. (p. 143)

Izard (2007, p. 264) noted that basic NA states typically "have a low base rate and a short duration." In contrast, this client, with persistent NA at Level 3 (e.g., *Anxious, Moderately sad*), may be experiencing long-standing problems in her social environments (e.g., family issues); another plausible hypothesis is a personality disorder.

Studies of the **improvement probabilities** (Meier, 2014) of scores on the *DANA* indicate that clients with an initial HIL score of Level 2 are likely to increase to Level 3 when reassessed in five sessions. Similarly, two thirds of clients with initial HIL scores of Level 3 are likely to remain at Level 3 in five sessions. Thus, both clinical and empirical perspectives suggest this client has been stable and failed to improve.

These scores also demonstrate some of the advantages and disadvantages of employing quantitative data for PMOA purposes. First, they provide a more objective perspective on the amount of change a client is experiencing. Although a therapist might be tempted to see at least small amounts of progress within and across sessions, the NA data basically indicate that for these 10 sessions, the client did not change. The disadvantage of viewing quantitative data alone, however, is that PMOA scores typically do not provide potential explanations for the observed pattern of data. In other words, therapists may not know why this person is failing to improve; the chosen therapy may be ineffective, for example, or the client may be avoidant of therapeutic procedures (suggested by the low HIL level in Session 1) and/or unmotivated to change. It is also possible that the client began to make progress on her presenting problem (Sessions 8 and 9) but experienced increased NA when terminating with her therapist (Session 10) and planned to return to therapy the following semester. Progress notes might provide a useful context for interpreting these HIL data.

TRACKING STABILITY AND CHANGE IN A CLIENT'S DEPRESSION WITH THE BECK DEPRESSION INVENTORY

A graduate student therapist provided a supervisor with PMOA data about a female depressed client over 7 months of therapy. This included periodic administration of the *Beck Depression Inventory* (*BDI*; Beck & Steer, 1987). Each item refers to different aspects of depression and contains four statements of increasing severity. Depression symptoms and attitudes include mood, guilt feelings, suicidal wishes, irritability, sleep disturbance, and appetite changes. *BDI* scores in previous studies have shown high internal consistency (reliability), high correlations with other measures of depression, and **sensitivity to change** resulting from a variety of medication and counseling interventions (Kendall, Hollon, Beck, Hammen, & Ingram, 1987). Hatfield and Ogles's (2004) survey of practicing psychologists found the *BDI* to be the most frequently measure employed for outcome assessment.

The client is a 45-year-old Caucasian woman named Susan, diagnosed with chronic depression who also had abused alcohol and cocaine. Sober after completing an inpatient substance abuse treatment program, she now attends daily AA meetings. A long-term psychotherapy client, Susan has struggled with depression since she was an adolescent and has made several suicide attempts by overdosing on prescription medication. Susan completed the *BDI* at the start of this current round of treatment in October, and then the therapist in training began giving the *BDI* to the client regularly as treatment progressed from January through April. Figure 2.6 displays the *BDI* scores and subscale scores for a total of 10 sessions. In addition to the PMOA scores, a brief summary of key elements from progress notes was available. These notes (and accompanying *BDI* scores) are provided in Table 2.3 for sessions completed from January through April.

Callahan, Almstrom, Swift, Borja, and Heath (2009) reviewed research indicating that the therapy of trainees produces improvements at slower rates and with higher occurrences of premature termination. If you are Susan's supervisor, what questions would you address with her about the case? For example:

1. What aspects of these data would you pay attention to?
2. How could you provide this trainee with useful feedback about Susan, her progress in therapy, and likely outcomes?
3. Does the PMOA data suggest treatment should be adjusted?
4. How could you help the student therapist conceptualize this case?

In terms of change in the *BDI* data, Susan evidenced a noticeable decrease in depression over two of the measured time intervals. First, her *BDI* total scores

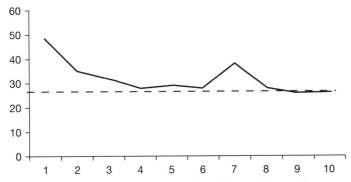

Figure 2.6 Susan's *Beck Depression Inventory* (*BDI*) Scores Across Therapy Sessions. *The client completed the BDI at the start of treatment in October (Session 1) and then again the following January (Session 2). The therapist in training then began giving the BDI to the client regularly as treatment progressed from February through April (Sessions 3 through 10). The dotted line shows where **BDI** Total Score equals 28, indicating a demarcation between moderate and severe depression.*

decreased from a total of 48 in October to 35 in January; the January score, however, still indicates severe depression. Second, in March her *BDI* total score bumped from 28 to 38 and back to 28. Although therapy notes are unavailable for the October–January period, the higher *BDI* scores in October may reflect Susan's reactions to her suicide attempt and hospitalization. The March *BDI* increase is accompanied by progress notes indicating that Susan stopped taking her medication at this time because of her concerns about cloudy thinking and weight.

Interestingly, many seemingly significant interpersonal events in Susan's life do not appear to be associated with changes on *BDI* total scores. The time series in Figure 2.6 indicates that Susan's depression remained largely stable during the January–April period. Her therapy had relatively little effect on further decreasing her depression during this period, despite the presence of positive life events such as the start of a romantic relationship and positive attention from her family. On the other hand, noticeable in the progress notes are Susan's negative **self-beliefs**, which include expectations that good things never last and she would perform poorly in school because of lack of intelligence (**outcome** and **self-efficacy expectations**, respectively, in Bandura's [1977] terms). Susan was surprised when the therapist asked her what it would take for her depression to abate; this suggests that Susan's depression was so chronic that she could not imagine that her depression could significantly lessen. She also failed her final session with her therapist, raising questions about the **working alliance** and **attachment issues** with her therapist.

One consideration is that with the chronic, traitlike depression that Susan evidenced over 7 months of treatment, relative stability over time with no hospitalizations may be the most realistic positive outcome possible. Psychologists distinguish between psychological **states** and **traits**. Often assumed to be hereditary, traits are enduring, stable characteristics, whereas states are transitory

Table 2.3. SUMMARY OF PROGRESS NOTES WITH A DEPRESSED CLIENT

Session (BDI Score, category)	Key Issues
1. October Intake (*Beck Depression Inventory* [*BDI*] = 48, *severe depression*)	Susan has been chronically depressed and a substance abuser. She has completed substance abuse treatment and attends AA meetings daily. She also participates in psychotherapy and has made several suicide attempts by overdosing on prescription medication. After the latest suicide attempt, she was hospitalized for 1 week; the therapist began treatment after her release.
2. January Therapy Session (*BDI* = 35, *severe depression*)	The therapist saw the client again after the midyear academic break. Susan presented as depressed but reported positive experiences over the holidays when she spent time with family and friends. Her *BDI* score this week indicated that she had fewer somatic complaints and more positive feelings about herself.
3. February Therapy Session (*BDI* = 32, *severe depression*)	Susan reported this week that she had begun a romantic relationship with a man. She reported having had difficult relationships with men in the past.
4. February Therapy Session (*BDI* = 28, *moderate depression*)	Susan reported feeling "the best [she had] felt in years." Situational factors again contributed to her improved mood: Her mother threw her a surprise party with all her siblings, important because she believed her family no longer cared about her after her last suicide attempt. Her romantic relationship was also going well and Susan stated that she had a "glimmer of hope."
5. February Therapy Session (*BDI* = 29, *severe depression*)	Susan was unhappy that she had a bad cold and an unproductive week that included canceling a date with her boyfriend. She was worried her boyfriend might break up with her because she did not see him one night. This led to a therapy discussion about all-or-none cognitions and her beliefs that all normal people work even when sick and that all men are angry when their girlfriends do not see them when they'd like. After the therapist challenged her to provide evidence for and against those statements, she conceded that the depression was clouding her thinking: She describes her depression as external to herself, as "tricking me."
6. March Therapy Session (*BDI* = 28, *severe depression*)	Susan was getting over an illness. Her psychiatrist had made a change in her medications so that she would not feel so "numb."

(*continued*)

Table 2.3. (Continued)

Session (BDI Score, category)	Key Issues
7. March Therapy Session (*BDI* = 38, *severe depression*)	Nothing situational had changed, according to her self-report, in terms of relationships with family and friends. Susan reported that she just felt terrible, that her thinking was "cloudy" and she knew it would affect her work. Susan eventually revealed that she had stopped taking her medication several weeks ago because she thought it had caused her to gain weight. She also believed the medication was causing her to feel "flat." However, she realized she could not cope without the meds and began retaking them several days before this therapy session.
8. April Therapy Session (*BDI* = 28, *severe depression*)	Susan indicated she became excited about an upcoming internship. In preparation for leaving his training assignment, the student therapist began to discuss with Susan her transfer to another clinician at the end of the month.
9. April Therapy Session (*BDI* = 26, *moderate depression*)	Susan stated this is the best she has felt in years. She did, however, almost immediately begin catastrophizing that when things are good, they never last. She fears she will fail in her schoolwork because she "is not that smart."
10. April Therapy Session (*BDI* = 26, *moderate depression*)	Susan reported feeling very good again this week; she stated she especially liked that it was sunny. Susan also reported everything in her life was going "the exact same" as last week. She said it was kind of "eerie" and she just knew something bad was going to happen soon. Asked what it would take for her not to be depressed, she was surprised by the question. Susan indicated that she was unsure because she could not really remember a time when she was not depressed.
11. April Therapy Session (No *BDI* completed)	This was her last scheduled appointment with the student therapist. She called and cancelled, indicating she had the flu. She did not complete the *BDI*.

phenomena influenced by situations and environments (Cattell & Scheier, 1961; Spielberger, 1991). Traits remain stable over time and across situations; that is, they exhibit **cross-situational consistency**. Most psychological phenomena are thought to evidence both trait and state characteristics, and test developers have accordingly developed measures such as the *State-Trait Anxiety Inventory* (Spielberger, Gorsuch, & Lushene, 1970) and the *State-Trait Anger Expression Inventory* (Spielberger, 1991). In the case of Susan, her depression scores on the *BDI* evidenced a significant decrease over the October–January time period, a period in which her social circumstances showed noticeable improvement over the Christmas holidays. Yet from January through April, Susan's *BDI* scores remained relatively stable, except for a worsening when she briefly discontinued her antidepressant medication.

Therapy provided by this graduate student may have maintained Susan and helped her to notice the life improvements that occurred during the gradual periods of decreasing depression. Equally plausible, however, is the possibility that the provided therapy had little or no effect on either the improvement in depression or stability over time. Susan had been in therapy for many years, and her current therapist believed that one reason for the lack of improvement was that Susan avoided awareness of the physical abuse she suffered as a child. Those experiences left her with a deeply ingrained sense of hopelessness and worthlessness; she did not feel loved and felt like she was a burden who would never amount to anything. She had used drugs and alcohol to cope, but participating in therapy and AA helped Susan to learn new coping skills that included calling her sponsor, support at AA meetings, positive self-talk and cognitive restructuring, distraction, and physical exercise.

Given that Susan's *BDI* scores remained stuck in the moderately depressed range, additional case conceptualization and treatment approaches (that focused on her avoidance of the childhood physical abuse, for example) might be considered. Given that many graduate students focus on techniques and procedures, supervisors can be particularly helpful in providing trainees with deeper ideas about how to think about difficult clients. Resources such as Berman (1997), Eells (2013), Fishman (2013), Meier (2003), and Persons (2013) can be useful for teaching and learning about case conceptualizations and PMOA data.

IDIOGRAPHIC ANALYSIS OF CLINICAL NOTES TO TRACK PROGRESS AND OUTCOMES

Currently most therapists do not collect quantitative PMOA data, but write progress notes for each psychotherapy session. These notes are typically **idiographic** in that they describe relatively unique aspects of the client's history, problems, and response to treatment. Similarly, most case conceptualizations can be considered a mixture of idiographic and nomothetic elements for a particular client. Analyses of PMOA data can also be considered idiographic when comparisons with an individual client's scores are made across time (as compared to evaluating an individual's scores to others in a normative way). Most of the PMOA analyses described in this chapter are idiographic in that they involve an analysis of potential change over time and sessions for an individual in counseling and psychotherapy.

From an idiographic perspective, progress notes can be employed in a more structured manner to produce PMOA qualitative data for use in clinical feedback and case conceptualization. Table 2.4 displays themes extracted from a qualitative analysis of progress notes with a depressed client over 20 sessions

Table 2.4. Qualitative Analysis of Progress Notes With a Depressed/Anxious Client

Session Number	Key Issues
1	Presenting problem centers on **depression and anxiety**; agrees to referral for possible medication; reports history of conflicted family relationships, particularly with long-deceased alcoholic father
2	Has started medication and will continue counseling; reports difficulty at work with "crazy" customers; we establish a schedule of activities designed to increase positive reinforcement for him
3	Reports *a history of trying to re-create a family life*, but with people other than immediate family of origin; for example, becomes a physical, emotional caretaker for distant relatives, older neighbors; reports no effect from reinforcement activities
4	**Reports that he is very angry** with *many past incidents with family of origin*, particularly father, and some current events with mother
5	**Is much less anxious, moderately less depressed, but seems almost manic**; very strong emotional reactions to many current events
6	Agrees to start a journal where he writes thoughts, feelings, and related events
7	Reports that he has come to the conclusion that **he hates himself**; reading books about identity development; **now frequent, angry arguments with partner**
8	Reports becoming **easily angry with coworkers**, even when their behavior does not affect him directly, as well as with partner and family members
9	Reads for 30 minutes from a journal about *past family incidents* that provoked **anger, rage, and sadness in him**; question arises whether he should pursue family therapy with mother and siblings
10	Notes that **he is angry with his mother** but *cannot express those feelings to her or even explore much in session; family culture indicates that being angry with parents is equivalent to disobeying them*
11	Despite father's death 15 years ago, reports that he still **wishes there was some way he could be emotionally close to father**; I confronted about this unrealistic idea; he later cancels next session
12	Some processing in session of *how he experiences emotion*; relates stories that provide evidence (to him) that his role was to function as *emotional caretaker in his family; tried to protect mother from abusive, alcoholic father*
13	No-show; later reported that he forgot about the session
14	*Wondering whether to stay in current relationship*; debating financial security versus partner's treatment of him as a child
15	Considering whether to leave town, start a new life elsewhere; now spending much time considering therapy issues between sessions

(continued)

Table 2.4. (Continued)

Session Number	Key Issues
16	Same issues as Session 15
17	Ran into his brother's friend who had no idea that client's father was alcoholic; *confirmed for client that mother and siblings denied family difficulties*; I noted that in the past he had denied such problems as well
18	Clearly has changed locus of responsibility for family conflict away from himself; **anger and rumination about family has decreased**; more focus on work, other people
19	*Discusses buying a house with partner; one brother is now contacting him for social interactions*
20	Termination; **client reports greater self-confidence, emotional independence from family**, stable work performance; describes himself as "better integrated"

NOTE: Bold text indicates material conceptualized as relevant to outcome, whereas italicized content relates to process. Sources are Meier (1999, 2003), reprinted by permission.

(Meier, 1999, 2003). For each session, Table 2.4 contains two or three sentences summarizing key issues during the psychotherapy of this young depressed man. Progress and outcomes can be tracked by examining the notes for themes indicative of the client's psychological status. Over the course of therapy, changes in or persistence of these themes can indicate sign of improvement, worsening, and stability.

Relevant information highlighted in Table 2.4 indicates that this client expressed intense anxiety and depression in Session 1 that began to lessen by Session 5. Sessions 7 through 10 suggest that this client is becoming aware of and experiencing anger, and in Sessions 10 through 12 the clinical discussion focused on the role of anger in his family and his awareness about how he experiences emotion. Session 12 appeared to represent a **critical incident** in that the focus was on how he experienced emotion and his role as the family's emotional caretaker. Regarding the latter, he appeared to avoid experiencing NA and tended to express NA only in the form of intense feelings such as anger, rage, and depression. The client failed to attend the next session, saying he had forgotten about it; he had attended previous sessions on a regular basis. The client appeared to process emotions more openly in the following sessions, and this appeared to be a turning point.

After Session 14, with anger and rumination about family issues abating, the client appeared to be paying more attention to current issues with relationships and work. He also appeared to be processing important issues outside of therapy sessions. Finally, in Session 20, he concluded therapy by reporting greater self-confidence, emotional independence, and stable work performance. Depression was no longer mentioned as a problem.

The themes in Figure 2.7 also provide information useful for a case conceptualization depicted in terms of important process and outcome elements (Meier, 2003). A case conceptualization is a verbal and graphic depiction of important process (causes) and outcome (effects) elements for a specific client (Meier, 2003). The client's description of relevant history and events indicates potential causes of the client's problems, and the client's presenting problem provides information relevant to desired outcomes (Meier, 2003). In general, an ideal case conceptualization includes a brief list of process and outcome elements included in a graphical depiction of the relationship among those elements. The conceptualization can also include a depiction of the **treatment plan** describing interventions aimed at particular process–outcome relations. As noted earlier in this chapter, more detailed guidelines about creating a case conceptualization can be found in other sources (Eells, 2013; Fishman, 2013; Meier, 2003; Persons, 2013).

A graphic conceptualization of client processes and outcomes can be useful as a quick map for thinking about clients both in session and for treatment planning. As shown in Figure 2.7, the client's history of conflicted family relationships (e.g., denigration by his alcoholic father) and the accompanying NA (e.g., anger, depression, anxiety) can be considered his major process and outcome elements, respectively. Figure 2.7 also depicts that his difficulties with current relationships (arguments with coworkers, partner) stem from his learning history with his family. Finally, the client's avoidance of discussing and experiencing these difficult topics means that his NA will continue to appear because the originating problems had been unresolved. The therapeutic interventions primarily focus on conflicted family relationships, current relationships, and avoidance of experiencing around these conflicts. The interventions appeared to be effective in that the client's NA decreased, as did his focus on family relationships.

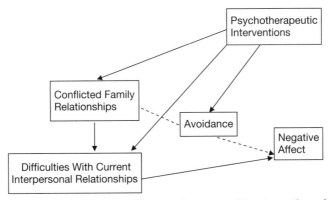

Figure 2.7 Graphic Case Conceptualization of Depressed/Anxious Client from Table 2.4.

MULTIPLE IDIOGRAPHIC MEASURES:
THE CASE OF MR. F

While most PMOA measures are **nomothetic** in origin—that is, the constructs measured are intended to be applicable with all clients—**idiographic** measurement assesses relatively unique aspects of an individual case. For example, Mr. F, a 19-year-old Asian American who sought counseling because of **intrusive thoughts** (Abramowitz, 2002), had ruminations about cursing at others during class, looking at people's genitals, and raping a female friend. Mr. F feared he might take such actions but maintained that he would never do so. A year before he enrolled at the university, Mr. F began having intrusive thoughts about killing his parents in their sleep. Mr. F also reported anxiety, depression, frequent indigestion, and sleep loss. Mr. F avoided objects and locations such as knives, the dormitory balcony where he would have thoughts of jumping, classes where he was afraid he would curse, and his computer because he was afraid of sending inappropriate e-mail messages. Rituals intended to help cope with his anxiety about the intrusive thoughts included whispering curse words in public and reasoning about the possibility that he would actually do an inappropriate act. Mr. F met *Diagnostic and Statistical Manual of Mental Disorders*, 5th edition (DSM-IV) criteria for obsessive-compulsive disorder (OCD) and major depressive episode (Abramowitz, 2002).

Twice-weekly sessions over 8 weeks focused on in vivo and imaginal **exposure** to the aversive thoughts. In one session Mr. F was instructed to *not* think of pink elephants; he subsequently reported thinking about numerous pink elephants, demonstrating to Mr. F that attempts to suppress thoughts resulted in an increase in the unwanted thought. Other work included completing standard measures of OCD symptoms, depression (i.e., *BDI*), unwanted thoughts, and strategies for controlling thoughts at the beginning, middle, and end of treatment and at follow-up to treatment. Such an assessment schedule, however, may not provide data timely enough to adjust the treatment as it progresses.

Given this complex clinical picture, how might a therapist track Mr. F's progress over the course of therapy? Abramowitz (2002) created idiographic rating scales for three constructs specific to Mr. F that he labeled *Fear of intrusive thoughts, Avoidance* (of situations associated with intrusive thoughts), and *Neutralizing rituals* (i.e., behaviors believed to lessen anxiety). The therapist completed these scales using a 0 (None) to 8 (Severe) assessment. Abramowitz (2002) collected baseline data for the three idiographic measures for three sessions (where no intervention occurred) and then continued to collect data after each of 13 subsequent treatment sessions. Table 2.5 displays values for the three measures by session.

Figure 2.8 provides a time series of the improvement apparent in Table 2.5 for one of the three measures, *Fear of intrusive thoughts*. The data indicate a quick decrease in problem severity over time. Other analytic techniques, such as the trend analyses described in Chapter 7, can provide additional useful information

Table 2.5. IDIOGRAPHIC THERAPIST RATINGS FOR
MR. F's FEAR OF THOUGHTS, AVOIDANCE, AND
RITUALS

Session	Fear of Thoughts	Avoidance	Rituals
BASELINE SESSIONS			
1	7	7	6
2	6	6	5
3	6	7	5
THERAPY SESSIONS			
1	5	5	4
2	5	6	4
3	4	5	1
4	4	2	2
5	3	2	1
6	2	1	1
7	2	0	1
8	2	0	0
9	1	0	1
10	2	0	0
11	1	1	1
12	2	0	0
13	1	0	0

NOTE: Therapist ratings on the scale could range from
0 (None) to 8 (Severe).

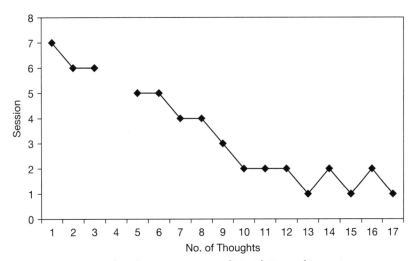

Figure 2.8 Time Series for Therapist Ratings of Mr. F's Fear of Intrusive Thoughts. *Mr. F's improvement over time. The vertical phase change line differentiates between the baseline sessions (left of line) and intervention sessions (right of line).*

about the overall impact of the intervention. These measures, tailored to Mr. F's problems, indicate that the therapy was quickly effective and that his OCD symptoms had largely diminished after five to seven therapy sessions. Therapy could now conclude after five to seven sessions, but other factors may influence that decision. These could include whether the client can accept his occasional OCD symptoms and the possibility that the client is cycling through up-and-down periods of symptoms (e.g., Hoffman & Meier, 2001).

MULTIPLE IDIOGRAPHIC MEASURES: THE COMPLEX CASE OF DORIS

Hoffman and Meier (2001) described the case of Doris, a 30-year-old Caucasian student who presented at a university counseling center. Doris constituted a **complex case** in terms of multiple problems: In addition to scoring 35 on the *BDI* at intake (indicating severe depression), she had difficulty sleeping and concentrating, reported previous emotional and physical abuse (including violence in her family of origin), had been a crime victim, suffered the recent loss of a relationship, was socially isolated, and had poor academic grades. She also indicated that she smoked marijuana daily and had done so for years. After she recently broke off a long-term romantic relationship with a physically abusive man, memories of the abuse kept her awake at night and created strong NA throughout the day. In response, Doris isolated herself and increased her use of marijuana.

A complex case such as Doris poses a challenge both for therapy and PMOA assessment. Therapists who treat clients who present with numerous problems must decide which to target initially. From a substance abuse standpoint, some therapists (and insurance companies) believe that alcohol and drug abuse must be addressed first. Other therapists believe the substance abuse to be symptomatic of other problems, and that the substances medicate or alleviate the client's distress. Doris's problems included depression (with symptoms of sleep disturbance and concentration), past and recent emotional and physical abuse, relationship difficulties, crime, social isolation, and poor isolation. If you are Doris's therapist, how would you address her issues?

PMOA assessment may be able to assist in the therapy process of such complex cases. That is, if an underlying cause is responsible for the manifestation of multiple problems, tracking as many problems as feasible will reveal how many of them respond to the provided therapeutic procedures. If multiple problems show improvement, then therapy should proceed unchanged. If only a subset of problems evidence change, however, then different problems will need to be addressed sequentially in therapy. In Doris's case, how might you assess her multiple problems?

Based on cognitive-behavioral theory, Doris's therapist initially proposed that her depression was maintained and reinforced by Doris's negative self-talk and abusive choice of partners (Hoffman & Meier, 2001). The therapist instructed Doris to record her thoughts so that she could challenge her negative self-talk;

Doris also learned about the nature of domestic violence to help her choose non-violent partners and began antidepressant medication. However, after early sessions in which Doris reported impulsive and sometimes violent behavior, and after learning that the depression coincided with the end of the relationship with the abusive boyfriend, the therapist reconceptualized Doris in terms of **posttraumatic stress disorder (PTSD)**. Doris saw violence as normal in relationships and believed that the victim of violence was also the cause. When triggered by threatening thoughts and situations, Doris responded impulsively, sometimes violently. She tried to avoid the feelings associated with these situations and states through marijuana use and social isolation. Subsequently, the therapist provided Doris with education about marijuana's negative consequences and a self-care plan for regular sleep, increased social contact, and daily deep breathing exercises.

Derived from the case conceptualizations (Meier, 1999, 2003), the therapist also began to track idiographic indicators specific to Doris. As shown in Figure 2.9 (a to d), the therapist collected data on:

1. *Impulsivity/aggression*: the number of impulsive/aggressive themes mentioned in each session's case note (Figure 2.9 (a)). These themes included material describing physically violent behavior and/or emotionally explosive behavior such as yelling, screaming, or cursing.
2. The number of *negative experiences* reported by Doris that could potentially trigger inappropriate coping responses (Figure 2.9 (b)). Examples included depression, hostility, and arguments with others.
3. *Depression/anxiety* level, as coded from Doris's psychiatrist's notes (Figure 2.9 (c)). No concerns were coded as 0, some concerns as 1, and continued or worsening concerns as 2.
4. *Marijuana use*: the number of times per week that Doris self-reported smoking (Figure 2.9 (d)).

Several trends are visible in Figure 2.9 (a to d) (Hoffman & Meier, 2001). All four variables show their highest (worst) values during initial sessions; all variables also evidence general improvement from initial to last sessions. However, three of the four variables display a movement toward no problems around Sessions 8 through 10. Consequently, this may be a potentially appropriate time to terminate treatment; had this counseling center implemented a 10-session limit for all clients, as was common practice at the time, Doris's treatment would have ended. But most of Doris's scores worsened and remained moderately high between Sessions 10 and 14. Thus, Doris's case is complicated beyond her significant number of problems: She evidenced improvement during the first 10 sessions of therapy but worsened again, a common pattern in psychotherapy.

If the PMOA data had been employed to end therapy after Session 8, the therapist would have missed the opportunity to help Doris learn from subsequent events. Doris had a significant health crisis that started at Session 8; there was a break between semesters that occurred between Sessions 10 and 11, resulting

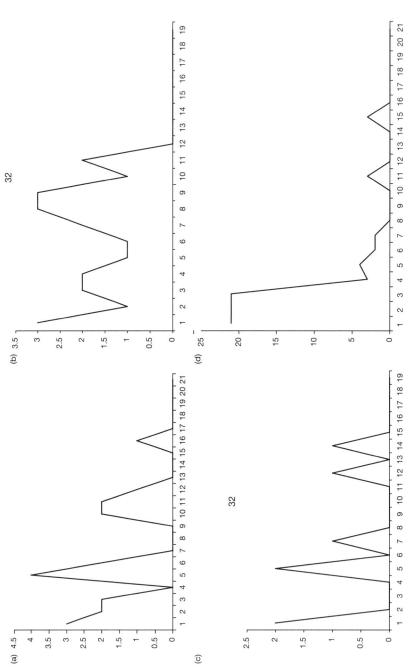

Figures 2.9 a. Doris Data: Impulsive/Aggressive Themes. *A count of the number of impulsive/aggressive themes for Doris per session is displayed.* **b. Doris Data: Negative Experiences.** *The number of negative experiences reported by Doris in a session is shown.* **c. Doris Data: Depression/Anxiety.** *The rating of depression/anxiety levels as indicated by a psychiatrist's notes is displayed.* **d. Doris Data: Marijuana Use.** *The number of times during the previous week that Doris had smoked marijuana is shown.*

in a month between sessions and, presumably, time to reflect on therapy content; and Doris suffered a death in her family before Session 13. Hoffman and Meier (2001) hypothesized that these events were critical incidents because they helped Doris gain a more realistic perspective about the limits of what she could control in the world. She began to relax and accept the people and circumstances around her and, importantly, to avoid being "triggered" by external events. At her final two to three sessions, PMOA data indicated that Doris had stabilized at low problem levels and was ready to terminate.

SUPERVISION INCORPORATING PROGRESS MONITORING DATA WITH AN AVOIDANT CLIENT

Clinical **supervision** refers to the process of oversight of a counselor trainee's work. Despite all of the considerable applied, research, and theoretical effort focused on supervision, little evidence exists to demonstrate that traditional supervision improves client outcomes (Sapyta, Riemer, & Bickman, 2005). Given that only about 30% of contemporary clinicians use PMOA measures (Hatfield & Ogles, 2004), one plausible explanation is that the feedback about client progress employed in most supervision is based primarily on the supervisees' subjective impressions about progress. Sapyta et al. (2005) noted that clinicians typically get little direct feedback about their work, particularly in training: "Therapists are trained, are supervised, and practice in the absence of information about client treatment response from objective sources" (p. 147). Thus, it is not surprising when research documents instances when practicing clinicians fail to accurately gauge clients' responses to counseling and psychotherapy (Gray & Lambert, 2001).

A supervisor's perspective on PMOA data can also provide supervisees with a more objective reaction to the data. As noted earlier, research indicates that the clients of trainees improve at slower rates and with higher occurrences of premature termination (Callahan et al., 2009). Supervisees may understandably view negative trends in client data as critical of their work; supervisors may more reasonably suggest that such data are feedback indicating that the case conceptualization and therapy approach be re-examined (Mash & Hunsley, 1993; Meier, 2003). Mash and Hunsley (1993) suggested that once failure to improve is evident, therapists should examine such factors as the quality of the working alliance, the degree to which the treatment was faithfully implemented, and the client's motivation, problems with affect, and verbal communication skills; these are essentially alternative conceptualizations to be considered. Signs of treatment failure appear particularly important to recognize because research suggests that many clinicians assume that if they implement generally accepted approaches, success must follow (Kendall, Kipnis, & Otto-Salaj, 1992). Even with **empirically supported treatments** (ESTs), therapists do not know if they will be successful with any particular client (Lambert, 2012; Streiner, 1998). Finally, supervisors who know the psychotherapy research literature may also help supervisees place

PMOA data in context by acknowledging the limits of any measurement device and the usefulness of obtaining additional information, from other methods or sources, when making important clinical decisions.

Table 2.6 displays a **persistence table** constructed by a supervisor as a result of audiotapes and supervisee reports of client behaviors. Clients tend to continue to discuss problems when those problems remain relevant for them; narrative therapists observe that clients present with a "problem-saturated description of life" (White & Epston, 1990, p. 45). Once resolved, however, clients stop talking about those problems. With this principle in mind, persistence tables track the topics that a client discusses across sessions.

Arry was a lesbian college student struggling with her family's rejection of her sexual identity; her parents dismissed Arry's preference for women as "a phase." She experienced this loss of family support as "overwhelming" and frequently avoided discussing this situation or her feelings. As shown in Table 2.6, the topic of her family's rejection of her lesbianism, along with avoidance behaviors, appears in all six initial sessions. Arry maintained intense NA throughout this set of sessions, suggesting that she was struggling greatly with her family's rejection and that avoidance of awareness of her feelings was a major method of coping (Lazarus & Folkman, 1984). A persistence table employed in supervision can also note themes related to the counselor's behavior; for example, Arry was also very funny and her jokes could distract the counselor trainee from staying with Arry's pain.

Viewing this table, one could reach the reasonable conclusion that although the sessions with Arry may have laid the foundation for future work, the client did not resolve her problems. The presenting problem(s) remained a key focus of the therapeutic conversation, and reports of avoidance also persisted across sessions. When clients evidence a range of avoidant behaviors, the therapist must make difficult judgments about how and how much to help these clients retain their focus on their painful issues; experienced supervisors can be particularly helpful for trainees learning to deal with client avoidance. Part of what may be happening with Arry is that in an academic setting, the end of the school year may result in an artificial stop to therapeutic work. Such clients may need more time to build a working alliance where they can safely express and experience painful feelings and situations.

What is useful from a supervisory standpoint about persistence tables is the picture they present about the consistency of the major client themes. Clearly, family issues should be the major focus of the therapeutic conversation and interventions with Arry, and the client's (and, sometimes, therapist's) avoidance

Table 2.6. SUPERVISOR'S PERSISTENCE TABLE FOR
ARRY

Session Number

Themes	1	2	3	4	5	6
Family issues	▦	▦	▦	▦	▦	▦
Avoidance	▦	▦	▦	▦	▦	▦

of such should be a major focus of the therapist's strategy. This table would also benefit from the addition of a few alternative themes that could be examined should the focus on family issues turn out to be misleading or unhelpful. Chapter 7 presents such a persistence table with more variability.

SUMMARY

Substantial literature exists that documents the limitations of clinical judgment in predicting future events (e.g., actuarial vs. clinical judgment; Meehl, 1954, 1957). In the current clinical context, where PMOA measures are seldom used and clinical judgment is relied on in terms of adjusting and continuing interventions, treatment failure rates can run as high as 50% (Persons & Mikami, 2002). The structured methods of PMOA measures can help to identify cases where treatment failure is possible. As illustrated by the seven case examples in this chapter, data from PMOA measures can provide feedback about a client's progress (or lack thereof) in counseling and psychotherapy. The primary utility of such feedback is to alert the therapist (and supervisor) to the need to adjust therapy.

PMOA scales are intended to tap into change-sensitive psychological states likely to be influenced by psychosocial and pharmacological interventions. Overall, use of scales such as the *BDI, BIMAS,* and *DANA*, as well as idiographic and qualitative PMOA measures, provides an empirical source of information that complements the clinician's judgment about how much and in what direction clients are changing. PMOA data can also help evaluate case conceptualizations, raise questions about the utility of the current treatment plan, and, in supervision, provide information relevant to teaching and improving therapist competencies.

In contrast to a predetermined number of sessions (e.g., 10 in college counseling centers) or utilization reviews (which may have the implicit purpose of limiting sessions), the use of PMOA measures enables the type and length of therapy to be tailored to the needs of the individual client. Thus, PMOA measures provide a method of treatment delivery that is more efficient than a one-size-fits-all allotment; such an approach is more likely to prevent premature termination (on the part of both client and therapist) and to minimize repeated treatment periods. And while the mental health field has generally embraced ESTs as the basis for treatment decisions, individual clients' varying responses to any type of intervention, including ESTs, means that clinicians cannot assume that even research-based treatments will be effective. Thus, PMOA measures are a logical and necessary component of interventions, particularly when clients do not improve or worsen when receiving an intervention.

The PMOA scales described in this chapter are representative of currently available measures and consequently also reflect current problems and unresolved issues. As described in subsequent chapters, PMOA data can vary by the source of information (e.g., clinician, self, teacher, parent, significant other); different techniques employed to analyze change in PMOA data (e.g., RCI, ES, time series) can sometimes lead to different conclusions about the amount of change; and the content of PMOA scales varies greatly, with little consensus about what is central to gauging client progress and outcome. On the basis of PMOA data alone, therapists typically cannot rule out all of the plausible explanations for trends in those data for any particular client. Progress notes and other material may inform explanations of those trends, but clinicians must ultimately act on the basis of the best available information in complex interpersonal situations with considerable uncertainty.

Exercise 1 *Identifying a Client's Negative Affect*

Below is a dialogue between therapist and patient (Alexander Street Press, 2009). Using this dialogue, search for *negative affect states* expressed by the client. Write what you find on the line below, and see answers in the appendix.

1. _____   2. _____

3. _____   4. _____

COUNSELOR: And how are you feeling about being in session and talking about the stuff you've been talking [about].... How are you feeling about how things are going here?

PATIENT: I think it...I mean I feel good. When I came in, I was feeling really hopeless about my relationship and feeling like I was doing everything wrong and here I think we've been able to identify what are the causes of the things that are making me upset. Maybe not necessarily as much what role I play in it, but at least targeting the incidences and why I'm feeling the way I'm feeling [and] instead of just feeling like nothing's working, I can say, "Well I feel upset because these things are happening." And it kind of helps me put a handle on it. I think I've seen myself become a little bit more assertive with him and stop...you know, if he says something to me, stop overreacting and assuming...like if he says something to me and it's very curt, I wouldn't (ph) generally start arguing back and been a little bit better about sitting back and thinking about how I'm feeling and expressing how I'm feeling. At least I can say what's on my mind. [0:06:38]

COUNSELOR: What would happen if you said you don't know?

PATIENT: Well he's telling me that it's okay with him if I'm just saying, "I don't know," or "No, I didn't do this." Most of the time, I think he would be frustrated that I didn't...what was it...I had to get a credit card from Lowe's because [we're going to get some of our] (ph) things on there, you know, the no finance charges whatever. I didn't do it, and he asked me and I was like, "Well, I was going to do it but blah-blah-blah-blah." And he's like, "You could have just said you didn't do it and left it at that." He was like, "I don't need a whole story about why it wasn't done."

COUNSELOR: So when you talk about this, do you have any sense of what it is for you, like what is it that happens for you that you feel kind of this need to say, "Yes I did do it" even though you haven't done it? [0:08:03]

PATIENT: I haven't but I do that at work too. If my boss says, "Well what about this?" and I'll come up with an answer and generally (inaudible) while I'm talking, I'll remember what's going on, but I don't think I need to do that and I don't know why.... It's almost like being like panicked, you know, like, whatever. I say it and then I'm like... [well at least I'm making like] (ph) that's kind of tough.

Exercise 2 *Using Qualitative Data for Clinical Feedback*

Watch a brief student role-play of "Jeremy," http://www.youtube.com/watch?v=7O45nSwxDJ8&feature=fvw, a social phobic (play 2:49 to about 8:00). As you watch, please complete these tasks:

1. Create a table listing what you see as the major themes discussed in the session. Once your list is created, interpret your themes in terms of a theoretical orientation.
2. Using the list of themes from the table and your theoretical interpretation of it, what feedback and suggestions could a supervisor provide the student therapist?

See the appendix for notes.

Literature Review

INTRODUCTION

This chapter provides a review of the major substantive and methodological literature relevant to progress monitoring and outcome assessment (PMOA). The first section summarizes research about the general efficacy of counseling and psychotherapy, with an emphasis on feedback-enhanced therapies, treatment failure, and the role of avoidance in treatment failure. Problems with traditional outcome measures are described as part of a section on how change-sensitive tests should be constructed and evaluated. The chapter concludes with literature relevant to errors applicable to a clinical rating scale.

Understanding this material provides the reader with a basis for deciding how best to select, use, and interpret scores on PMOA measures. Particularly important is understanding the problems and limitations involved with the use of the resulting data. For reasons explained later, PMOA test users need to employ caution in the interpretation and decision-making process with clients.

MONITORING CLIENT PROGRESS AND DETECTING TREATMENT FAILURE

Decades of research support several key findings about the **efficacy** of counseling and psychotherapy (Smith & Glass, 1977), including the following:

1. Most clients improve as a result of counseling and psychotherapy.
2. The level of this improvement exceeds that seen in control groups.
3. The strength of the therapeutic alliance is associated with improvement.
4. When examined in large clinical samples, gains across counseling approaches appear to be roughly equivalent (Kazdin, 2000; Smith & Glass, 1977).
5. Poorer outcomes are associated with more severe client problems and greater client **resistance** (Norcross, 2004).

Contemporary therapists also have the benefit of access to many empirically supported treatments (ESTs) that enjoy research support for particular approaches to specific mental health diagnoses and problems. Even with ESTs that demonstrate beneficial effects on average for a clinical category, however, some individuals will evidence no change and some will worsen. *This finding of individual differences in therapeutic benefits is the most critical result of psychotherapy research.* In actual practice, clinicians have no method for ascertaining whether a particular client will improve, remain unchanged, or worsen during the course of the prescribed EST. Consequently, it makes sense to track clients' progress over time in case clients worsen or fail to improve so that treatment can be adjusted as needed.

Feedback-Enhanced Therapies

Measures for monitoring progress and eventual outcomes, consequently, seem like a logical complement to therapy, even when implementing ESTs. In feedback-enhanced therapies (FETs), data from ongoing measurement of clinical progress provide feedback about the client's improvement, stability, or worsening during therapy. Progress monitoring data then become an integral part of the clinical decision-making process regarding whether to continue or alter therapeutic procedures. Ideally, the psychotherapy theory underlying treatment, as operationalized in a case conceptualization, would provide guidance about the choice of progress monitoring measure(s) as well as interpretation of client scores.

Evidence has been accumulating for decades regarding the effectiveness of FETs (Beutler & Harwood, 2000; Meier, 2008; Persons, 1989). Based on **Direct Observational Coding** (DOC) procedures, for example, Paul, Mariotto, and Redfield (1986) described a comprehensive assessment system, based on behavior therapy and behavioral assessment principles, designed to produce clinical and administrative data in residential treatment facilities (Meier, 2008). DOC procedures are based on the principle that the recording of the presence or absence of a behavior (e.g., "the client cried in session") enhances validity estimates. Using trained observers, the validity and relevance of behavioral observations can be maximized using multiple, discrete, and scheduled observations made as soon as possible following a behavioral event. Because DOC procedures require explicit sampling of individuals and occasions by trained observers, Paul's approach in inpatient facilities employs staff whose major function is to move about the facility and assess targeted behaviors.

Paul's work with data collection and feedback systems demonstrated that clinical information can be useful for adjusting therapy as well as for other purposes such as **effectiveness research** (i.e., outcome research in applied settings) and documenting the effects of staff training. Implemented with more than 600 clinical staff in 36 different treatment programs (Licht, Paul, & Power, 1986), DOC data systems have produced evidence of substantial differences in the behavior of different clinical staff and treatment programs. Staff–client interactions in studied agencies, for example, ranged from 43 to 459 interactions per hour; DOC data also demonstrated changes in staff behavior resulting from training procedures and the maintenance of such behavior. How staff interact with and intervene with clients was highly correlated with client functioning and improvement (correlations ranged from .5 to .9 on different variables; Licht et al., 1986). Research also indicated that the quality of staff–client interaction had more effect than the quantity of that interaction. Licht et al. (1986) emphasized that DOC information may be important both in the monitoring of treatment implementation and as feedback to adapt treatment to improve effectiveness.

More recently, Lambert et al. (2001) examined the effect of providing progress monitoring data to therapists working with college counseling clients who were evidencing improvement and those who were not. Clients completed the *Outcome Questionnaire-45* (*OQ45*) weekly. Therapists received progress reports to indicate which clients had an adequate rate of change, had an inadequate rate of change, or were failing to make any progress. Lambert et al. found that *OQ* scores at termination were higher for clients who were initially not making progress but whose therapist was receiving feedback compared to clients who were not making progress and whose therapist received no feedback. In contrast, clients who were not progressing and whose therapist received no feedback worsened over time.

Summarizing the results of four studies that evaluated the effects of clinical feedback with over 2,500 cases, Lambert, Harmon, Slade, Whipple, and Hawkins (2005) found that a feedback system enhances outcomes for patients with a negative response to intervention. For clients not making improvement at the beginning of therapy, those whose therapists received feedback about progress showed less deterioration and more improvement over time than clients with therapists not receiving feedback. More specifically, in these studies, 21% of clients who were not making progress continued to deteriorate when their therapist was not given feedback; in contrast, only 13% of clients deteriorated among those who were not making progress but whose therapist received feedback about that lack of progress. Twenty-one percent of clients improved who were not making progress and whose therapist was not given feedback, compared to 35% who were not making progress and whose therapist was given feedback. Lambert et al. (2005) concluded, "We recommend widespread application of feedback systems in routine care" (p. 171).

Other research groups have found similar positive results with clinician feedback systems (Brown & Jones, 2005; Miller, Duncan, Sorrell, & Brown, 2005; Reese et al., 2009). Miller et al. (2005) employed an outcome management system using a four-item outcome measure (*Outcome Rating Scale; ORS*) and a four-item therapeutic alliance scale (*Session Rating Scale; SRS*), both completed by the client. Providing outcome and alliance information to the clinician increased success rates (Miller et al., 2005). Individuals who completed the therapeutic alliance scale at intake were also more likely to evidence improvement than those who did not (Miller et al., 2005). Recent meta-analyses also confirm the positive effects on outcome of providing clinicians with feedback about progress (Boswell, Kraus, Miller, & Lambert, 2013; Carlier et al., 2012; Goodman, McKay, & DePhilippis, 2013; Knaup, Koesters, Schoefer, Becker, & Puschner, 2009; Poston & Hanson, 2010).

Treatment Failure

The need for progress monitoring appears even stronger when considering rates of estimated treatment failure. In the research and theoretical literature, the concept of treatment failure includes a lack of improvement despite sufficient dosage of therapy, clients dropping out of therapy after a few sessions, and harmful effects resulting from participation in psychotherapy (Barlow, 2010). Estimates of treatment failure and harmful effects vary widely: Persons and Mikami (2002), for example, indicated that treatment failures ranged between 10% and 50% of all clients.

Many therapists, however, appear to take treatment failure seriously only when it reaches the level of potential suicidal or homicidal behavior (Meier, 2008). Measurement issues may contribute to this situation: Historically, few systematic methods have been available for identifying clients' lack of progress or preventing treatment failure (Meier, 1994). Thus, a test score reflecting data relevant to identifying clients who are not making progress or are at higher risk of harmful effects would be very useful for clinical practice and research. Altering treatment depends on clinicians' ability to detect client deterioration as it occurs (Hatfield, McCullough, Frantz, & Krieger, 2010). Clinical judgment by itself may be insufficient: Stewart and Chambless (2008) found that therapists in private practice needed a median of 12 sessions before deciding that the provided intervention was not working. Hatfield et al. (2010) examined therapists' ability to recognize deterioration in university counseling center clients (as evidenced by repeated measurement of the OQ45). Therapists' progress notes mentioned deterioration in only 21% of the 70 cases where OQ scores declined by 14 points and in only 32% of the 41 cases where OQ scores declined by 30 points.

Why would therapists continue to implement the same treatment with clients who are failing to improve? Without structured feedback, clinicians appear to believe that continuing generally accepted procedures will eventually lead to positive change (Kendall, Kipnis, & Otto-Salaj, 1992). Kendall et al. (1992) surveyed 315 psychotherapists to investigate their levels of treatment failure and their explanations for such failure. Results indicated that (a) about 11% of each clinician's clients were not making progress; (b) most therapists who planned to continue treating failing clients had no alternative treatment plans; (c) clinicians' theoretical orientations influenced their judgments about lack of progress (i.e., psychodynamic therapists averaged 14 months before reaching this conclusion, while cognitive-behavioral therapists averaged 6 months); (d) most clinicians failed to cite severity of client problems as a reason for failure; and (e) in contrast to previous research, therapists rated clients' "inability to benefit from therapy" (p. 275) as the most important reason for their lack of progress, with these therapists rating themselves as the least likely cause.

Other reasons may also account for therapists' relative inattention to treatment failure. Defining treatment failure may partially depend on the therapeutic approach used to interpret therapeutic events (Mash & Hunsley, 1993); an initial increase in symptoms, for example, may be seen as indicative of progress in psychodynamic, paradoxical, behavioral, and other approaches (cf. Mergenthaler, 1996). Kendall et al. (1992) noted that the literature on treatment failure is relatively sparse; few guidelines exist about what to do when clients fail to make progress. Because objective criteria for defining progress or failure are often lacking, ascertaining the amount of change will depend on the source's perspective (i.e., therapist, client, significant other; Kendall et al., 1992). Kendall et al. (1992) concluded that a pressing need exists for therapists to consider alternative strategies when dealing with clients not making therapeutic progress.

Avoidance and Treatment Failure

Assessing a construct theoretically relevant to progress in psychotherapy should provide information about how to alter therapy when the need arises. Although in the psychotherapy literature clinicians and researchers employ a variety of related terms, client avoidance refers to efforts (often unconscious) to avoid experiencing particular affect, cognition, behaviors, or situations. Similarly, Acceptance and Commitment Therapy describes experiential avoidance as an inability or unwillingness to process inner experiences such as negative emotions and thoughts (Bardeen, Fergus, & Olcutt, 2013; Hayes, Wilson, Gifford, Follette, & Strosahl, 1996). Table 3.1 presents examples of client statements indicative of such behaviors. Clients, for example, may be openly hostile toward their therapist, may have difficulty talking about a particular topic (even bringing up the topic only at the end of sessions), or may avoid **emotional experiencing** in depth by talking rapidly or being verbose. Individuals who have experienced stressful and traumatic events may employ self-defensive strategies in an effort to cope with intrusive memories and their associated intense negative affect (NA). Discussing current research on intrusive thoughts and memories, Berntsen (2010) wrote:

> Any distinctive and highly emotional event will be extraordinarily well encoded and consolidated in memory. This will enhance its accessibility relative to other memories and thus increase the likelihood that it comes to mind involuntarily. (p. 141)

A key issue regarding avoidance of NA is the choice of method(s) individuals employ to cope. Methods that involve avoiding or incomplete processing of

NA appear to often have the paradoxical effect of maintaining or even increasing affective states such as depression and anxiety (Moses & Barlow, 2006). Cognitive-behavioral theories indicate that anxiety increases when individuals employ avoidant response strategies (Zvolensky & Otto, 2007); Kashdan and Breen (2007) observed that excessive social anxiety is related to individuals' "chronic, rigid tendencies to manage and conceal emotional experiences and

Table 3.1. EXAMPLES OF CLIENT AVOIDANCE

HOSTILE CLIENT

Counselor: Your progress has plateaued. Does that disappoint you?

Client: I'm ambivalent. In fact, that's my new favorite word.

Counselor: Do you know what that word means, ambivalence?

Client: I don't care.

Counselor: If it's your favorite word, I would've thought you –

Client: It means, "I don't care." That's what it means.

Counselor: On the contrary, Susanna. Ambivalence suggests strong feelings, in opposition. The prefix, as in "ambidextrous," means "both"; the rest of it, in Latin, means "vigor." The word suggests that you are torn, between two opposing courses of action.

Client: Will I stay or will I go?

Counselor: Am I sane…or am I crazy?

Client: Those aren't courses of action.

Counselor: They can be, dear, for some.

Client: Well then…it's the wrong word.

Counselor: No. I think it's perfect. "Quis hic locus, quae regio, quae mundi plaga? What world is this, what kingdom, what shores of what worlds?" It's a very big question you're faced with, Susanna. The choice of your life. How much will you indulge in your flaws? What are your flaws? Are they flaws? If you embrace them, will you commit yourself to hospital for life? Big questions, big decisions. Not surprising that you'd profess carelessness about them.

Client: Is that it?

Counselor: For now.

VERBOSE CLIENT

Patient: He called me and he's like, "What's wrong? You sound horrible." And I'm like, "I am. I really feel shitty today. I really feel lousy." And he's like, "Why?" And I was like, "It's just a lot of reasons." And he's like, "Because of me?" And I said, "Some of it." He said, "Do you want to break up?" I said, "No. Do you?" He said, "No." I said, "There's some things I need to talk to you about and I just am not happy anymore," I'm not happy with him. So he got really scared and he just…. Some of the reasons I told him, you know, "You really have to start being more supportive and understanding of my feelings." I said, "I've been here for three years, and no matter what, even if I don't understand the way you feel, I'm still supportive of you, and you, you don't give that back to me and I need that back." And, you know, he understood that.

(continued)

Table 3.1. (Continued)

And I talked to him about not really respecting my feelings, and he understood that too. But then later, like the next night when we had dinner, he—and I mean and he thought about it, for I didn't see him that night. And he called me and he's like, "I understand what you said and I love you and I—you know, you're right," and blah, blah, blah. Then the next night, when we talked about it more and I started to talk to him about my insecurities, and he's got this huge thing with people blaming him. He's like, "Not me, it's you." Because he thinks everybody's trying to blame him and point the finger at him, which I'm not. I'm just saying this is the way I feel and you have to understand it, you know, because he does. Because anybody who's going to deal with me has to understand the way I feel or accept the way I feel; they don't have a choice, just like I don't have a choice about anybody else's feelings. I can't control anybody else's feelings. So we kind of—he got all mad, I don't know, and then he started saying all this stuff that I love you and I don't know why, you know…so that I'm just confused. I'm not sure where my feelings are coming from, if it's just my nature to feel that way and he triggers them, which some people will and some people won't, and that's okay, you know, and acceptable.

NOTE: Sources: *Verbose Client* (Alexander Street Press, 2009) and *Hostile Client* (Mangold, 1999).

the situations that elicit them" (p. 2). Meta-analyses by Abramowitz, Tolin, and Street (2001) and Wenzlaff and Wegner (2000) also found that individuals' effort to suppress unwanted thoughts produced a **rebound effect** whereby individuals experience a larger number of such thoughts. Hayes et al. (1996) suggested that diverse problem behaviors share a common experiential avoidance function.

Shedler, Mayman, and Manis (1993) proposed that people who deny and repress personal psychological distress be labeled **defensive deniers**. These individuals can be identified through clinical interviews and their defensiveness would be associated with autonomic reactivity. In a series of studies, Shedler et al. (1993) instructed research participants to complete the *Beck Depression Inventory* (*BDI*), the *Eysenck Neuroticism* scale, and a written version of the *Early Memory Test* (*EMT*). On the *EMT*, participants provided reports of their earliest childhood memories as well as their impressions of themselves, other people, and the mood in the memory; an experienced clinician evaluated this material to determine each subject's mental health or distress. The experimenters also exposed subjects to laboratory stressors and recorded their changes in heart rate and blood pressure. Shedler et al. identified one group who reported themselves as distressed on the **self-report** scales and who were also rated as distressed by the clinician. However, another group who self-reported positive mental health were rated as distressed by the clinician; this second group of defensive deniers demonstrated greater reactivity on the physiological measures. Most important, Shedler et al. maintained that clinical interviewers could detect these deniers, whereas self-reports could not.

Campbell-Sills and Barlow (2007) maintained that individuals differ in their strategies for regulating emotion and that maladaptive choices can exacerbate anxiety and mood disorders. Similarly, McLaughlin, Borkovec, and Sibrava (2007) suggested that "both rumination about past events and worry about potential future events may…play a causal role in the creation of depressed and anxious affect" (p. 24). **Depressive rumination** (Nolen-Hoekseman, 1991), for example, refers to repetitive thoughts that focus on depressive symptoms and their implications; rumination has been found to be related to the development of depression and to increase the length of depressive episodes and intensity of depressive moods (McLaughlin et al., 2007). If NA essentially provides feedback about discrepancies between current and desired status, then worry and rumination are likely to be natural cognitive processes individuals employ to solve problems and achieve goals (cf. Martin & Tesser, 1996; McLaughlin et al., 2007). In fact, research indicates that (a) rumination occurs after feedback in laboratory studies and can enhance NA in depressed individuals but prevent it in nondepressed persons (Lyubomirsky & Nolen-Hoeksema, 1995; McIntosh & Martin, 1992; Nolen-Hoeksema & Morrow, 1993) and (b) rumination was equally associated with anxiety and depression in a student sample but more strongly associated with depression in a clinical sample (McLaughlin et al., 2007; Segerstrom, Tsao, Alden, & Craske, 2000).

Suppression, efforts to hide one's feelings from oneself and/or others, has been associated with increased physiological arousal and impaired memory performance (Campbell-Sills & Barlow, 2007; Moses & Barlow, 2006). Campbell-Sills and Barlow (2007) observed that thought suppression and obsessive-compulsive disorder (OCD) are strongly associated and that research indicates that thought suppression often leads to a rebound in unwanted thoughts. Campbell-Sills and Barlow (2007) maintain these avoidance behaviors are (a) most prevalent in individuals with panic and phobic problems who seek to avoid the experience of fear and (b) associated with increases in NA such as frustration and depression as individuals lose the positive experiences of their social relationships.

KEY CRITERIA FOR PROGRESS MONITORING AND OUTCOME ASSESSMENT MEASURES

Research over the past two decades has established that psychological tests differ in their ability to detect client change and provide PMOA feedback (Cronbach et al., 1980; Tryon, 1991). A second major concern is the content of PMOA measures: What should be measured with any particular client or therapy? Third, given the frequency with which avoidance and other self-report problems influence measurement, a PMOA measure that can provide data relevant to such domains would be useful. Fourth, a substantial body of research documents how clinicians can error during the process of providing clinically relevant data.

Change Sensitivity

Modern efforts in psychological testing essentially began after Binet and colleagues successfully developed intelligence tests in response to the French government's need for procedures to identify children with mental retardation (Meier, 2008). Binet's tests became the prototype for all psychological tests and established a paradigm that focused on the identification of individual differences in latent traits for the purposes of selection (Dawis, 1992; Meier, 2008). For example, in the early 1900s, Parsons (1909) believed that students required systematic help in choosing a vocation; he employed a matching model in which vocational requirements were matched against individuals' vocational traits to help produce the best vocational choices. Subsequent self-report surveys such as the Strong Vocational Interest Blank (Strong, 1943) included items and scales that focused on individual differences in factors measuring vocational traits of interest. Test scores were then employed to help individuals self-select potential vocations and occupations.

Although often implicit, the **trait selection approach** to measurement became the standard paradigm for psychological testing (Meier, 2008). Psychological tests were designed to be (a) measures of psychological traits believed to be present in all individuals, (b) as brief as possible, (c) administered to large groups, and (d) evaluated primarily by their ability to predict future criteria (often related to school or work performance). However, several of these criteria differ significantly from what contemporary experts recognize as needed for measurement of constructs that exhibit change over time. Collins (1991) concluded:

> Little in traditional measurement theory is of any help to those who desire an instrument that is sensitive to intraindividual differences. In fact, applying traditional methods to the development of a measure of a dynamic latent variable amounts to applying a set of largely irrelevant criteria. (pp. 138–139)

Similarly, Hill and Lambert (2004) observed that "most outcome measures have not been developed with an eye toward choosing items that are sensitive to change, and little is known about this aspect of test validity" (p. 117).

Yet most attempts to assess progress and outcomes in counseling and psychotherapy typically have involved traditional psychological tests such as the *BDI* or *Minnesota Multiphasic Personality Inventory* (*MMPI*) that were initially designed for screening and diagnosis (Froyd, Lambert, & Froyd, 1996). Ideally, the use of tests in counseling and psychotherapy should contribute to improved outcomes, particularly with individual clients. Early research on the **treatment utility** of measurement (Hayes, Nelson, & Jarrett, 1987) concluded that the use of traditional tests has little impact on treatment outcome (but see Finn, Fischer, & Handler, 2012, for a different approach). A likely explanation is that items on traditional tests are largely insensitive to detecting the amount and types of change that occur in counseling and psychotherapy: While the sum of items on any measure will likely reflect some degree of change resulting from psychosocial interventions, test scores will differ to the extent that they contain such change-sensitive items.

Kirshner and Guyatt (1985) observed that "in clinical practice, the introduction of new tests or measures often occurs without scientists feeling the need, when assessing an instrument's usefulness, to focus on the specific purpose of the test" (p. 28). Selecting a test without considering the specific purpose for which that test was developed may be problematic. The degree of apparent change resulting from counseling and psychotherapy, for example, can be significantly influenced by the method of assessment and the specific measure (Lambert, 1994). Thus, therapist and expert judge ratings produce larger effects than self-reports, global ratings produce larger effects than assessments of specific symptoms, measures based on specific targets of therapy produce greater effects than more distal assessments such as personality measures (Auerbach & Kilmann, 1977; Weisz, Weiss, Han, Granger, & Morton, 1995), and data collected soon after therapy ends produce greater effects than data collected at a later followup (Lambert, 1994). Lambert, Hatch, Kingston, and Edwards (1986) evaluated the *Zung Depression Scale, BDI*, and *Hamilton Rating Scale for Depression* for depression and concluded that "rating devices can by themselves produce differences larger than those ordinarily attributed to treatments" (p. 58). The choice of the outcome measure could strongly influence the estimate of the impact of the therapeutic effect, as Lambert (1994) summarized:

> There is a growing body of evidence to suggest that there are reliable differences in the sensitivity of instruments to change. In fact, the difference between measures is not trivial, but large enough to raise questions about the interpretation of research studies.... Meta-analytic results suggest that the most popular dependent measures used to assess depression following treatment provide reliably different pictures of change. (p. 85)

The adaptation and use of trait-focused tests for purposes for which they were not designed means that scores on these tests evidence **imprecision** because their scores include unintended information. Imprecise data resulting from a mismatch of test purpose and test construction procedures typically produces unexpected or surprising results.

Developed on the basis of observations of depressed and nondepressed individuals, the *BDI* (Beck & Steer, 1987) and *BDI-II* (Beck, Steer, & Brown, 1996) items assess a mix of cognitions, somatic responses, and affect related to depression; these include mood, guilt feelings, suicidal wishes, irritability, sleep disturbance, and appetite changes. Considerable psychometric evidence indicates that the *BDI* can function as a reliable and valid measure for the purpose of diagnosing and screening for depression (Segal, Williams, & Teasdale 2002). Scores on the *BDI* have shown high internal consistency, high correlations with other measures of depression, and sensitivity to change resulting from medication and psychotherapeutic interventions (Kendall, Hollon, Beck, Hammen, & Ingram, 1987). Yet research results have raised questions about the validity of the *BDI* when the intended purpose is to measure change. Kendall et al. (1987) found that over 50% of individuals classified as depressed by the *BDI* change depression categories when retested, even when the retesting period consisted of only a few hours or days. Scores on the *BDI* have also been shown to exhibit sudden, unexplained increases and decreases between psychotherapy sessions (Kelly, Roberts, & Ciesla, 2005). One explanation is that the *BDI* is too sensitive to mood and distress (i.e., change sensitivity) to be able to separate and detect smaller effects from psychosocial interventions (i.e., **treatment sensitivity**). These results raise questions about the ability of this major self-report to provide valid data for assessing progress and outcome, particularly over relatively short periods of time.

Research has demonstrated that specific items on psychological tests can be differentially sensitive to change. For example, different item properties relative to psychotherapy change were evident in a study of the *Symptom Checklist* (*SCL-90-R*) completed by psychotherapy outpatients. Kopta, Howard, Lowry, and Beutler (1994) found differences between *SCL-90-R* items displaying sensitivity to change and items selected via traditional approaches. Kopta et al. (1994) found that the items could be grouped differentially on the basis of the amount of change displayed in response to treatment, classifying items into three temporal categories: acute (i.e., quick response to treatment), chronic distress (moderate response rate), and characterological (slow response rate). The items grouped in these three categories did not correspond to the single category found in factor analyses of the *SCL-90-R* conducted at a single time point (e.g., Cyr, McKenna-Foley, & Peacock, 1985) or to the nine symptom dimensions reported by Derogatis (1983; Kopta et al., 1994). Instead, these different item changes can be considered **phase/time effects**; that is, the items were sensitive to change at different phases or times of psychotherapy. Similarly, the three scales of the *OQ45*—symptom reduction, interpersonal functioning, and social role functioning—may show change at different phases of the therapeutic process.

Psychotherapy researchers also discuss change in terms of **short-term, intermediate,** and **long-term outcomes** (cf. Meier, 2003). This suggests that constructs relevant to measuring change may be variable over short-term to long-term periods or sensitive to change during specific intervals (e.g., first three sessions). Mash and Hunsley (1993), for example, indicated that treatment failure may become evident in as little as three sessions, so a short-term indicator of such would be highly valued in clinical settings. Research also demonstrates that persons completing psychotherapy evidence differential rates of change over time on different items within the same syndrome (Kopta et al., 1994). Howard's **phase model** proposes that the expected direction of therapeutic movement across sessions is *remoralization* (i.e., removal of distress), followed by *symptom reduction,* and then *improved life functioning* (Howard, Moras, Brill, Martinovich, & Lutz, 1996).

Finally, **intervention characteristics** influence the capacity of a measure to detect change resulting from an intervention. Essentially, psychotherapy must produce some degree of change in clients for a measure to be able to detect it. The type of intervention (particularly as matched with a particular problem or diagnosis), the duration and dosage of the provided intervention, and the frequency (e.g., daily, weekly, monthly) can all influence the strength of client change. Interventions that produce weak change are inappropriate for testing new measures because there may be little or no change to detect (cf. Meier, McDougal, & Bardos, 2008). In contrast, interventions that produce large effects (e.g., targeted at particular problems in homogeneous client groups who know what should change) may result in the selection of a subset of items that cannot detect change when employed with interventions and clients with different characteristics.

In summary, the key criterion for evaluating PMOA measures is change sensitivity. As Vermeersch et al. (2004, p. 38) observed:

> *Sensitivity to change* refers to the degree to which an instrument accurately reflects client changes that occur following participation in therapy. . . . Therefore, the sensitivity to change of a measure is directly related to the construct validity of the instrument, because the primary purpose of outcome measures is to document client changes following a course of therapy.

Although the field currently has no standard with which to assess the accuracy of change, we can make reasonable inferences about whether change has occurred. Evidence that observed change results specifically from a therapeutic intervention, however, can be difficult to obtain.

Content Validity

Content validity refers to the extent to which a test measures the important domain(s) of a construct; a test should be evaluated on the extent to which it taps into a construct's important characteristics. The problem of content validity lies at the heart of the difficulties of designing a measure for assessment of psychotherapeutic progress and outcome. Urban and Ford (1971) observed that although hundreds of outcome measures have been developed, the most difficult problem has been "determining what to measure and in which instance it is appropriate to do so" (p. 21). Despite the field's increasingly impressive and sophisticated psychometric and statistical methods, the basic problem still remains *what* should be measured to detect the effects of counseling and psychotherapy.

Theory and research findings are typically important sources of information about a test construct's key content and domains. Tests with items based on theory and research often generalize better across samples and interventions;

items selected for such tests are less likely to result from random error. For tests of constructs thought to be amenable to influence from psychosocial interventions, theories describing how particular interventions lead to specific outcomes ideally would provide the basis for item selection and evaluation of progress and outcome measures (Meier, 1997). Unfortunately, the state of psychotherapy theory and related research often does not provide specific linkages, but only general conclusions about the beneficial effects of psychotherapy or the ability of a particular therapy to produce more beneficial effects than control groups (Hawkins & Meier, 2012). The result is that hundreds of therapeutic approaches exist (Kazdin, 1994; Perez, 1999), as well as thousands of psychological tests potentially relevant to the psychotherapy process and outcome, but with little linkage between the two. As Faust (1986, p. 423) described this situation:

> There is a universe of potentially available information about patients. One must decide what information is most relevant, how to obtain it, how to integrate what is obtained, and how to relate it to what are often nebulous and ill-defined categories.

Determining the content validity of a measure designed to assess progress and outcome in psychotherapy is further complicated by factors inherent in the psychotherapy process. Persons (1991) noted that "the most demanding clinical task of any therapist is to choose a problem and an attack on that problem that will be helpful to that particular patient for that particular problem at that particular moment" (p. 101). Thus, it is not uncommon for different therapists (e.g., the intake counselor vs. the providing counselor) to focus on different problems (i.e., content) with the same client. Relatedly, Beutler and Hamblin (1986) employed the term **persistent relevance** to refer to whether clients' key problems at the beginning of therapy remain the chief issues throughout the course of therapy. Many clients shift their focus over time in terms of what they present as their key problem(s), and the choice of an outcome measure that focuses on a particular issue prominent at intake may be problematic if the client later shifts focus to a different issue. Many clients also present with what they consider more common problems (e.g., trouble studying) and then at some later point self-disclose to their therapist their more central or sensitive issue (e.g., sexual orientation). In this context, what is needed is test content that remains relevant across time, problem domains, different individuals, and treatment types.

Data Collection Frequency and Source

Traditional psychological testing typically involves a single administration of a lengthy measure. With progress monitoring, measures are administered frequently, as often as once a week or more. Outcome measures are given at least twice, at the beginning and end of therapy; typically outcome measures are completed with a considerable time period between administrations, which makes it more difficult for respondents to remember their initial responses. Repeated administration of any psychotherapy-related self-report measure may result in self-monitoring, a reactive method known to change the monitored behavior, typically in the same direction as an intervention (Craske & Tsao, 1999; Nelson, 1977). As discussed further in Chapter 5, self-reports may be too reactive if employed frequently but may be appropriate if spaced over time. The **source** of clinical information may also result in different types of errors; clinical raters may be influenced by error sources such as confirmation bias and range restriction errors (Meier, 2008). Rater errors are also discussed in more detail in Chapter 5.

Brevity

A final practicality is to balance the need for brief tests, completed repeatedly in clinical settings, with a sufficient number of items for adequate psychometric properties. **Brevity** refers to the length of time needed to complete PMOA measures. Tests employed repeatedly in psychotherapy settings must be brief to be useful (Berman, Rosen, Hurt, & Kolarz, 1998). Traditional tests such as the *MMPI*, with its 1.5 hours to complete, are inappropriate for progress monitoring purposes because of their length (Gresham et al., 2010; Vermeersch et al., 2004). Some research suggests that psychotherapists have a 5-minute limit for completing progress and outcome measures (Miller et al., 2005). Even a relatively brief measure such as the *Outcome Questionnaire* and its 45 items may be too lengthy for use with some clinical populations or in some clinical settings. For example, the compliance rate for the *OQ45* in a psychotherapy training clinic was only 25% (Miller, Duncan, Brown, Sparks, & Claud, 2003). On the other hand, very brief measures (e.g., fewer than 10 items) may be too short to be psychometrically sound; in general, reliability estimates increase as the number of items increases.

TEST DEVELOPMENT PROCEDURES FOR PROGRESS MONITORING AND OUTCOME ASSESSMENT MEASURES

The criteria for evaluating PMOA measures, and their associated errors, should inform test construction procedures for PMOA measures so that they provide the best possible data for feedback purposes. Test users are ultimately concerned with interpreting the meaning of test scores, but that interpretation step depends on the methods employed to create, administer, and score the test. This section describes aspects of test construction that should maximize the psychometric properties of any test whose primary purpose is to measure change resulting from psychosocial interventions. Some of the guidelines described here are identical or similar to those employed with traditional tests, whereas others are unique to developing change-sensitive tests. Knowledge of these guidelines and procedures should inform the reader who must choose and use a PMOA measure in clinical practice.

Construct Validity

The central concept in modern test theory, **construct validity**, has two meanings. First, construct validity historically has referred to whether a test measures what it is supposed to measure. If a test developer creates a test intended to measure intelligence, for example, what evidence is there that the test actually measures intelligence? The empirical reality is that test scores never reflect the single construct intended; scores on a test of intelligence, for example, never simply measure the construct of intelligence, but other constructs as well. With any test, multiple factors influence test scores, to a greater or lesser degree, and those factors represent **error** in that they influence test scores in ways unintended by the test developer.

Given this history, the second, contemporary definition of construct validity is simpler and more practical. That is, a test can be said to have construct validity if evidence exists that it can be employed for a particular purpose. To do so, test developers may first review relevant literature to get a sense of the key content domains for test and purpose (e.g., psychotherapy theory for a test of PMOA). They will also evaluate item ceiling and floor effects to assess for sufficient variation in preparation for other analyses such as (a) correlations to estimate convergent and discriminant validity or (b) an evaluation to assess if scales have sufficient range to demonstrate change. Test developers also evaluate the reliability of test items in a manner appropriate to the test purpose (e.g., test–retest for stable traits). Next, test developers evaluate the content, **convergent** (i.e., covariation with another test of a similar construct), and **discriminant validity** (i.e., lack of covariation with another test of a similar construct) of test items and scores. Reliability and validity analyses may also examine the potential influences of error sources (such as rater errors) on test scores.

Content Validity

As Urban and Ford (1971) noted, settling on content for a universal (i.e., nomothetic) PMOA measure has been a very difficult task. This content should evidence change across a wide variety of client problems and intervention types.

One direction suggested by the theoretical and empirical literature regarding the content validity of a nomothetic PMOA measure is NA. As Persons and Fresco (2008) observed, the clinical specialties in psychology and mental health are "beginning to consider and understand the importance of emotional systems in adaptive human functioning and experience" (p. 98). That is because emotions are central to human functioning (Izard, 2007; Persons, 1991); emotions appear to function as signals of an individual's condition within a perceived environment (Campbell-Sills & Barlow, 2007). Feelings inform individuals about their status in an actual or perceived environment, and these signals function as powerful motivators for human activity. Izard (2007, p. 269) proposed that "emotions are the primary motivational system" and that research indicates that emotions influence "perception, cognition, decision making, judgment, and action" (p. 270). Evidence from psychophysical experimental research also indicates that affective intensity is a universal category (Gracely & Naliboff, 1996).

Although some disagreement exists about the number of basic human emotions, most emotion researchers have found the constructs of positive affect (PA) and NA to be useful descriptions of emotion characteristics found across cultures. PA refers to emotions experienced as pleasant states (such as happiness), whereas NA refers to emotions experienced as unpleasant (such as sadness). Tables 3.2 and 3.3 display a partial list of NA terms used in two PMOA measures, the *Depression/Anxiety Negative Affect* scale (*DANA*; Meier, 2012) and the *Behavior Intervention Monitoring Assessment System* (*BIMAS*; McDougal, Bardos, & Meier, 2012). Emotions can also be characterized as either **universal basic emotions**, such as PA and NA, or **emotion schemas**, in which individuals think idiosyncratically about their emotions as well as the situations that elicited those emotions (Izard, 2007). Izard (2007) suggested that in comparison to basic emotions, emotion schemas are greater in frequency and longer in duration. For example, an individual with a fear of flying may, while actually flying on an airplane, occasionally experience the basic emotion of fear. This individual, however, will more frequently feel slightly to moderately anxious while thinking about an upcoming trip that involves flying (i.e., an emotion schema in which anxiety is elicited when thinking about flying).

Two key components of NA are **depression** and **anxiety**. Although a variety of definitions exist for both constructs, depression generally refers to feelings of sadness typically triggered by past events such as a significant loss. In contrast, anxiety is future focused; Bandura (1977), for example, defined anxiety as "a state of anticipatory apprehension over possible deleterious happenings" (p. 137). Carter (2007, p. 28) maintained that "depression and anxiety are the

Table 3.2. LIST OF NEGATIVE AFFECT TERMS ON THE DANA LEVEL 3, MODERATE NEGATIVE AFFECT

__ Embarrassed	__ Worried
__ Pressured	__ Moderately angry
__ Anxious	__ Frustrated
__ Ruminating	__ Moderately sad
__ Scared	__ Agitated
__ Depressed	__ Distressed
__ Vulnerable	

NOTE: *DANA* refers to the *Depression/Anxiety Negative Affect* scale (Meier, 2012).

Table 3.3. NEGATIVE AFFECT TERMS ON THE BIMAS

Sleepy/tired
Depressed
Sad/withdrawn
Embarrassed/ashamed
Anxious/worried/nervous
Thoughts of hurting self
Emotional/easily upset

NOTE: *BIMAS* refers to the *Behavior Intervention Monitoring Assessment System* (McDougal et al., 2012).

most common reactions to stressful life events." Research indicates that depression and anxiety are present with most, if not all, psychological disorders (Crawley, Beidas, Benjamin, Martin, & Kendall, 2007; Hill & Lambert, 2004); for example, researchers have linked depression and anxiety with problems ranging from OCD (Abramowitz, 2002) to kleptomania (McElroy, Hudson, Pope, & Keck, 1991). Hill and Lambert (2004, p. 107) noted that the most widely used instruments for measuring change resulting from counseling and psychotherapy, such as the *BDI, State-Trait Anxiety Inventory* (STAI; Spielberger, Gorsuch, & Lushene, 1970), and *SCL-90-R*, "are popular probably because symptoms of anxiety and depression occur across a wide variety of disorders."

Research literature on psychotherapeutic outcomes also suggests that client improvement in depression and anxiety will be associated with progress in counseling and psychotherapy (Safran & Greenberg, 1989). Meier (2008) reviewed outcome studies conducted by Vermeersch, Lambert, and Burlingame (2000), Weinstock and Meier (2003), and Vermeersch et al. (2004) examining change in a total of 7,344 clients who received services at university counseling centers, an outpatient clinic, private practices, and employee assistance programs. Given this heterogeneous set of clients, presenting problems, counselors, and therapeutic interventions, the counseling and psychotherapy literature indicates that change across problem domains should be roughly equivalent (e.g., Smith & Glass, 1977). Depression- and anxiety-related items, however, evidenced larger effect sizes than items assessing any other domain. Figure 3.1 shows these findings for clients who completed the *OQ45* in the Vermeersch et al. (2000) study.

Although the presence of a therapeutic relationship and the establishment of hope may represent important **common process factors** (Wampold, 2001), these results suggest that depression and anxiety represent **common outcome elements**. That is, some alleviation of depression and anxiety may be present as a ubiquitous effect of all counseling interventions; thus, all interventions may produce improvement on outcome measures that contain depression- and anxiety-related content. Even for clients who present with problems in other domains, decreases in depression and anxiety should be secondary effects resulting from processes that commonly occur in counseling (Grove & Andreasen, 1992; Wells, Sturm, Sherbourne, & Meredith, 1996). These include the establishment of a therapeutic

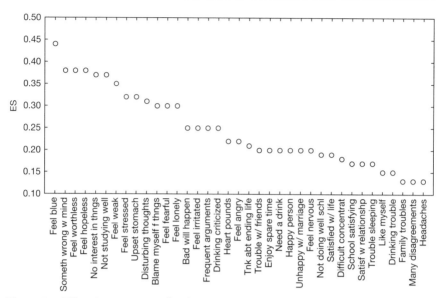

Figure 3.1 Effect Sizes per Item for the *Outcome Questionnaire-45* (OQ45). *This figure displays an effect size (d) for the 37 OQ items that displayed statistically significant differences in slope between treatment and controls as reported by Vermeersch et al. (2000). Abbreviated item wording is reported in the figure.*

relationship, new learning, changes in expectations, and catharsis (Bandura, 1977; Coyne, 1990).

Mergenthaler's (1996) research documents the important role of affect in psychotherapy process and outcome. Studying a single case, as well as samples of improved and not improved clients, Mergenthaler found evidence that client change depended on **therapeutic cycles** that involve shifting between degrees of high and low emotion and high and low abstraction/reflection. Successful therapy, at least for experiential and insight approaches, consists of moving through these four states, roughly sequentially: Relaxing, Experiencing, Connecting, Reflecting, and Relaxing again. Mergenthaler (1996) observed that clients first build emotion (often by discussing an event or symptoms), followed by increased reflection. The key to client change and progress in therapy is one or more Connecting states, where clients reflect on emotional material. Mergenthaler's analyses of clinical data did find that improved clients evidenced a higher proportion of Connecting states and fewer Relaxing states than did clients who did not improve.

The idea of cycling through periods of high and low levels of emotion and cognition certainly fits the psychotherapy experience of many clients. Few, if any, clients evidence linear improvement over the course of therapy. Even in behavioral approaches, clients typically demonstrate some variability in their rate and direction of progress over time. One score on the *DANA* is Highest Intensity Level (HIL), which refers to the highest affective intensity level exhibited or reported by the client in session. Figure 3.2 shows HIL values over sessions with

Figure 3.2 One Client's Cycling Through Affective Intensity Levels Over Eight Sessions. *One interpretation of these scores, using Mergenthaler's (1996) research on successful cases, suggests this client completed one cycle of the emotion-reflection process over the first five sessions of psychotherapy.*

an individual client. The client exhibits the highest intensity level possible (5, *Extreme NA*) in Session 1, followed by Levels 4, 3, 2, and 1 (*Transient NA*) in the subsequent four sessions. As indicated by the high to low NA progression, Mergenthaler's (1996) research on successful cases indicates this client completed one cycle of the emotion-reflection process over these five sessions. The NA levels still remain at a moderate intensity level at Sessions 6, 7, and 8, suggesting that the client still has at least one more cycle to process before the problem focus of these therapy sessions resolves.

In contrast, recall the case of Susan from Chapter 2 who completed the *BDI* over several months. As shown in Figure 3.3, Susan's *BDI* scores evidenced a substantial decline from the start of treatment in October (Session 1) until the following January (Session 2). Those scores, however, remained relatively stable when assessed from February through April (Sessions 3 through 10). These scores indicate that Susan was not cycling through periods of emotion and reflection in therapy. As described previously, her therapist believed that a major reason for the lack of improvement was that Susan avoided awareness of the physical abuse she suffered as a child, leaving her with a deeply ingrained sense of hopelessness and worthlessness.

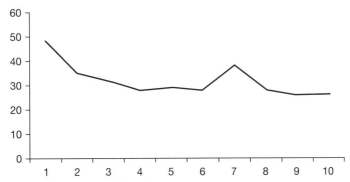

Figure 3.3 Susan's *Beck Depression Inventory* **Scores Across Therapy Sessions.** *The client's score evidences a large drop from Sessions 1 to 2 but stability in the subsequent sessions. Note that this is the same graphic as Figure 2.7.*

Change Sensitivity

Clinicians and researchers have increasingly recognized the importance of employing measures specifically developed to be intervention sensitive or responsive to treatment (e.g., Guyatt, Walter, & Norman, 1987; Lipsey, 1983, 1990; Vermeersch et al., 2000; Vermeersch et al., 2004). Recent approaches to test development with outcome measures have focused on methods of selecting change-sensitive items that display desired psychometric properties (Meier, 1997, 2000; Vermeersch et al., 2000; Vermeersch et al., 2004). Vermeersch et al. (2004), for example, examined scores on the 45-item *OQ* completed by 5,553 students receiving treatment at 40 university counseling centers nationwide and 248 university student controls. Thirty-four of 45 individual items as well as the *OQ* total score and three subscales evidenced faster rates of change in the treated than untreated groups.

Meier (1997, 1998, 2000) and McDougal et al. (2012) proposed a set of **Intervention Item Selection Rules** (IISRs; see Table 3.4) designed to identify intervention-sensitive items during either test construction or item evaluation. The major assumptions of this approach are that (a) test items and tasks differ along a trait-state continuum and (b) different test construction and item analysis procedures are necessary to select items with a high state loading that reflect the results of interventions. IISRs test two competing claims regarding change at the item level: that such change is the result of an intervention or results from other factors that constitute error in the context of scores intended for a particular purpose. The key IISR principles are that intervention-sensitive items should change in response to an intervention and remain relatively stable over time when no intervention is present. The following criteria are contrasted with potential alternative explanations for item and scale score change.

Table 3.4. BRIEF DESCRIPTION OF INTERVENTION ITEM
SELECTION RULES (IISRs)

Rule	Description
1	Aggregate item scores at appropriate levels
2	Ground scale items in theoretical and empirical literature
3	Assess range of item scores at pretest
4	Detect change in an item's score after an intervention
5	Assess whether change occurs in the expected direction
6	Examine whether differences in change exist between intervention and comparison groups
7	Examine whether intake differences exist between comparison groups
8	Examine relations between item scores and systematic error sources
9	Cross-validate results to minimize chance effects

NOTE: See Meier (1997, 1998, 2000) for a full description and several empirical applications of IISRs.

1. *Aggregate at appropriate units.* The construction of a psychological test typically involves a set of decisions regarding the selection and aggregation of items and scales. With traditional tests, the test construction process involves collection of data with many items and large samples. This step is followed by item analyses that eliminate some items and eventually result in a set of selected items that can be aggregated into a total score and associated subscales (Burisch, 1984). For traditional tests developed to identify stable traits for selection purposes, aggregation of individual item responses into a summary scale increases the reliability and validity of measurement of the studied construct (Epstein, 1979, 1980). Because aggregation of item responses reduces random error (Messick, 1989), scores on traditional trait-based tests may be aggregated across items, individuals, and occasions before item analyses are conducted. For intervention-based tests, however, change across occasions (i.e., time and sessions) is the major focus of interest, so aggregation of scores across time (at least in a pretest/posttest design) should not occur during the development of change sensitive tests.

With traditional tests, the **aggregated score** across all items is almost always the comparison point for evaluating item and scale scores. One major problem that results, however, is that individuals who possess the same score, in the low to middle distribution of scores, may have endorsed different items. Two individuals with the same score of 30 on the *BDI*, for example, may have endorsed (a) items in entirely different domains (cf. Dohrenwend, 2006), (b) a different number of items, and (c) different levels of intensity on those items. The use of different PMOA measures is comparable to employing different thermometers that show the current room temperature as 60, 65, 70, and 75. These similar temperature readings are sufficient for judging whether the room is hot, cool, or cold but lack the necessary precision to specify the actual room temperature or to conduct research, for example, investigating the freezing or boiling points of water. Similarly, scores on current PMOA measures that aggregate items into total scores will provide a basic differentiation (e.g., high vs. low) on the PMOA construct of interest, but they will not offer the precision of a scale where designation of a score at a particular level has the same or similar meaning across individuals. PMOA measures developed with traditional test construction methods are likely to confound content and intensity levels.

The use of aggregated items for total scores in PMOA measures may result in additional problems. First, application of traditional test development criteria to a PMOA test may result in the deletion of items with low variability; items that detect low frequency items that occur at the top or bottom of a true scale will not be retained with traditional test construction methods. The resulting total score, composed mainly of moderate levels of frequency/severity, may create a ceiling effect for clinical samples who cannot endorse items of sufficient frequency/severity. Frequency counts employed in behavioral assessment may also miss **interval-level properties** if the sampled behaviors do not reflect the full range of possible intensities for a construct such as fear or anxiety. Finally, normative comparisons may be misleading when they are based on ordinal scales whose scores do not correspond to interval levels. Persons who score in a midrange, for example, may possess different amounts, types, and severities of the tested construct.

2. *Ground items in theory and research.* To the extent possible, change-sensitive items should be grounded in relevant psychological and psychotherapy theory and research. Theoretical grounding does not exclude practical importance, but provides an important context for understanding the meaning of changing scores on an intervention-sensitive measure. Ideally, items should be grounded in a theory of the psychotherapeutic intervention(s) being used. In other words, what item content will reflect the effects of the intervention(s) being employed? For example, considerable research and theory exist to suggest that over time, most clients should evidence decreases in NA intensity if they improve.

Test developers should conduct a literature review of theoretically expected and empirically derived psychotherapy effects in preparation for creating items and tasks thought to be affected by a particular intervention. Thorough explication of the constructs expected to be influenced and unaffected by the intervention should result in a large initial item pool with the capacity to investigate specific intervention effects. Similarly, clinicians familiar with the interventions in question may be able to describe the types of effects commonly experienced by clients receiving these interventions. Other potential sources of information about intervention effects are clients themselves, parents, teachers, and significant others.

3. *Avoid ceiling, floor, and underestimation effects.* **Ceiling** and **floor effects** restrict the potential range of scores and therefore inhibit detection of desired changes in intervention-sensitive tests. Ideally, mean scores for an item should not be at the top or bottom of the possible range of scores at the initial testing. With interventions intended to increase scores, initial item scores with ceiling effects (e.g., 1 or 2 standard deviations greater than the mean) should be dropped; items with floor effects should be dropped in interventions intended to decrease scores. While these analyses are typically conducted with preintervention scores, they might also be conducted with follow-up or termination scores if the purpose of subsequent measurement is to evaluate further improvement after the intervention.

4. *Detect change.* This rule specifies that a major criterion for inclusion in a test is that an item detect change over time; scores on intervention-sensitive items should demonstrate change in individuals who receive an intervention. Statistical significance is an appropriate indicator of such change, although its dependence on sample size suggests that (a) the alpha level should be set

higher (e.g., .10) in test development studies with smaller clinical samples or (b) an effect size threshold (e.g., 0.50 *SD*) may be more relevant in clinical research. The time period of interest may be brief, moderate, or long term and may include periods within therapy (for progress monitoring) as well as pre- and posttest performance (outcome assessment). Psychotherapy theory and research may be helpful in identifying items reflecting constructs that may differentially change by time period.

5. *Change in the expected direction.* An item that shows significant change over time in intervention participants should change in the expected direction. However, items that display changes in an unexpected direction may be retained if the test developer is interested in identifying negative effects of the intervention (Mash & Hunsley, 1993). Similarly, some or all items that evidence no change may be retained if the test developer wishes to employ these items to detect such errors as acquiescence or criticalness errors in test takers. Again, psychotherapy theory and research may help identify items that, for example, are expected to evidence worsening at the beginning of psychotherapy but later improvement.

6. *Change relative to a comparison group.* Change in items completed by an intervention group can be compared to change in items completed by participants in the best available **control** or **comparison group** (Rounds & Tinsley, 1984). This does not directly address the issue of change over time but provides information about items' ability to distinguish between the amounts of change in two groups. This can be important in situations where all groups are expected to improve; for example, items assessing change in children receiving a psychosocial intervention may be compared to developmental changes over time in a group of children of a comparable age. Use of a best available control group may be important because in many clinical situations, **no-treatment control groups** may be impractical or unethical. Comparisons between intervention and comparison group scores will enable test developers to determine whether certain items show more change resulting from an intervention in relation to a comparison condition. For example, two or more interventions may produce patterns of differential item change, results that can be of practical importance for matching client problems and interventions.

Finally, if the PMOA measure has also been developed to function as a screening or selection instrument (e.g., the *BIMAS*; McDougal et al., 2012), **normative data** may be employed for comparison. In a **normal distribution**, individuals who score at the top of the scale (indicating more problems) are likely to be the individuals who self-select or are selected for psychotherapy. One way to determine whether change has occurred is to track PMOA scores until those scores reach the middle levels of the normal distribution. One can then argue that although these individuals may still possess some moderate amount of the problem, they are comparable to the average person and thus no longer in need of therapy. Normative data may be reported in the test manuals of commercially published tests and in published articles about the specific measure.

Finally, dividing clients into more homogeneous groups prior to data analysis may enhance the sensitivity of that analysis to determine if item scores show change from psychotherapy. That is, small **sample sizes** and more **heterogeneous samples** hinder the ability to find statistically significant changes over time with any measure. When a sufficiently large sample is available (which can be determined through a **power analysis**), test developers can create more homogeneous datasets (e.g., comparing men vs. women) through **client characteristics** such as race/ethnicity, gender, and age. Theoretical predictions that a particular psychotherapeutic intervention should be more effective for a particular group enhances the possibility that any found effects actually result from the treatment–demographic interaction instead of chance.

7. *No difference at preintervention.* Item scores should be equivalent between intervention and comparison groups before an intervention is implemented; item scores should not show differences between groups presumably drawn from the same population. In IISR studies, **random assignment** should be employed when possible to equate intervention and comparison groups (Shadish, Cook, & Campbell, 2001). Instructions, experimenter expectancies, or self-selection in different groups might produce a pretest item difference independent of any subsequent intervention effects, and items that show pretest differences between groups should be deleted during item analysis.

8. *No relation to relevant systematic errors.* Initial and follow-up item scores should not be associated with **systematic error**. If a subset of items that appear more **socially desirable** behave differently over time, for example, these item means may be distorted and decrease the chances of detecting intervention effects. Other potential errors include self-report items that show change with repeated administrations independent of treatment, or items reflecting avoidance content that evidence low endorsements or little change over time. Items that reflect such errors should be identified and dropped during test construction unless the errors are a source of interest for that particular PMOA measure.

9. *Cross-validate.* IISR studies that emphasize empirical analyses over theoretically predicted item change may be capitalizing on chance. To combat chance effects, Steps 3 through 8 should be repeated in a **cross-validation** study of new samples from the population of interest.

IISRs reflect a combination of correlation and experimental methodologies that Cronbach (1957) noted as largely distinct research traditions in psychology. IISR analyses focus on whether the effects of psychosocial interventions can be identified in individual item responses. A key question about this type of item selection method is whether other effects will overwhelm intervention effects. That is, intervention effects must compete with the following:

1. State influences, such as situational and developmental factors (Cronbach & Snow, 1977);
2. Trait effects such as intelligence;
3. Systematic errors, such as memory errors and social desirability bias; and
4. **Sampling error** arising from the heterogeneity of subjects (Kazdin, 2003). Large samples may be necessary to find generalizable change items and to cross-validate them; smaller samples with homogeneous clients may have more **statistical power** but less generalizability (Lipsey, 1990). This may be difficult in clinical situations where the practical problems of collecting repeated data measures are substantial.

SUMMARY

Research indicates that most clients improve as a result of counseling and psychotherapy, yet treatment failure rates can be as high as 50% (Persons & Mikami, 2002). This variability in individual response to therapy means that even when clinicians employ empirically supported treatments, some clients will evidence no change and some will worsen. Research also documents that one way to decrease treatment failures is to employ clinically relevant feedback during therapy. Lambert et al. (2005) found that a feedback system enhances outcomes for patients with a negative response to intervention. For clients who were failing to improve, clients whose therapists received feedback about progress showed less deterioration and more improvement over time than clients of therapists who received no feedback.

The theory and empirical findings described in this chapter suggest a set of principles that can be employed to evaluate change-sensitive PMOA measures. Based on the major topics in this chapter, Table 3.5 summarizes a set of 10 criteria for PMOA measures. Each criterion is relevant on its own, but many are most important when evaluated in conjunction with another. The purpose of evaluating the stability of scores on a PMOA measure, for example, is not simply that the scores are invariant over time, but that they are stable in the absence of an intervention and yet sensitive to change when participants complete an intervention. Similarly, evaluating whether a PMOA measure can detect phase/time effects matters principally when employed with an intervention expected to produce such effects.

These criteria provide the reader with a basic methodology to evaluate and compare different PMOA measures. In Chapter 6, these evaluation criteria are illustrated and applied to a sample of PMOA measures.

Table 3.5. TEN CRITERIA FOR EVALUATION OF PROGRESS MONITORING AND OUTCOME ASSESSMENT (PMOA) SCALES

Criterion	Brief Explanation
Reliability/stability	Does scale demonstrate stability in the absence of intervention? Coefficient alpha also helpful for internal consistency estimates.
Ceiling/floor effects	Does scale mean, plus or minus 1 standard deviation, exceed the scale range?
Content validity	Does scale content relate to the theoretically expected effects of psychosocial interventions?
Change sensitivity	The major criteria for assessing the construct validity of a PMOA measure: Scale score evidences change over time. Score may also differentiate between groups (e.g., clinical and nonclinical, treatment and control).
Phase/time effects	Scale can detect change at different phases or times of psychotherapy (e.g., short term, intermediate, long term).
Intervention characteristics	Aspect of intervention expected to influence change on a specific PMOA scale, including approach/type, duration, dosage, and frequency.
Client characteristics	Participant characteristics such as race/ethnicity, age, and gender that may influence the type and amount of change resulting from an intervention and evidenced on the scale.
Data source	PMOA measurement methods will influence scale scores.
Avoidance	A set of constructs that influence progress in psychotherapy and/or the valid reporting of data on the PMOA scale.
Brevity	Is scale brief enough to encourage completion of repeated measurement by clients, clinicians, and others?

4

Test Score Interpretation

INTRODUCTION

Progress monitoring and outcome assessment (PMOA) measures are designed
to provide clinical information relevant to the purposes of PMOA. These scores
should aid clinicians in their judgments about the type, direction, and amount of
progress made by clients. In turn, these data can inform decisions about whether
to continue with the current psychotherapeutic approach and whether the client
has improved to the extent that she or he is ready to terminate. In the case of a
client whose scores indicate worsening or a lack of improvement, these scores are
intended to alert the clinician and/or supervisor of the need to consider changing the therapeutic approach.

PMOA scores should not be the sole source of information in such decisions,
but employed in conjunction with the clinician's judgment as well as appropriate
and available data from other sources, including psychological tests, supervisors, and other individuals with knowledge of the client's functioning. Using
a research metaphor, PMOA data are the **dependent variables** in the design of
the therapeutic study, with therapeutic interventions as one of the known **independent variables**. Typically casual factors cannot be known on the basis of
the PMOA data alone; explanations for the PMOA data patterns must be found
elsewhere.

TYPES OF REPORTS

The competent clinician must combine her or his experience and theoretical and clinical knowledge to interpret PMOA data for purposes of feedback
and clinical decision making. To this end, the next section provides simple
examples of the types of data provided in PMOA reports; more complex issues
and methods are described in Chapter 7. Progress monitoring involves interpreting multiple data points as they change across sessions and time, while
outcome assessment interpretations focus on measurement of a few (e.g., one

to three) data points between the beginning and end of therapy. Methods for describing and analyzing both types of change are described in the following sections.

Progress Monitoring: Change Across Sessions and Time

Recall that progress monitoring (PM) refers to the use of test scores, typically quantitative scores, for feedback about the progress of a client who is receiving therapy. Typically these quantitative data are displayed across all sessions of interest, often via a time series that allows the test interpreter to view all data points at once. Clinicians find PM data useful for a variety of questions, such as knowing whether the client has improved, worsened, cycled, or remained stable since therapy began. The amount of progress can also be addressed with PM data, particularly when answering the question of whether the client has improved to a degree that she or he is ready to end therapy. PM data are particularly useful when they indicate that the client has failed to improve. As noted in previous chapters, the work of Lambert (e.g., Lambert, 2007) and colleagues has demonstrated the usefulness of PM data to signal to clinicians that more attention (and perhaps different interventions) should be paid to the nonimproving client.

As described in Chapter 2, one of the *Depression/Anxiety Negative Affect* (*DANA*; Meier, 2012) scale's key scores is Highest Intensity Level (HIL), the most intense level for any negative affect (NA) descriptor endorsed per session. Recall that NA is associated with most client problems, and as problems resolve, NA decreases. If a rater endorsed the NA terms *Anxious, Fearful*, and *Actively suicidal*, the corresponding intensity levels would be 3, 4, and 5, respectively. Level 5 is the highest level of the endorsed terms, so HIL for this session would be 5. In Figure 4.1, time series for HIL are displayed for three clients. In example (a), the client evidences a clear step-down pattern on HIL, moving from Level 4 (Sessions 1 and 2) to Level 2 (Sessions 3 and 4) and then Level 1 (Session 5). Given the relatively quick improvement evident, the client potentially could be ready to terminate therapy if the client and therapist agreed, based on the client's response to treatment and circumstances. However, meeting for another session or two (or checking in via some other method, such as a telephone call or e-mail) may be strategic to determine if the improvement holds.

One reason that continued contact with client (a) may be necessary is the pattern of data evident with client (b). This client also evidenced rapid improvement, from Level 5 to Level 2, but then rebounded back to Level 3 (also recall the case of Doris from Chapter 2, who evidenced a similar pattern over 20 sessions). This **cycling** of higher and lower affective states may be indicative of the therapeutic process described by Mergenthaler (1996; see Chapter 2). Mergenthaler's research-based depiction of the therapeutic process suggests that at least in therapies that focus on emotional experiencing, most clients move through states of high and low emotional processing and abstraction/reflection. Client (b) may

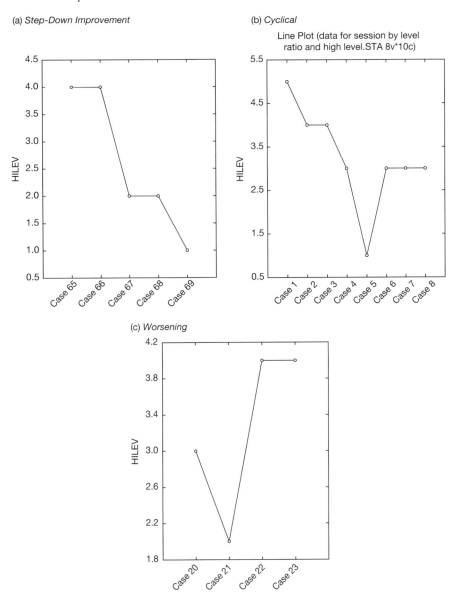

Figure 4.1 Three Examples of Highest Intensity Level Data Patterns.

have taken a **vacation session** during the fifth meeting, returning the following week to take up emotional processing again.

With client (c), knowledge of this particular client's background and/or current situations might provide an explanation of the significant worsening of NA intensity levels. This short slice of PM data may be indicative, for example, of the client's cycling of moods, the effects of a negative external event in the client's life, or an impasse in therapy. In any event, understanding potential causes is important when clients evidence worsening or lack of progress in PMOA data.

Knowing why a client improves is potentially important even when it is unclear whether the improvement is a result of therapeutic interventions. With improvement, the client's uptick on PMOA data may be more an effect of external events, suggesting that the need for therapy will return if external circumstances change for the worse. In general, more data translates into less error in interpretation of client change over time and across sessions.

Outcome Assessments: Change From Beginning to End

With outcome assessments, clinicians typically are trying to make a final decision or statement about the client's status. This decision is usually context dependent. College students who are participating in therapy in a college counseling center may stop therapy because a semester is ending and they are leaving campus. In private practice, an insurance company or government agency may deny additional payment. In both cases client and therapist may believe more progress can be achieved with additional sessions.

One method of deciding whether therapy has been sufficiently successful, and whether therapy should be ended or continued, is to compare the client's current score to desired scores in another group. This normative comparison, where clients are typically evaluated with a nonclinical population, suggests that individuals whose scores approach the normal range of scores for nonclinical samples are ready to terminate. Tests such as the *Outcome Questionnaire-45* (*OQ45*) and the *Behavior Intervention Monitoring Assessment System* (*BIMAS*) provide normative scores so that this kind of comparison can be made with individual scales and individual clients. A **t score** or another standardized score is typically employed for this comparison.

With the *BIMAS* (McDougal, Bardos, & Meier, 2012), scores were transformed by age group. On the Conduct scale of the *BIMAS*, for example, a score of 4 for a 5-year-old equals a *t* score of 50, indicating that the raw score of 4 (and the *t* score of 50) represents the mean or average score for 5-year-olds in the *BIMAS* normative sample. These *t* scores have a mean of 50 and a standard deviation of 10. Recall the case from Chapter 2 of John, a sixth grader, who was evidencing problems on the *BIMAS* on the Negative Affect (NA; where high scores indicate more problems) and Academic Functioning (AF; low scores indicate more problems) subscales. Specifically, John's initial *t* score of 78 for the teacher-rated NA scale put him at *High Risk* (category range, 70 to 85, well above the mean of 50). John's *t* score of 23 (well below the mean of 50) on the teacher-rated AF scale indicated that John was not prepared for class, often had failing grades, and was absent from school. John's mother (*t* score of 75) and John (*t* score of 68) also reported higher scores for NA; low *t* scores for *AF* were similarly uniformly low across raters (23 for teacher, 28 for parent, and 34 for self-report).

As shown in Figure 4.2, these scores indicate that John did not meet average levels when compared to his peers and thus should be considered for intervention(s). On the basis of the *BIMAS* scores, the assessor suggested interventions for John

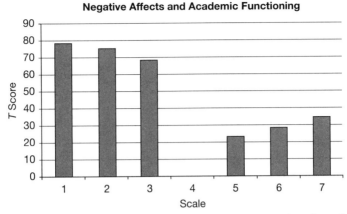

Figure 4.2 John's Initial BIMAS *T* Scores for Negative Affect (NA) and Academic Functioning (AF) Scales as Rated by Teacher, Mother, and Himself. *Scales 1, 2, and 3 refer to John's NA t scores as initially rated by his teacher, mother, and self; low scores indicate lower NA. Scales 5, 6, and 7 show John's AF t scores, again as rated by teacher, mother, and self; higher scores indicate better functioning.*

that focused on group interactions; academic work around class preparation, homework, and attendance; and peer mentoring. John participated in the school psychologist's weekly support group, received daily academic services, and began working as a peer tutor to read books to younger children.

Readministration of the *BIMAS* Teacher Form approximately 2 and 4 months later provided data to gauge John's status in relation to norms. If one of the goals of therapy was to return John to a normal range, that is, within 1 standard deviation (SD) from the mean (40 to 60), no final scores at 2 and 4 months, respectively, for NA (teacher 68, 63) or AF (teacher 29, 37) meet the target range. Using the norm group criterion, John should continue in therapy until his scores decline to 60 for NA (1 SD above 50) and reach 40 for AF (1 SD below 50).

Normative comparisons are essentially a static evaluation of a client's PMOA score within a distribution of scores. In contrast, effect size (ES) is a statistic that can be employed to evaluate the size of the change between two scores over time. For example, we can compare John's scores on the *BIMAS* administered in December of the school year and the following April. ES involves subtracting the two scores and dividing by a standard deviation (often the pooled standard deviation of scores from the first and last sample). John's NA scores went from 14 to 8 on the *NA* scale and his AF scores went from 5 to 13 (McDougal et al., 2012). Incorporating the appropriate SD values, we can calculate ES as follows:

$$\text{ES}(NA)(8-14)/9.09 = -0.66$$

$$\text{ES}(AF)(13-5)/3.53 = 2.26$$

How should ESs of –0.66 and 2.26 be interpreted? As shown in Table 4.1, McDougal et al. (2012) employed a scheme proposed by Clement (1999). Using this method, John's NA score indicates slight improvement, and his AF score indicates much improvement.

Like ES, the Reliable Change Index (RCI) can be employed to gauge whether change has occurred between two time points (Jacobson & Truax, 1991). The RCI is calculated for each specific PMOA scale, comparing the difference in two test scores by the standard error of difference between them. The RCI formula takes into account a reliability estimate for the PMOA measure. The amount of change on the PMOA measure is statistically significant if the absolute difference between two administrations is equal to or greater than the corresponding RCI value (McDougal et al., 2012). The measured change is then assumed to result from a real difference between the two scores (presumably as a result of an intervention), not from random fluctuations or measurement error.

Table 4.2 displays the RCI values for the *BIMAS* scales (McDougal et al., 2012). A difference equal to or greater than the value shown for each *BIMAS* scale would be considered a statistically significant difference. Recall the earlier example of John whose teacher-rated *NA t* scores for two administrations were 78 and 68. The difference of 10 is greater than the RCI value of 9 for the Teacher Form, NA scale, shown in Table 4.2; this indicates that the difference is a statistically significant decrease between the two sessions. The change in *t* scores between the first and second administrations of the AF (23 and 29, a difference of 6), however, is not large enough to be considered trustworthy. That is, the RCI analysis indicates that random changes and measurement error, not the intervention, may be causing scale scores to change. Finally, Figure 4.3 displays time series graphs for NA and AF scales, with John evidencing improvement on both scales (i.e., decreasing on NA and increasing on AF). To use a RCI calculator that can be employed with any PMOA scale, go to http://www.psyctc.org/stats/rcsc1.htm.

Another method for gauging outcome is the theoretical or natural **endpoint** on some PMOA measures. *BIMAS* items (McDougal et al., 2012), for example, use a scoring format that asks respondents to rate the frequency over the past week of

Table 4.1. INTERPRETATION OF ES

Range	NA Scale	AF Scale
<–1.50	Much improved	Much worse
–0.51 to –1.49	Improved	Worse
–0.50 to +0.50	No change	No change
0.51 to 1.49	Worse	Improved
>1.50	Much worse	Much Improved

NOTE: Interpretation of positive or negative ESs depends on scoring on the scale. For NA, negative ESs indicate a decrease in scores and improvement. For AF, positive ESs indicate an increase in scores and improvement. Source is Clement (1999).

ES = effect size; NA = Negative Affect; AF = Affective Functioning.

Table 4.2. RELIABLE CHANGE INDEX VALUES FOR BEHAVIOR INTERVENTION
MONITORING ASSESSMENT SYSTEM (BIMAS) SCALES

	BIMAS Form		
Scale	*Teacher*	*Parent*	*Self-Report*
Conduct	8	11	11
Negative Affect	9	8	9
Cognitive/Attention	7	10	10
Social	7	5	8
Academic Functioning	8	11	9

NOTE: Differences between two administrations of an individual's *BIMAS* scale scores should equal or exceed these values to be considered statistically significant. Source is McDougal et al. (2012), Appendix C.

a child's behavior. Responses can range from *Never* (behavior occurred 0 times over the past week), to *Rarely* (1 to 2 times), to *Sometimes* (3 to 4 times), to *Often* (5 to 6 times), to *Very Often* (7 or more times a week). If a therapist is tracking one or more items over time (or the sum of those items, on a scale), examination of the frequency of problem items provides an interpretable sign about the need for continued therapy. A client with obsessive-compulsive disorder who checks whether the toaster is unplugged before leaving for work, for example, may do this a dozen or more times per week. While a reduction to zero may be unlikely, a frequency of 1 to 2 times per week may indicate that therapeutic effects have been maximized.

Similarly, the *DANA*'s lowest intensity level (1, *Transient NA*) represents a natural endpoint for therapy. Given that most people experience transient NA, clients whose HIL scores are predominantly 1 or 2 after intervention are candidates for termination. Given the endpoint criterion, however, clients can make progress and still not be ready to end. The client in Figure 4.4, for example,

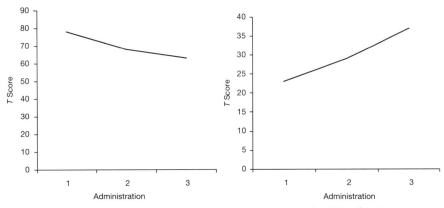

Figure 4.3 Negative Affect (NA) and Academic Functioning (AF) Teacher Ratings Across 6 Months. *John's scores on NA and AF, respectively, show improvement over time.*

Figure 4.4. Highest Intensity Level Data Suggesting Improvement, but Not Termination.

shows a decrease in HIL, but HIL in the final rated sessions (Sessions 37 through 39) remains at intensity level 3. This suggests clinical progress but not completion of therapeutic work: In most cases this client would continue therapeutic work until HIL scores persist at level 1 or 2.

Finally, the simple criterion of change of at least **1 standard deviation** (1SD) on PMOA data can be employed for both progress monitoring and outcome assessment. This approach assumes that if treatment is ineffective, and no other substantial factor is influencing clients, differences between two PMOA scores at selected time periods (e.g., baseline vs. final session) will scatter around 0. However, if a PMOA score changes more than 1 standard deviation and no other plausible explanation exists for the change, the change can be attributed to treatment. Once the 1SD threshold has been met, the interpretation of improvement or worsening simply depends on the direction of change on the particular PMOA scale. As long as a dataset exists that enables a calculation of means and standard deviations for each relevant PMOA score, this approach can be employed in both nomothetic (e.g., comparing a client's scores to others) and idiographic (e.g., comparing a client's scores to her or his own scores) situations.

Table 4.3 displays descriptive statistics for two *DANA* scores (Highest Intensity Level [HIL] and Total Number of Endorsed Items [TOT]) reported for clinical

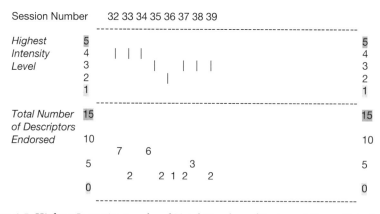

Figure 4.5 Highest Intensity Level and Total Number of Endorsed Items Data for an Individual Client in Sessions 32 through 39.

Table 4.3. DESCRIPTIVE STATISTICS FOR THREE DEPRESSION/ANXIETY NEGATIVE
AFFECT (DANA) SCORES FOR THE TOTAL SAMPLE

Score	M	SD	Min	Max
Highest Intensity Level (HIL)	3.46	0.79	1	5
Average Intensity Level (AIL)	2.40	0.54	1	4.29
Total Number of Endorsed Items (TOT)	5.67	4.17	0	27

NOTE: Sample size equals 380 for HIL and AIL and 383 for TOT. Scores are calculated on *DANA* ratings collected for each session.

samples employed during test development (Meier, 2012). Figure 4.5 provides data for an individual client that can be employed to assess change with the 1SD method using these descriptive statistics. As shown in Figure 4.5, HIL for this client declined from 4 (Session 32) to 3 (Session 39), a difference of one intensity level that exceeds 1SD (0.79) for HIL. Similarly, TOT declined from 7 at Session 32 to 2 at Session 39, a difference of 5 that exceeds 1SD (4.17). Thus, both measures suggest that this client experienced change in the direction of improvement during the therapeutic intervention.

INTEGRATING QUALITATIVE AND QUANTITATIVE INFORMATION

A mixed-methods approach using both quantitative and qualitative data can provide feedback about client progress as well as possible explanations for that progress or lack thereof. For example, *DANA* HIL ratings for an adult college student client who completed eight sessions in an outpatient mental health clinic over an academic trimester are shown in Figure 4.6. HIL ranged from 5 (Sessions 3, 4, and 7) to 1 (Session 8), indicating that the client experienced periods of intense and moderate NA until the final session. Based on Mergenthaler's (1996) finding that successful clients experience alternate phases of high and low emotion and reflection, the HIL pattern suggests a client who is cycling through processing and reflecting on emotional material. The client appeared to have experienced

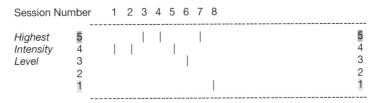

Figure 4.6 *Depression/Anxiety Negative Affect* (DANA) **Ratings for an Adult Client Over Eight Sessions.** *Tick marks indicate DANA Highest Intensity Level endorsed for that session. Higher ratings indicate more intense negative affect.*

two periods of intense emotion (Sessions 1 through 4 and another at Session 7), likely interspersed by a single interval (around Sessions 5 to 6) of high abstraction where the client reflected on emotional material.

Although the NA data suggest that one cycle of abstraction–emotion was completed, did the client resolve the presenting problem(s)? And does the low HIL level at Session 8 indicate the client should terminate therapy?

One way to answer these questions is to review progress notes. Most therapists conclude each session with a summary of key issues related to treatment progress and planning. One strategy is to use those notes to track the perseverance of client themes over time: Major themes should have persistent relevance (Beutler & Hamblin, 1986); that is, the topic should appear repeatedly across sessions. What may have been a pressing topic when a client began therapy will lose its sense of urgency with effective therapy. In general, a decrease in the presentation and length of discussion of a clinically relevant theme, as well as a decrease in NA around that theme, suggests that the client is ready for closure on these topics.

Table 4.4 displays a persistence table constructed by a supervisor using audiotapes and supervisee reports of the same adult client. Eight themes are listed across the eight sessions, with the major themes designated by a solid box. Six themes related to client problems are listed, including *avoidance of affect, affect expressed, self-injurious behaviors, in crisis, academic problems, relationships,* and *coping skills exhibited* by the client. The client appears to avoid experiencing or expressing affect across all sessions; the emotions the client did express were primarily anger and hostility (all sessions except Session 8). Given that this client had a diagnosis of Borderline Personality Disorder, it is not surprising that self-injurious behaviors and relationship issues were frequent topics of the therapeutic conversations. Similarly, relationship issues are discussed in seven of the eight sessions. This suggests that this client primarily continues to struggle with experiencing, moderating, and expressing affect, particularly in relationships with others.

The *DANA* data, coupled with the observed continuation of themes related to affect, avoidance, and relationships, indicate the client should continue therapy.

Table 4.4. PERSISTENT THEMES FOR ADULT CLIENT ACROSS EIGHT SESSIONS

	Session Number							
Themes	1	2	3	4	5	6	7	8
Avoid affect	■	■	■	■	■	■	■	■
Affect expressed	■	■	■	■	■	■	■	
Self-injurious behavior	■	■	■		■		■	
In crisis	■	■	■			■		■
Academic problem		■				■		
Relation issues	■	■	■	■	■	■	■	■
Coping skills		■		■		■		

The qualitative data suggest that relationship issues and the experiencing of affect around those relationships should be a major focus. Helping this client to learn emotional experiencing and regulation, perhaps as part of assertiveness and coping skills training, might be one useful approach (Linehan, 1993).

CAUTIONS AND LIMITATIONS WHEN INTERPRETING PROGRESS MONITORING AND OUTCOME ASSESSMENT DATA

Researchers who describe feedback-enhanced therapies (FETs) typically focus on the alert function of PMOA data. That is, PMOA data provide a yes/no type of alert that a client is not making expected progress or not meeting a standard of some sort (Lambert, Harmon, Slade, Whipple, & Hawkins, 2005; Lambert et al., 2001; Saptya, Riemer, & Bickman, 2005). Lambert and Hawkins (2001) described the case of a young bipolar patient who had received medication and experienced a decrease in symptoms, but then appeared to stop taking the medication after the symptoms decreased. The symptoms then returned and were evident in the *OQ45* data. In this case, the appropriate action was to persuade the client to resume taking the medications, the original intervention.

Typically, the best options that most PMOA interpretations can provide are generic, research-based suggestions when clients evidence a negative response to treatment. Worthen and Lambert (2007, p. 50), for example, reported the suggestions provided by the interpretative component of the *OQ45* when a client shows a negative response to treatment:

> Steps should be taken to carefully review this case and identify reasons for poor progress. It is recommended that you be alert to the possible need to improve the therapeutic alliance, reconsider the client's readiness for change and the need to renegotiate the therapeutic contract, intervene to strengthen social supports, or possibly alter your treatment plan by intensifying treatment, shifting intervention strategies, or decide upon a new course of action, such as referral for medication. Continuous monitoring of future progress is highly recommended.

Usually, PMOA data alone cannot inform the clinician about how to interpret the observed data or what alternative intervention(s) may be useful for a particular client.

In general, interpreting PMOA score changes as a result of psychosocial intervention(s) should be done with caution. Interpreting PMOA data without an understanding of possible causes represents a **black box design** that cannot provide hypotheses or explanations useful for improving interventions or methodologies (Posavac, 2011). Attributing change to therapy will be problematic without a control group or a baseline period of no change. Consequently, decisions about whether to continue, stop, or alter therapy should never be taken *only* on the basis of test data, but by decision makers (such as the therapist, supervisor, client, and significant others) who have the best interests of the client at heart. With the case of John, for example, a case can be made that he has made improvement and his interventions be stopped since his *t* scores are approaching a normal or average range (in relation to the *BIMAS* norm groups). Even with the *BIMAS* data, however, it is unclear in John's case whether (a) therapy is primarily driving those gains, (b) gains can be maintained in the absence of therapy, and (c) John can function adequately even if his scores are equivalent to others in a normal range.

SUMMARY

The primary information clinicians seek from progress and outcome assessments is progress since intake and determining the need to alter treatment (Hatfield & Ogles, 2004). PMOA scores provide feedback to clinicians about which clients are and are not making progress. Armed with these data, clinicians can consider whether and when to adjust the provided intervention(s).

PMOA measures can be employed to create data, graphics, and interpretative reports to aid in knowing whether a client is making progress in therapy as well as a more final answer to the question of client outcome. Time series displays, discussed in detail in Chapter 7, are perhaps the most frequently employed graphical display for showing progress over time with a single or multiple variables. Similarly, outcome assessment interpretations may employ indices such as ES and the RCI to depict how much a client changed on one or more mental health variables over the course of therapy. And while quantitative measures and analytic methods indicate the amount and direction of change, they typically provide little direct information about why clients change or do not. Here qualitative methods such as analysis of progress notes can provide clues, particularly about the persistence of client focus on one or more problems. The combination of quantitative and qualitative methods can offer a useful, but still limited, approach to interpreting PMOA scores in terms of informing treatment decisions.

Regardless of the purpose of the test, most test users are primarily interested in knowing what scores on a test mean, the test interpretation component. Interpretation of test scores, however, depends on preceding steps, including test construction procedures, the conditions of administration, and how scores are created. The next chapter addresses the test administration conditions that can influence PMOA scores.

5

Administration and Data Collection

INTRODUCTION

This chapter addresses the preparation and procedures needed to produce valid clinical data for progress monitoring and outcome assessment (PMOA) measures. Compared to typical psychological testing where the test procedure usually involves only a single administration, with PMOA's repeated testing a different set of conditions is present. Repeated measurement, particularly with self-reports, can complicate the conditions in which clients and clinicians produce and report clinical data.

Instructions for test administration of PMOA measures are designed to increase the likelihood that the rater can provide data valid for PMOA. Typically these ratings require both (a) some amount of preparation and/or training for the rater and (b) focused attention and recall during the brief period when the rater provides data. In the PMOA context, **standardization** refers to providing approximately equivalent conditions under which an individual reports information. These conditions are described later.

To ensure that ethical and legal guidelines are followed, this chapter also provides information about informed consent, confidentiality, and debriefing. Regarding preparation for PMOA test administration, the next section describes a series of problems that can arise if the rater is not prepared to perform the ratings. These are procedural problems and errors that could influence the rater's ability to provide valid data.

ISSUES WITH SELF-REPORTS

Like most psychological tests, the majority of PMOA measures are self-reports where the client provides data relevant to progress and outcomes. Well-known scales such as the *Outcome Questionnaire, Beck Depression Inventory (BDI),* and *Outcome Rating Scales* are self-reports. The widespread use of self-reports is inevitable given their ease of development, administration, and scoring

(Meier, 1994): A 1992 American Psychological Association advertisement in the *APA Monitor* estimated that 20,000 psychological, behavioral, and cognitive measures were created annually.

Researchers, however, have suggested limitations for the use of self-reports, particularly when providing sensitive information relevant for PMOA measurement. Shedler, Mayman, and Manis (1993) concluded from their research that clinicians could detect defensiveness that standard mental health scales could not. Monroe and Reid (2008) noted that "in general it is unsound to relinquish decisions about what counts as life stress to the idiosyncratic interpretations of study participants" (p. 951). Monroe and Reid also maintained that researchers who favor self-reports assume "erroneously that study participants fully comprehend what information is required and can report the information with methodological fidelity" (p. 951). From a clinical perspective, Meier and Davis (2011; see also Barrett, 2006) noted that many clients initially cannot differentiate their emotions other than to describe them as "good" or "bad." Consequently, with many clients new to counseling and psychotherapy, one of the first therapeutic tasks involves instructing them about how to recognize and report such feelings as anger, sadness, job, and fear. Addressing the two versions of the *BDI*, Coyne (1994, p. 33) criticized the assumption that depressed individuals could validly report their affective condition:

> Either version appears sensitive to a histrionic reaction to a minor event. Moreover, a person in a state of acute but transient distress may react to the tone of the items without the specific, differentiated feelings and attitudes actually being applicable to them. It is a dubious assumption that acutely upset respondents have such a complex view of their immediate emotional state.

Other studies find discrepancies between self-reports of psychological phenomena and overt behavior indicative of or related to the phenomena (e.g., Doleys, Meredith, Poire, Campbell, & Cook, 1977; Schroeder & Rakos, 1978). Summarizing a variation on this perspective, Kagan (1988) wrote:

> A serious limitation of self-report information is that each person has only a limited awareness of his or her moods, motives, and bases for behavior, and it is not obvious that only conscious intentions and moods make up the main basis for variation in behavior.... Less conscious indexes, including facial expressions, voice quality, and physiological reactions, occasionally have a stronger relation to a set of theoretically predicted behaviors than do self-reports. The reader will remember that when a large number of investigations were derived from psychoanalytic theory, the concept of unconscious ideas was prominent and self-report was treated as replete with error. (p. 617)

Pennebaker, Mehl, and Niederhoffer (2003) reviewed research indicating that persons with **alexithymia**, a personality characteristic associated with difficulties in the identification and verbalization of emotional experiences, have difficulty sharing emotions with others, particularly for negative events. Mergenthaler (1996) also noted that clients in therapy differ in their ability to verbalize their internal states, including emotion. Thus, clinicians who have been trained to recognize affect in nonverbal communication (such as facial expressions and voice tone) may be able to produce more valid affective information than individuals' self-report.

Studying a sample of 1,578 soldiers who returned from a 12-month tour in Iraq, Bliese, Wright, Adler, Thomas, and Hoge (2007) assessed symptoms related to posttraumatic stress disorder, depression, anger, relationship problems, and general psychological distress in 509 randomly selected soldiers who provided data at immediate postdeployment and 120 days later. Bliese et al. found that prevalence rates for most mental health problems were 2 to 5 times higher at 120 days postdeployment than at immediate postdeployment. Milliken, Auchterlonie, and Hoge (2007) replicated these results in a sample of 88,235 soldiers returning from Iraq who evidenced more mental health problems 6 months after return than at their immediate postdeployment. These studies indicate that individuals underreported their mental health issues when initially tested.

With social desirability bias, individuals may over- or underreport characteristics that make them appear to be unattractive to others. The direction of the distortion will reflect the social context of measurement for the tested individual. Teyber and McClure (2011) noted that clinical theorists have recently focused on the importance of shame in the therapeutic process; certainly clients may be initially reluctant to reveal shameful or embarrassing information. Clients may also malinger or exaggerate their negative affect (NA) or other symptoms to obtain associated benefits such as disability payments or continuation of the therapeutic relationship.

An additional complication for self-reports when used for the purposes of progress monitoring and, to a lesser extent, outcome assessment is that repeated administrations may introduce error. Citing the work of Longwell and Truax (2005) and Sharpe and Gilbert (1998), Persons and Fresco (2008) noted that researchers have found "that repeated administration of the *BDI* consistently resulted in a lower score, even when research participants were not depressed and were not receiving treatment" (p. 115). Repeated administration of any psychotherapy-related self-report measure may result in self-monitoring, a reactive method known to change the monitored behavior, typically in the same direction as an intervention (Craske & Tsao, 1999; Nelson, 1977). Questionnaire length may also affect completion rates, as some research suggests that the 45 items of the *Outcome Questionnaire* may be too long for repeated administration. Miller, Duncan, Brown, Sparks, and Claud (2003), for example, reported a usage rate of only 25% for the *OQ* at an outpatient community agency over a 1-year period.

ISSUES WITH CLINICAL RATERS

Clinical raters may be influenced by systematic factors other than those intended to occur during the rating process (Meier, 2008). Murphy and Davidshofer (2005), for example, described **halo, leniency**, and **range restriction errors**. Halo errors occur when a rater's overall impressions about the ratee influence ratings about specific aspects of the person; a rater holds a stereotype about a ratee, and that global impression hinders a more precise or valid rating in specific domains. With leniency and criticalness errors, the rater is either under- or overestimating the performance of the ratee. Leniency errors may be a cause of ceiling or floor effects (Kazdin, 2003): In a ceiling effect, all ratings cluster near the top of the scale; with a floor effect, they cluster at the bottom. When an intervention is implemented, ceiling and floor effects can hinder the detection of the intervention's impact. For example, suppose a researcher designs a pretest/posttest study examining the effects of a stress reduction program. If an observer's judgments of participants' stress significantly underestimate those levels at the pretest, how could a decrease resulting from the intervention be detected at posttest? In fact, if the observer underestimated stress at pretest, even an effective intervention might be found to have no effect or a negative effect.

Raters' inability or unwillingness to observe the range of ratees' performance is reflected in range restriction errors. Raters who make this error fail to discriminate ratees' level of performance, instead consistently choosing a rating near the scale midpoint. Halo, leniency criticalness, and range restriction errors all result in scores that do not reflect actual variation in ratees' performance. Instead, raters show too much consistency and not enough valid variation relevant to the assessment's intended purpose.

Behavioral assessors have described two rater errors called **drift** and **decay** that both negatively influence the reliability of assessments (Paul, 1986). Rater drift occurs when the raters make systematic changes in definition or interpretation of a construct over time; decay occurs with similar but random changes in definition. Decay may result from delays in the time period between when an event occurs and its observation or recording. As the amount of time increases between when a person observes an event and records the event, the reliability of the observation decreases (Paul, 1986). The longer the clinician takes to record data, the more likely she or he is to forget or distort data. Swezey (1981) employed the term **error of standards** to describe inconsistencies among raters who all employ different standards when assessing individuals' behaviors.

Clinical ratings typically occur in the context of a counseling or psychotherapy session where the clinician has an opportunity to observe and interact with the client for an extended period of time. The observation might occur in the clinician's office, but it may also take place in other settings, such as a school, home, or hospital. Traditionally, the interaction occurs in a therapy session of 45 to 50 minutes; an intake or initial session is of similar or slightly longer length. When ratings occur repeatedly over multiple sessions, clinical rating using a PMOA measure presumes similar or identical rating conditions. If these conditions change, it is the test user's responsibility to describe the changes and potential effects as part of the interpretation of PMOA scores. These in-session effects are described in the following paragraphs and summarized in Table 5.1.

Rating sessions could be for individual, group, couples/marital, or family counseling and psychotherapy. Changing this **modality** of counseling and psychotherapy, however, may influence the behavior of the client in terms of psychological states such as emotional awareness and expression. Thus, scores derived from clinical ratings across sessions assume that the modality remains identical over time, providing roughly equivalent conditions for the client to experience and express psychological states. If the modality changes across sessions, the test user should account for session differences, if any, in the interpretation of test scores.

The **observation period** (i.e., therapy session) is presumed to be approximately 45 to 50 minutes, but the period could be for a shorter or longer length of time. Comparing ratings across multiple sessions assumes that the length of each session is roughly equivalent. Sessions of different lengths may influence the behavior of the client (e.g., emotional awareness and expression) and consequently the sample available for the rater to consider.

Clinical raters should complete the rating procedure as soon as possible during or after the session ends. Research suggests that as the length of time grows between observation of client behavior and the actual rating, **recall errors** may occur (Meier, 2008). The more time that elapses between observation of the psychological behavior/characteristic and the rating itself, the more likely that recall

Table 5.1. In-Session Conditions That Can Influence Progress Monitoring and Outcome Assessment Ratings

Condition That Changes	Example
Modality of psychotherapy	A client who moves from individual to group counseling may have less opportunity to express in session
Observation period(s)	School counselor observes and rates the client in time periods of different lengths
Time between behavior and recording	Clinical rater sometimes completes rating immediately after session, sometimes hours or days later, with resulting errors in recall/memory
Time period of interest	Reports older than 1 week may be susceptible to memory/recall errors
Modality of negative affect expression	Verbal reports may be more likely to be distorted than nonverbal indicators
Avoidance	Client may be unwilling to experience or express psychological conditions such as negative affect
Confirmation bias	Tendency for clinicians and other assessors to notice information that conforms to expectations and dismiss disconfirming data

errors will influence the rating. Ideally, the clinician should complete his or her ratings working alone in a quiet setting with few distractions. If the clinician writes progress notes immediately after a session, for example, that would be an appropriate time to produce ratings about in-session observations. Ratings in other conditions should be avoided or performed with caution. Completing a rating along with the client, for example, might be useful as an intervention designed to increase self-awareness but would also decrease the number of items endorsed if the client objected to endorsements of particular items.

For many PMOA measures, the rater is instructed to provide data that were most salient for a client during the past week. When ratings are completed repeatedly for this time period, the resulting comparisons of multiple ratings over time for this **standard time period** allow the detection of change. Traditionally, 1 week is the approximate length of time between sessions for many psychotherapy clients, although one of the major influences of managed care has been to increase the length of time between sessions (Davis & Meier, 2001). If the time between the client sessions is less than 1 week, to avoid rating overlapping days, the rating period could be the length of time between sessions. Client reports of psychological states from longer than 1 week should be considered with caution, given the memory errors that may arise with longer recall (Meier, 2008).

Similarly, the clinical rater can attend to both the client's **verbal reports** and **nonverbal communications** in session. Psychotherapists and other clinical raters may have access to information sources, such as client nonverbals, that provide more unbiased information about client traits and states (Shedler et al., 1993). Clinical observations can be made on the basis of both verbal reports and nonverbal expressions of affect during the session. Many clinicians, however, trust nonverbal indicators of affect because of clients' ability to censor verbal reports (Meier & Davis, 2011). Many clients who are avoidant of NA, for example, may express more affect nonverbally than through verbal reports (e.g., see the Jeremy video employed for *Depression/Anxiety Negative Affect* [*DANA*] training in Chapter 8).

Note that sources of information other than the client can be utilized. Particularly for clients who are children, these sources can include parents, teachers, and other adults who spend significant time with the client. Issues with these raters are discussed in detail in the next section, Parents, Teachers, and Other Adult Raters as Data Sources.

Two additional problems for raters may appear. First, as described in Chapter 3, clients may exhibit avoidance of intense NA as well as certain thoughts and behaviors. Particularly before the therapeutic alliance has formed, clients may avoid awareness of problems containing intense NA or shift topics when beginning to experience intense NA. When this occurs frequently, raters may need to rely on nonverbal indicators of NA such as facial expressions and tone of voice, instead of client verbal reports, to assess NA. Even client dreams may be useful as an emotionally safe way to discuss intense affect (Hill, 2003).

Instructions

On the next page you will find descriptive terms for 5 levels of Negative Affective states of increasing intensity and/or severity. Descriptors within each set are of approximately equal intensity and/or severity.

For each level, check one or more terms that were most salient for your patient <u>during the past week</u>. If a different term of roughly equal intensity applies, write in that term on the blank line.

For the term(s) checked at the most intense/severe level, please estimate how often your client expressed or experienced the negative affective state during the past week. For term(s) that are difficult to estimate, provide your best guess.

Note that your ratings can be made on the basis of both verbal and non-verbal expressions of affect. Also, improvement for different clients may be evidenced by a variety of patterns, including an initial increase in negative affect, maintenance of negative affect, or a decrease in negative affect.

Finally, please indicate whether the individual appears to be avoiding expressing or experiencing negative affect (e.g., denial).

Please complete your rating as soon as possible after the session ends.

Figure 5.1 Instructions for *Depression/Anxiety Negative Affect* (*DANA*) Raters. *These are the instructions for the DANA employed in the test development phase.*

Figure 5.1 displays the instructions for raters who complete the *DANA* scale (Meier, 2012). These instructions offer specific guidance for raters related to avoidance of NA and some of the rater issues described previously. With the *DANA*, the avoidance rating provides information that can help to identify clients who are unlikely to make progress in many psychotherapeutic interventions (Meier, 2012).

An additional problem that can affect both self-report and rating by other methodologies is **confirmation bias** (Meier, 2008). Confirmation bias refers to the tendency to pay attention to information that validates initial expectations and beliefs and to ignore other, disconfirming information; observers hold a belief or impression that causes them to ignore the full range of the phenomena in question. Applying this logic to clinical situations, clinicians' theories and beliefs can prevent them from noticing relevant clinical information that could potentially be useful for modifying and improving counseling interventions (Hoshmand, 1994; Meier, 2003). A clinician who believes that a particular type of psychotherapy must be successful if continually applied, for example, may ignore or dismiss evidence (such as a client's intense feelings of anxiety, recurring instances of avoidant behavior, or ruminations) to the contrary. Similarly, confirmation bias is a potential explanation for the finding of Bickman et al. (2000) that many clinicians do not have alternative treatment plans for failing clients: These clinicians appear unaware that they can conceive of other ways of thinking about and intervening with failing clients.

PARENTS, TEACHERS, AND OTHER ADULT RATERS AS DATA SOURCES

Although clinicians may frequently provide data about their clients, other adults may be appropriate sources of information, when certain conditions occur. Teachers, for example, may often have less motivation to distort ratings in a favorable or unfavorable direction than sources such as clinicians or clients (Dadds, Perrin, & Yule, 1998). One of the major issues with such raters, however, is the reading level required by PMOA measures. The *Behavior Intervention Monitoring Assessment System* (*BIMAS*; McDougal et al., 2012), for example, was designed to provide progress monitoring and outcome data with children and adolescents ages 5 to 18 receiving mental health services. The *BIMAS* contains language that requires a reading ability at the fifth to sixth grade level. The reading level criterion also presumes that the rater also understands the language in which the test material is written. McDougal et al. (2012) noted that the best data typically come from the caregiver who spends the most time with the child. That may be a parent, but it might also be a grandparent or a teacher. It may also be useful to ask multiple individuals to provide data about a child, although research suggests that different raters may provide different information (Meier, 2008). Similarly, multiple teachers can assess a single child for progress and outcome information. Data from different sources may provide clues about situational influences on the child's behaviors, thoughts, and feelings but also present difficulties when attempting to create a coherent picture of a child's or adolescent's mental health status.

ETHICAL AND LEGAL GUIDELINES

In accord with principles offered by professional organizations, McDougal et al. (2012) summarized ethical and legal guidelines that apply to the administration phase of psychological testing. These guidelines include **informed consent, confidentiality,** and **debriefing.**

Informed consent refers to helping clients understand the types and effects of the procedures, including treatment, employed in the provision of care. With PMOA measures, informed consent will be influenced by the typical procedures employed in any particular therapy setting. Some private practitioners, for example, ask beginning clients to read and sign a written form that explains all therapy procedures, including the collection and use of clinical data. In other settings it may be more appropriate for a clinician to describe the test, the rating procedure, and potential uses of test scores to every client. Thus, clients should understand and provide informed consent about all assessment procedures, even if the particular procedures vary by setting.

When part of informed consent, confidentiality should address who will have access to the information, how the information will be shared, and with whom the information will be shared. Clients should also be informed about the limits to confidentiality involved with assessment data. With PMOA measures that contain questions about suicide and homicide, for example, endorsement of such items raises questions about potential harm to self and others and the clinician's responsibilities in those instances (Meier & Davis, 2011).

Finally, clinicians should carefully consider the extent to which they will share and debrief clients about test data and uses of that data (e.g., sharing with insurance companies). Explaining and interpreting test information with a client is essentially an intervention (cf. Finn, Fischer, & Handler, 2012), and its potential effects on the client should be considered before the information is shared.

SUMMARY

The methods and contexts in which PMOA data are administered and collected are critical to understanding how to interpret the resulting scores. Transparent self-report inventories, for example, may be subject to underreporting or exaggeration when respondents gain something (e.g., additional treatment) from distorted reports. Similarly, reports from individuals operating in different contexts, such as the client, clinician, or significant other, will diverge to the extent that those contexts differ (Meier, 2008). Two matching contexts in which reporting is likely to be most valid are (a) a working alliance where the client and therapist have developed a trusting, empathic relationship in which the client feels safe in reporting potentially shameful, embarrassing, and socially undesirable information and (b) an anonymous setting where the client feels confident about confidentiality, such as can occur with computer-administered interviews (Jennings, Lucenko, Malow, & Devieux, 2002).

Clearly written and well-explained informed consent procedures should enhance the working alliance and clients' confidence about confidentiality. Enhancing or measuring the rapport between client and therapist may be important for understanding when clients feel comfortable enough to respond more honestly as compared to socially desirable responses. Providing more structure for interviews and more training for raters may also improve test reliability and subsequently enhance validity.

Other contextual factors include the time period on which PMOA reports are based (e.g., past hour, day, week, month, year) as well as the interval between event occurrence and PMOA report. Regarding the former, events that occur in a recent, short, discrete period are more likely to be remembered and reported accurately (Meier, 2008). Clinical reports, for example, about in-session events and behaviors will be more accurate if data are recorded as the events/behaviors occur or immediately after a session. Standardization of PMOA data collection and administration procedures is a final context that bears emphasis for its potential effects on PMOA reliability and validity estimates. Variability in data source, time of data collection, and type and amount of rater training (as explained in Chapter 8) may decrease psychometric estimates.

Exercise 3 *Assessing Client Nonverbals*

If a client is unable or unwilling to report valid information about sensitive topic(s) in therapy, what options does an assessor have? Many therapists' training includes learning how to assess nonverbal communication. The assumption is that clients may be able to cognitively select their verbal language but that nonverbals are more difficult to censor, particularly around affect. Thus, nonverbals offer another window into process and outcome constructs.

For this brief exercise, watch time period 4:11–6:20, Perls working with Gloria (https://www.youtube.com/watch?v=it0j6FIxIog). Fritz Perls was a well-known Gestalt therapist highly skilled in working with client nonverbals. Answer the following questions:

1. What are some nonverbal indicators of Gloria's affect?
2. What are some of Gloria's likely feelings?
3. If Gloria made progress in therapy, how might these feelings change? How might her avoidance of these feelings change?

Answers are in the appendix.

6

Evaluating Progress Monitoring and Outcome Assessment Measures

INTRODUCTION

This chapter describes criteria for evaluating progress monitoring and outcome assessment (PMOA) measures for use in clinical practice and research. Evaluating PMOA measures involves a combination of traditional psychometric criteria and criteria appropriate to experimental methods. PMOA measures, for example, should be highly correlated with each other and demonstrate change over time when exposed to efficacious psychosocial interventions, but evidence stability in conditions where no intervention is present. PMOA measures should be designed and/or evaluated explicitly for the purposes of progress monitoring and/or outcome assessment; construct validity should be evaluated in the context of the testing purpose.

In many clinical settings, the default decision when choosing a PMOA measure has been to simply employ a familiar, traditional instrument such as the *Beck Depression Inventory* (*BDI*) or *Minnesota Multiphasic Personality Inventory* (*MMPI*). Hill and Lambert (2004) observed that "most outcome measures have not been developed with an eye toward choosing items that are sensitive to change, and little is known about this aspect of test validity" (p. 117). The problem with tests that have not been created and evaluated explicitly for PMOA purposes is that they may contain a subset of items and measures that are insensitive to change. Such tests may fail to detect the small to moderate effects often associated with psychotherapy, and statistical estimates based on their scores may underestimate psychotherapy's effects. Essentially, the inclusion of a subset of insensitive items adds noise and imprecision to the test score. These tests will also be longer than necessary for PMOA purposes; lengthy measures are problematic for the repeated testing that occurs with progress monitoring and may lead clients and clinicians to fail to use lengthy measures (Miller, Duncan, Brown, Sparks, & Claud, 2003).

EVALUATING RELIABILITY AND VALIDITY ESTIMATES OF PROGRESS MONITORING AND OUTCOME ASSESSMENT MEASURES

Traditional test development procedures employ item selection guidelines that implicitly or explicitly have been designed to measure trait-based constructs (Meier, 1994, 2008). As described in Chapter 3, test developers often begin the process by reviewing relevant theoretical and empirical literature to get a sense of the key content domains for test and purpose. In pilot studies, they will evaluate item ceiling and floor effects to assess for sufficient variation in preparation for other analyses such as (a) correlations to estimate convergent and discriminant validity or (b) evaluations to assess whether scales have sufficient range to demonstrate change. Test developers also evaluate the **reliability** of test items in a manner appropriate to the test purpose (e.g., coefficient alpha or test–retest). Reliability and validity analyses may also examine the potential influences of error sources (such as social desirability and rater errors) on test scores. Typically many of these analyses are performed using correlations of test scores to determine if the developed test correlates highly with scores of similar measures (i.e., convergent validity) or has a low correlation with dissimilar test scores (i.e., discriminant validity). Factor analysis is also a favored technique if the test developer assumes that a latent (underlying) construct will be reflected in the correlations of items on the test.

Developers of PMOA measures will follow some similar steps but differ in several key respects. They are likely to pursue a literature review but may find little in psychotherapy theory for guidance since such theories usually describe few or no specific expected outcomes (Hawkins & Meier, 2013). Pilot studies will still be useful to evaluate item means, ceiling and floor effects, and variation to see if the examined item scores have the potential to change in response to an intervention. Determining if items remain stable in the absence of an intervention should constitute the primary assessment of reliability; for a measure of depression or anxiety, for example, these measures may be affected by mood in the absence of any formal psychosocial intervention. Construct validity would be enhanced by demonstrating that the PMOA measure evidences larger change when completed by participants experiencing an intervention targeting the specific content of the PMOA measure. For PMOA test development, traditional analyses such as coefficient alpha and correlational analyses may be useful but secondary to analyses that examine the type and amount of change. Most PMOA measures, for example, are very likely to correlate moderately to highly with measures tapping similar content; however, such information would be most useful for evaluating construct validity if the found correlations were surprisingly small.

Traditional test developmental procedures are likely to produce measures that do not optimize change-sensitive item or scale scores. Weinstock and Meier (2003) compared two types of test development procedures, principal components analysis (PCA, a type of factor analysis) and the Intervention Item Selection Rules (IISRs) described in Chapter 3, with 615 clients who completed a 56-item self-report checklist at intake and termination at a large university counseling center. Weinstock and Meier found that as predicted, the two test development procedures produced item sets with different psychometric properties. Table 6.1 displays descriptive statistics, coefficient alpha, and effect sizes for the PCA and IISR items. Both scales displayed high internal consistency (around .90) and the absence of ceiling or floor effects (defined as whether the mean, plus or minus 1 standard deviation, reaches either limit of the scale). The IISR effect size, however, was considerably higher, near the 0.68 found for average intervention effects by Smith and Glass (1977). This indicates that the 25 IISR selected items are more sensitive to psychosocial intervention effects than the eight PCA items.

This example also illustrates the importance of effect size (ES) for evaluating item and scale scores during the test development and evaluation of PMOA measures. As described in more detail in Chapter 7, an ES estimate is a measure of the strength of change, based on raw scores on a PMOA measure administered at two different points in time. ES can be employed, for example, to learn if groups (e.g., intervention vs. control) show differences over time or between each other on PMOA measures.

EVALUATION OF THE FAMILY LIFE QUESTIONNAIRE AS A PROGRESS MONITORING AND OUTCOME ASSESSMENT MEASURE

Reports appear sporadically across journals in mental health–related disciplines that examine the change sensitivity and related PMOA criteria of clinically related measures. As a recent example, Last, Miles, Wills, Brownhill, and Ford (2012) reported reliability and validity estimates for the *Family Life Questionnaire (FaLQ)*, a new self-report measure completed by parents. The

Table 6.1. *Psychometric Properties of Principal Components Analysis (PCA) and Intervention Item Selection Rule (IISR) Scales*

Scale	M	SD	alpha	Effect Size
EIGHT-ITEM PCA				
Intake	21.21	7.36	.84	
Termination	17.79	6.57	.88	0.47
25-ITEM IISR				
Intake	69.34	17.91	.90	
Termination	55.01	17.89	.93	0.74

NOTE: Source is Weinstock and Meier (2003).

Table 6.2. FAMILY LIFE QUESTIONNAIRE COEFFICIENT ALPHAS AND TIME 1–TIME 2 CORRELATIONS

	Coefficient alpha			Correlations
Scale	T1	T2	T3	T1–T2
Affirmation	.70	.64	.61	.80
Rules	.61	.74	.68	.70
Special Allow	.23	.01	.27	.50
Discipline	.40	.40	.30	.60

NOTE: The T1–T2 correlations are intraclass correlations between Time 1 and Time 2.

14-item *FaLQ* focuses on a parent's assessment of an individual child in terms of four scales: Affirmation (four items; e.g., "gets love and affection"), Discipline (four items; "Told of or corrected for things s/he does wrong"), Special Allowances (three items; "Leads a very protected life"), and Rules (two items; "These family rules are applied consistently"). Last et al. (2012) collected data at three time points during parenting courses, with the sample size decreasing at each interval (n = 91, 71, and 55 for parents completing questionnaires at Times 1, 2, and 3, respectively). Table 6.2 displays coefficient alpha and intraclass correlations for the Time1–Time2 period; Table 6.3 displays ESs for the four scales. Last et al. calculated ES by subtracting Time 1 from Time 3 scores and dividing by the standard deviation of the scale as found in a normative sample.

Reliability and stability. Coefficient alphas are below .5 for the Special Allowances and Disciplines subscales, most likely because of the small number of items (three and two, respectively) in the scales. These scale alphas indicate that items within these scales do not correlate with a total subscale score and that additional analyses are essentially uninterpretable. Alphas for Affirmation and Rules subscales are borderline (four of six values below .7) and again raise questions about whether scale items measure a unitary construct. Similarly, the Time1–Time2 correlations (1 week apart) were higher for Affirmation and Rules, but these values were calculated during an intervention period. Stability for change-sensitive items should be estimated with a control group or with an intervention group before participants receive an intervention.

Ceiling/floor effects. Although a description of the response format was provided, no information was given about the numeric values of the potential responses or the potential range of scores. Although Last et al. (2012) reported

Table 6.3. EFFECT SIZES AND DESCRIPTIVE STATISTICS FOR FAMILY LIFE QUESTIONNAIRE

Scale	M (SD)		Effect Size
	T1	T3	
Affirmation	14.13 (1.84)	15.09 (1.22)	0.50
Rules	6.43 (1.26)	6.14 (1.37)	0.17

means and standard deviations, calculations of the mean plus or minus 1 standard deviation cannot be compared to the top or bottom of possible scores. Given that parents evaluate their child with the *FaLQ*, ceiling effects (where the child is positively rated) would appear a likely problem.

Content validity. No information was provided about the source of the *FaLQ* items, nor was a theoretical basis for the scale described.

Change sensitivity. As shown in Table 6.3, the largest ES for any *FaLQ* scale, Affirmation, did not reach the mean ES of 0.68 reported in Smith and Glass's (1977) meta-analysis of psychotherapy outcome studies. Last et al. (2012) performed a *t* test to check for statistical significance between Time 1 and Time 3 scores and found a statistically significant difference for Affirmation only.

Phase/time effects. No information was provided about whether particular *FaLQ* scales would be expected to show differential change over short, moderate, or longer intervals of time.

Intervention characteristics. Last et al. provided little information about the content of the provided intervention, a parenting course, and no linkage between relevant theory and the *FaLQ* item content or sources. Relatively little impact would be expected for a psychoeducational course beyond an increase on knowledge measures, and the small ESs reported in the study match this expectation. No information was provided about the length of the parenting course or whether improvement should be maintained beyond the end of the intervention.

Demographics. ESs by gender and age were not reported.

Data source. Of 91 parents who initially provided information, only six were male (7%). Given research showing that parents can differ substantially in their reports about children's behavior (e.g., Christensen, Margolin, & Sullaway, 1992), *FaLQ* results should not be generalized beyond mothers.

Avoidance. No information was reported regarding avoidance-related constructs and *FaLQ* scores; a social desirability bias would appear plausible when a parent reports about her or his child. The *FaLQ* appears to have no method for detecting or estimating error in parent reports.

Additional information. Last et al. reported two correlations of (a) .56 between the *Affirmation* scale and a positive parenting scale and (b) –.45 between the *Rules* scale and another scale measuring inconsistent discipline. Although potentially important in evaluation of traditional trait-based scales, these convergent validity correlations add relatively little value to evaluating the *FaLQ* because most scales, particularly if they share method variance (e.g., self-report), correlate moderately to highly with scales measuring similar content.

Summary. One of the potential uses for the *FaLQ* is evaluating the impact of parent and family interventions. However, the low to moderate alphas for all four FaLQ scales raise cautions about the use of this scale as a PMOA measure in clinical practice. Last et al. (2012, p. 124) proceeded with their change analyses with all four scales and concluded that "the FalQ Affirmation and Discipline subscales can detect change." The items on the Discipline scale may be able to detect change over time, but whether the single construct of discipline applies to

Table 6.4. EVALUATION OF THE *FAMILY LIFE QUESTIONNAIRE (FaLQ)* ON PROGRESS
MONITORING AND OUTCOME ASSESSMENT CRITERIA

Criterion	*Brief Explanation*
Reliability/Stability	Moderate coefficient alphas for two of four scales; no information about score stability in the absence of intervention.
Ceiling/Floor Effects	Insufficient information to evaluate.
Content Validity	Insufficient information to evaluate.
Change Sensitivity	*FaLQ* scales display low to moderate effect sizes (ESs), indicating some ability to detect change.
Phase/Time Effects	Insufficient information to evaluate.
Intervention Characteristics	Minimal information about parenting intervention.
Demographics	No assessment of gender or age effects on *FaLQ* ESs.
Avoidance	No relevant data collected with *FaLQ*.
Data Source	Parent report; 93% of *FaLQ* data supplied by mothers.
Brevity	A total of 14 items indicates minimal completion time.

the sum of these item scores is in doubt based on the coefficient alpha analyses. In addition, the reported ESs are small, raising questions about the ability of the *FaLQ* scales to detect change from interventions that produce small to moderate effects.

The Last et al. (2012) report is a useful initial study but contains limited data related to *FaLQ*'s use as a PMOA measure in clinical practice. No information was available, for example, for evaluating five of the 10 PMOA criteria for the *FaLQ* (see Table 6.4). Given the field's lack of consensus about PMOA criteria, this is likely to be typical for many published measures. At this stage of study, clinicians should employ the *FaLQ* as a tool for clinical feedback or decision making with caution.

CONTEMPORARY PROGRESS MONITORING AND OUTCOME ASSESSMENT MEASURES

Traditional psychological tests such as the *MMPI* are lengthy measures initially designed for diagnostic and screening purposes. This does not disqualify these measures for PMOA purposes, but does raise questions about their fit for measuring change in practice settings where brevity is required (Gresham et al., 2010; Vermeersch et al., 2004). In this section, PMOA measures employed to assess progress and outcome in clinical research and practice will be described and evaluated in terms of the 10 criteria outlined at the end of Chapter 3. The psychometric information reported in this chapter is representative of major findings with these scales and is not intended to be comprehensive in the manner of a meta-analysis.

Beck Depression Inventory

A self-report scale, the *BDI* contains 21 multiple-choice items assessing 21 different aspects of depression (*BDI* and *BDI-II*; Beck & Steer, 1987; Beck, Steer, & Brown, 1996). The scales were developed on the basis of observations of depressed and nondepressed individuals, and each item refers to different aspects of depression and contains four statements of increasing severity. The *BDI-II* (Beck et al., 1996) conforms to diagnostic criteria listed in the *Diagnostic and Statistical Manual of Mental Disorders*, fourth edition (DSM-IV; Nezu, Ronan, Meadows, & McClure, 2000). Depression symptoms and attitudes include mood, guilt feelings, suicidal wishes, irritability, sleep disturbance, and appetite changes. Hatfield and Ogles's (2004) survey of psychologists found the *BDI* to be the most frequently employed measure for outcome assessment.

Scores on the *BDI* in previous research have shown high internal consistency, high correlations with other measures of depression, and sensitivity to change resulting from a variety of medication and counseling interventions (Kendall, Hollon, Beck, Hammen, & Ingram, 1987). On the other hand, some research indicates that over 50% of individuals classified as depressed by the *BDI* change categories when retested, even when the retesting period consisted of only a few hours or days (Kendall et al., 1987). In addition, the *BDI* has been shown to exhibit sudden, substantial increases and decreases between psychotherapy sessions (Kelly, Roberts, & Ciesla, 2005). The instability of some *BDI* items raises questions, when assessing counseling outcome, about attributing change in scores on this instrument to psychosocial interventions. Table 6.5 summarizes its psychometric properties in relation to PMOA purposes.

One explanation is that the some *BDI* items are too sensitive to mood or distress to separate and detect smaller effects from psychosocial interventions (i.e., treatment sensitivity). As noted previously, Persons and Fresco (2008) observed that researchers have found that repeated administration of the *BDI* is associated with a trend toward decreasing scores. It is likely that repeated administration of any psychotherapy-related self-report measure may result in self-monitoring, a reactive method known to change the monitored behavior, typically in the same direction as an intervention (Craske & Tsao, 1999; Nelson, 1977).

Using the *BDI* as an outcome measure, Richter et al. (1997) reported a study of 103 inpatients who received medication (those diagnosed with major depressive disorder [MDD]) or psychotherapy and some medication (those diagnosed with adjustment disorder/dysthymia [ADD]). The mean length of inpatient treatment was 42 days. Table 6.6 shows means, standard deviations, and ESs for both diagnostic groups and all measurement periods. For both groups, ES exceeded 0.70 when comparing the first and last administrations, suggesting that the *BDI* was sensitive to change at least partially resulting from the provided treatments. Two of the findings in Table 6.6 are unexpected. First, the ES (0.92) of the less severe diagnostic group (ADD) was smaller than the ES (1.37) of the patients with a more severe diagnosis (MDD). One possible explanation is that the medication administered to the MDD group produced beneficial effects more quickly than the psychotherapy received by the ADD group (cf. Sperry, Brill, Howard, & Grissom, 1996). Second, the ADD group evidenced a statistically significant decrease during the first two *BDI* administrations (Times 1 and 2; ES = 0.31). These results confirm the general trends found in other *BDI* research: The *BDI*

Table 6.5. Evaluation of the Beck Depression Inventory (BDI) on Progress Monitoring and Outcome Assessment Criteria

Criterion	Brief Explanation
Reliability/ Stability	Mixed: Many reports of high internal consistency, but also many reports that *BDI* scores change over short periods independent of any psychosocial interventions (e.g., Kelly, Roberts, & Ciesla, 2005; Kendall, Hollon, Beck, Hammen, & Ingram, 1987; Longwell & Truax, 2005; Richter et al., 1997; Sharpe & Gilbert, 1998).
Ceiling/Floor Effects	Studies with clinical samples suggest *BDI* scores have ample range to increase and decrease.
Content Validity	Items developed on basis of clinical observations of depressed clients; items correspond to *Diagnostic and Statistical Manual of Mental Disorders* depression symptoms (Richter, Werner, Heerlein, Kraus, & Sauer, 1998); no theoretical or empirical basis for why some items may be more change sensitive than others.
Change Sensitivity	*BDI* evidences change across psychotherapy and medication modalities, effect sizes (ESs > 0.70) (Richter et al., 1997).
Phase/Time Effects	*BDI* appears sensitive to quick medication effects (Richter et al., 1997).
Intervention Characteristics	*BDI* shows change across broad range of treatment modalities (Richter et al., 1998). BDI should evidence largest change with intervention aimed at depressed/anxious clients, but all clients are likely to evidence change on negative affect measures like the *BDI*.
Demographics	Richter et al. (1997) diagnostic groups results are reversed.
Client Characteristics	Perhaps *BDI* more sensitive to changes in individuals with less severe depression.
Data Source	The self-report *BDI* appears to be reactive; that is, research indicates "that repeated administration of the BDI consistently resulted in a lower score, even when research participants were not depressed and were not receiving treatment" (Persons & Fresco, 2008, p. 115; Longwell & Truax, 2005; Sharpe & Gilbert, 1998).
Avoidance	No information found.
Brevity	21-item scale.

Table 6.6. BECK DEPRESSION INVENTORY TOTAL SCORE DESCRIPTIVE STATISTICS AND
EFFECT SIZES (ESs) FOR 103 INPATIENTS

Time	M	SD	ES (Comparison Periods)
	MAJOR DEPRESSIVE DISORDER ($n = 39$)		
1	25.5	9.48	
2	23.0	11.48	0.16 (Time 1–Time 2)
3	12.4	11.00	
4	11.5	10.70	1.37 (Time 1–Time 4)
	ADJUSTMENT/DYSTHYMIC DISORDER ($n = 37$)		
1	24.9	10.52	
2	21.6	11.92	0.31 (Time 1–Time 2)
3	14.4	10.63	
4	15.2	11.38	0.92 (Time 1–Time 4)

NOTE: Time 1 and Time 2 administrations were consecutive days at the beginning of inpatient treatment, whereas Time 3 and Time 4 administrations were consecutive days at the end of treatment. ES was computed using the standard deviation at Time 1.

Total Score shows small decreases over very short intervals (even in the absence of an intervention) but also larger changes over the course of psychotherapeutic and medication interventions.

Although the *BDI* is one of the major tests employed to measure outcome, these results suggest that clinicians and researchers who employ the *BDI* for PMOA purposes, particularly over relatively short periods of time, should be cautious when interpreting these scores for assessing progress and outcome.

Outcome Rating Scale

The *Outcome Rating Scale* (*ORS*; Miller et al., 2003) and its companion scale, the *Session Rating Scale* (*SRS*), each contain four self-report items that employ a visual analog response format (a rating along a 10-cm line). On the *ORS*, the client reports functioning for the past week for overall well-being, personal well-being, interpersonal relationships (family and other close relations), and social relationships (work, school). The *SRS* focuses primarily on the working alliance.

Relatively little information has been published to support the change sensitivity of the *ORS* items or total score. Even when published research purports to show the *ORS*'s change sensitivity, insufficient information was presented to document this claim (e.g., lack of means, standard deviations, and effect size; Miller, Duncan, Sorrell, & Brown, 2005). It is possible that the *ORS* suffers from **publication bias**: Given that most journals tend to publish studies with statistically significant results, researchers using the *ORS* may not have submitted nonsignificant findings for publication. As shown in Table 6.7, research documents high coefficient alphas for the *ORS*, leading Miller et al. (2003) to conclude that "the measure perhaps can best be thought of as a global measure of distress rather than one possessing subscales for separate dimensions" (p. 95). If the *ORS* is primarily a measure of distress, it may be insensitive to detecting other types of psychotherapeutic change beyond the acute distress decreases detected by some PMOA measures (e.g., the *Behavioral Health Questionnaire*, Kopta & Lowry, 2002, and

Table 6.7. EVALUATION OF THE OUTCOME RATING SCALE (ORS) ON PROGRESS MONITORING AND OUTCOME ASSESSMENT CRITERIA

Criterion	*Brief Explanation*
Reliability/ Stability	Reports of high internal consistency (alphas >.90) but low test–retest reliability (*rs* of.66,.58,.53,.49) over periods of 10 days to 5 weeks, and effect size (ES) of 0.22 in untreated controls, suggest *ORS* scores are likely to evidence small improvements even in nonintervention conditions. Higher test–retest correlations found in study with undergraduate and graduate student respondents (Bringhurt, Watson, Miller, & Duncan, 2006; Campbell & Hemsley, 2009; Hafkenscheid, Duncan, & Miller, 2010; Miller et al., 2003).
Ceiling/Floor Effects	Clinical samples suggest *ORS* scores have ample range to increase and decrease (Miller et al., 2003).
Content Validity	Content based on the scale titles of the *Outcome Questionnaire-45* (individual, relational, social; Miller et al., 2003). No theoretical basis.
Change Sensitivity	Evidence that *ORS* total score shows change across 10 sessions of psychotherapy with 77 clients, ES = 0.70; *ORS* scores distinguish clinical and nonclinical groups (Miller et al., 2003; also Hafkenscheid et al., 2010); *ORS* does not differentiate between feedback and no-feedback groups (Murphy et al., 2012).
Phase/Time Effects	No information found, but indirect evidence that *ORS* is primarily sensitive to acute distress in early sessions.
Intervention Characteristics	No theoretical basis for predicting that *ORS* will detect change from particular interventions.
Client Characteristics	No information found.
Data Source	The self-report *ORS* appears to be moderately reactive, with small score improvements upon repeated testing (Miller et al., 2003).
Avoidance	No information found.
Brevity	Four-item self-report encourages repeated use; compliance rate near 90% in community family service agency (Miller et al., 2003).

the *COMPASS*, Sperry, Brill, Howard, & Grissom, 1996) in the first few sessions of psychotherapy.

Particularly in relation to other PMOA measures, the *ORS* has low test–retest reliability estimates (Miller et al., 2003). Psychometrically, this makes sense given the small number of items on the scale. In addition, one study found that using the *ORS* for feedback in therapy did not produce a statistically significant difference with a no-feedback group for improving outcome (Murphy, Rashleigh, & Timulak, 2012). Given that most studies employing other PMOA measures have found a beneficial effect for feedback groups, this result suggests that the *ORS* may be less sensitive for detecting treatment effects. While the brevity of the *ORS* and *SRS* has been touted as a strength (Boswell, Kraus, Miller, & Lambert, 2013), the small number of items suggests their scores will reflect less change-sensitive variance. Thus, the *ORS*'s best use may be as a technique for discussing progress with clients rather than as a change-sensitive indicator of therapeutic progress.

Outcome Questionnaire

The *Outcome Questionnaire-45* (*OQ45*) is a comprehensive outcome scale explicitly developed for PMOA purposes (Lambert & Finch, 1999). The *OQ* was designed to be easy to score, low cost, sensitive to change over short periods, and able to measure a range of symptoms and characteristics associated with mental health functioning. Intended for individuals ages 18 and older, the 45-item test can be completed in about 5 to 10 minutes. Sample items include *I feel blue* and *I am satisfied with my relationships with others*. The *OQ* produces a total score and three subscales: The Symptom Distress subscale contains items related to anxiety and depression; Interpersonal Relations items assess satisfaction with and problems in interpersonal functioning; and Social Role Performance items relate to satisfaction and competence in employment, family, and leisure roles.

As shown in Table 6.8, studies indicate that the *OQ45* has adequate test–retest reliability and internal consistency and correlates in expected directions and magnitudes with related scales such as the *SCL-90-R, BDI, State-Trait Anxiety Inventory*, and *Inventory of Interpersonal Problems*. Although research indicates that some *OQ45* items evidence change in response to treatment (e. g., Vermeersch et al., 2004), a study with college students found that students show improvement on *OQ* items even when they are not in counseling, but not at the same rate as treated individuals. In addition, factor analytic research has suggested that *OQ* items measure a single mental health construct (Lambert, 2007); all three subscales of the *OQ45* are highly intercorrelated, suggesting that the total score on the scale, like the *ORS*, can be considered an indication of general distress. The *OQ* has also been employed as a PMOA measure in research that used *OQ* scores as feedback to therapists, thereby reducing the rate of client failure.

Table 6.8. EVALUATION OF THE OUTCOME QUESTIONNAIRE-45 (OQ45) ON PROGRESS MONITORING AND OUTCOME ASSESSMENT (PMOA) CRITERIA

Criterion	Brief Explanation
Reliability/ Stability	Many reports of high internal consistency; total and scale scores evidence stability over time, but some items show improvement in untreated conditions (Miller et al., 2003; Vermeersch et al., 2004; Vermeersch, Lambert, & Burlingame, 2000).
Ceiling/Floor Effects	Studies with clinical samples suggest *OQ-45* scores and most items have ample range to increase and decrease (e.g., Vermeersch et al., 2000).
Content Validity	Items tapping symptom distress and interpersonal/social relationships reflect general symptoms and functioning areas. No explicit connections to psychotherapy theory.
Change Sensitivity	Numerous studies that *OQ* total and subscale scores change in response to treatment, although evidence that some items are insensitive to change (Vermeersch et al., 2004; Vermeersch et al., 2000).
Phase/Time Effects	Like other PMOA scales, for causes unknown symptom distress items show more change in early sessions than other social role functioning, followed by change on interpersonal functioning items (Lambert, 2007).
Intervention Characteristics	*OQ* shows change across broad range of treatment modalities (Vermeersch et al., 2000; Vermeersch et al., 2004).
Client Characteristics	No information found about different effect sizes (ESs) for demographic variables.
Data Source	The self-report *OQ* appears to be moderately reactive, with small item improvements upon repeated testing in both treated and untreated conditions.
Avoidance	No information found.
Brevity	5–10 minutes to complete, but some data and anecdotal evidence indicate that some clients find *OQ*'s 45 items too long for repeated administration; usage rate of only 25% at an outpatient community agency over a 1-year period (Miller et al., 2003).

Behavioral Intervention Monitoring Assessment System

Intended for use with children and adolescents ages 5 through 18, the *Behavioral Intervention Monitoring Assessment System* (*BIMAS*; McDougal, Bardos, & Meier, 2012) is a brief PMOA that includes rating forms for teachers, clinicians, parents, and youth. The *BIMAS*'s primary purposes are to screen children and adolescents for mental health problems and then assess progress and outcomes in young clients receiving psychosocial interventions in outpatient settings such as schools and clinics. Sample items include *Was impulsive* and *Acted sad or withdrawn*. The *BIMAS* is based on the Response To Intervention (RTI) model that begins with universal screening on domains of interest, identifying youth who would benefit from increasingly intense interventions, with accompanying progress monitoring (McDougal et al., 2012). The *BIMAS* items cluster into three Behavior Concern scales (Conduct, Negative Affect, and Cognition/Attention) and two Adaptive Functioning scales (Social Functioning and Academic Functioning); these scales show expected correlations with similar measures such as Conners ratings forms (McDougal et al., 2012).

As part of the validation process, McDougal et al. (2012) employed the teacher, parent, and self-report forms of the *BIMAS* to examine the outcomes of 46 students who participated in an anger management intervention. The clinical sample consisted of 32 males (70%) and 14 females (30%); included 30 African American (65%), two Hispanic (4%), and 14 Caucasian (30%) students; and included individuals who were 12 to 18 years old. *BIMAS* forms were completed before and after the intervention. Figure 6.1 displays ESs indicating that participants in the anger management group evidenced improvement (all effect sizes $\geq |0.8|$) across all rater types and all scales. The exception is the Social Functioning scale on the *BIMAS*-Teacher form where a moderate effect was found ($d = -0.7$).

As shown in Figure 6.1, the scale most likely to show change from an anger management treatment, the Conduct scale, does evidence the largest ESs across the different raters. A more general scale, Negative Affect, also shows a large ES, which makes sense because there should be decreases in negative affect as accompanying problems resolve. These results are instructive as a PMOA assessment strategy. When available resources permit, PMOA assessment in any clinical situation should include a measure specific to the client's target problem (anger and other conduct issues in this example) as well as a general measure

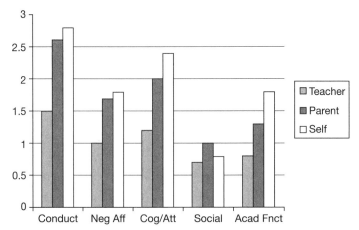

Figure 6.1 Effect Sizes (ESs) for Behavioral Intervention Monitoring Assessment System (BIMAS) Scores for an Anger Management Group. *Negative signs have been removed from the ES scores because all changes indicate improvement.*

indicative of the client's overall status (negative affect, symptoms, and/or functioning). If the relative changes of scores on targeted and general scales match those expected to be produced by intervention(s) with a particular client sample, greater confidence can be placed in both the validity of measurement and the delivered intervention. Time and resources may not always permit a combination of targeted and general measures, but the use of a measure like the *BIMAS*, which includes diverse scales assessing common problems for children and adolescents, makes such a combined strategy more practical and efficient. Table 6.9 summarizes the PMOA criteria for the *BIMAS*.

Table 6.9. EVALUATION OF THE BEHAVIORAL INTERVENTION MONITORING ASSESSMENT SYSTEM (BIMAS) ON PROGRESS MONITORING AND OUTCOME ASSESSMENT CRITERIA

Criterion	Brief Explanation
Reliability/ Stability	Scales evidence moderate to high internal consistency across parent, teacher, and self-report forms as well as gender and age (alphas >.8); scores also evidence moderate to high (rs >.8) stability with 2- to 4-week test–retest period (McDougal et al., 2012).
Ceiling/Floor Effects	Studies with clinical and normative samples suggest *BIMAS* scores have ample range to increase and decrease, but items on preliminary versions show ceiling effects (McDougal et al., 2012; Meier, McDougal, & Bardos, 2008).
Content Validity	Items developed based on review of literature, similar scales, and expert suggestions. Scales conform to accepted constructs classifying children's problem behaviors and important areas of functioning. No explicit link to psychotherapy theory.
Change Sensitivity	*BIMAS* scale scores change in response to treatment; scores distinguish between clinical groups and normative samples; anger management intervention produces highest effect sizes (ESs; > 1.4) on *Conduct* scale (McDougal et al., 2012; Meier, 2004; Meier, McDougal, & Bardos, 2008).
Phase/Time Effects	No information reported.
Intervention Characteristics	Evidence that scales respond to target treatment (e.g., anger management intervention produces highest ESs [> 1.4] on Conduct scale; McDougal et al., 2012)
Client Characteristics	Items on preliminary versions show larger ESs for boys (Meier et al., 2008).
Data Source	Repeated testing does not affect mean scale scores for teacher, parent, or self-report forms (McDougal et al., 2012).
Avoidance	No information reported about avoidance or rater errors.
Brevity	5–10 minutes to complete; forms have about 34 items each, with reading level about fifth grade (McDougal et al., 2012).

Depression/Anxiety Negative Affect Scale

Described in previous chapters, the *Depression/Anxiety Negative Affect* scale (*DANA*; Meier, 2012) is based on the idea that problem resolution in psychotherapy will be accompanied by decreasing reports of negative affect, particularly its intensity or strength (Diener, Larsen, Levine, & Emmons, 1985). The *DANA*'s 51 items describe negative affect (NA) in five item clusters representing increasing intensities: *Transient NA* (Level 1), *Increasing NA* (2), *Moderate NA* (3), *Intense NA* (4), and *Extreme NA* (5). The scores resulting from the endorsement of these items include (a) Total NA (TOT), the sum of the total number of NA terms endorsed per session, (b) Highest Intensity Level (HIL), the highest intensity level of any NA descriptor endorsed per session, and (c) Average Intensity Level (AIL), the mean intensity level for all NA terms endorsed per session.

Unlike an aggregated score, where a particular score can reflect responses or ratings to multiple, *different* items or tasks, HIL reflects a point on the *DANA*'s 5-point intensity scale that signifies a *unique* level of NA intensity. Thus, *DANA* scores should be a more precise measurement of the construct of interest than an aggregated score. In addition, the *DANA* asks the clinical rater to assess whether or not the client was avoiding NA. As described in Chapter 3, avoidance and its related theoretical constructs have the potential to influence both the progress of therapy and the validity of the collected PMOA data. Information about avoidance provides a potentially important alert to clinicians about when and why therapy progress may be impeded. Table 6.10 displays ESs evidencing differences in both the size and direction of change for clients whose therapists rated them as avoiding or experiencing NA.

Table 6.11 shows the evaluation of the *DANA* on the 10 PMOA criteria. Initial evidence indicates that *DANA* scores show internal consistency, strong content validity, and sensitivity to change. The *DANA*'s avoidance score also distinguishes between clients who make progress and those who fail to improve or who worsen. Evidence for the stability of *DANA* scores is weak, however, and the avoidance rating consists of only a single item. Like all new PMOA measures, replication and extension of these results are needed.

Table 6.10. Change Sensitivity for Depression/Anxiety Negative Affect (DANA) Variables by Gender and Avoidance Status

	HIL ES	AIL ES	TOT ES
Males	0.68	0.23	0.58
Females	0.93	0.83	0.62
Avoided NA	0	−0.94	−1.07
Experienced NA	1.37	1.08	1.31

NOTE: HIL refers to Highest Intensity Level, the highest intensity level of any DANA descriptor endorsed per session; AIL refers to Average Intensity Level, the mean intensity level for all NA terms endorsed per session; and TOT refers to the sum of the total number of negative affect terms endorsed per session. Adapted from Table 3 in Meier (2012).

Table 6.11. EVALUATION OF THE DEPRESSION/ANXIETY NEGATIVE AFFECT (DANA) ON
PROGRESS MONITORING AND OUTCOME ASSESSMENT CRITERIA

Criterion	Brief Explanation
Reliability/ Stability	Moderate internal consistency estimate (.76) for Total Negative Affect (NA) score; self-report version shows stability over time with graduate students (Keating, 2012; Meier, 2012).
Ceiling/Floor Effects	Clinical samples suggest DANA scores (but not items) have ample range to increase and decrease (Meier, 2012).
Content Validity	DANA items selected after review of relevant literature about emotion science and psychotherapy outcomes, related tests, and feedback from psychotherapists. Theoretical connection to most psychotherapy theories, but closest with experiential and narrative therapies (Meier, 2012).
Change Sensitivity	DANA scores change in response to treatment (Meier, 2012).
Phase/Time Effects	No information found, but research suggests DANA scores are likely to be cyclical for many clients, particularly those in experiential therapies (Mergenthaler, 1996).
Intervention Characteristics	DANA scores evidence change across range of treatment modalities (Meier, 2012).
Client Characteristics	As shown in Table 6.10, women evidence greater change on DANA scales (Meier, 2012).
Data Source	Literature suggests clinician-rated scores may be more valid than self-report with NA and avoidance constructs.
Avoidance	Matching theoretical expectations, clients experiencing NA show larger effect sizes (> 1) than clients avoiding NA (Meier, 2012).
Brevity	Data show a median of four to seven items completed in Sessions 1–8 (Meier, 2012), indicating quick completion time by clinicians.

DEVELOPMENT OF A CHANGE-SENSITIVE TEST: THE BEHAVIORAL INTERVENTION MONITORING ASSESSMENT SYSTEM

The key to developing a reliable and valid PMOA measure is the test construction and revision process. Although clinicians are concerned with the interpretation of scores on PMOA measures, interpretation depends on the procedures and decisions made about how the measure's items are selected (e.g., theoretical and empirical basis), administered (e.g., instructions to raters and respondents, training for raters), scored (e.g., response format), and validated (e.g., selection of data and participants in relation to test purpose). Problems in any one of these steps can result in misleading interpretations of data from the constructed test.

The BIMAS (McDougal et al., 2012) has complementary 30+ item forms that are completed by parents, teachers, clinicians, and children/adolescents. As an example of the test development process, this section describes one of the item selection studies that led to the creation of the parent form. As described earlier in this chapter, the *BIMAS*'s primary purposes are to screen children and adolescents for mental health problems and then assess progress and outcomes in young clients receiving psychosocial interventions in outpatient settings such as schools and clinics.

Parent Elementary Form

Meier, McDougal, and Bardos (2008) investigated the change sensitivity of the items on a preliminary version of the Parent Elementary form of the *BIMAS* (PE-BIMAS). All parents or guardians of children and adolescents who sought counseling at two multiple-branch community mental health agencies completed an intake version of the PE-BIMAS at their first visit; these agencies provide individual, family, and group interventions to children, adolescents, and families in urban, suburban, and rural communities. Students' presenting issues included peer difficulties, family conflict, illegal activities that brought children into court, emotional and physical problems, lack of self-confidence, child abuse, and hyperactivity. Because of difficulty obtaining outcome assessments at termination, follow-up forms were administered at quarterly intervals to all clients receiving services (i.e., approximately four times a year; cf. Lewis & Magoon, 1987). The mean amount of time between intake and follow-up with the collected PE-BIMAS forms equaled 7.2 months (SD = 5.1, range 1 to 38 months).

Of those 896 parents who completed both intake and follow-up forms, 66% identified as male and 34% as female. Race/ethnicity data included 60% Caucasian, 20% African American, 8% Hispanic, 4% Biracial, 2% Native American, 3% Asian, and 3% Other, and school grade was reported as 12% in Kindergarten, 14% in Grade 1, 13% in Grade 2, 14% in Grade 3, 19% in Grade 4, 15% in Grade 5, 11% in Grade 6, and the remaining 2% in Grades 7 through 10. To address possible chance effects, the scale analyses reported were cross-validated. To do so, study participants were randomly assigned to one of two groups, resulting in subsample A and subsample B, both with a sample size of 448. Randomization succeeded in creating two roughly equivalent groups with regard to gender (subsample A had 69% males, subsample B 64% males), relation to client (66% mother in A, 68% mother in B), and race (62% Caucasian and 20% African American in A compared to 58% and 19%, respectively, in B).

Potential items for this preliminary form of the PE-BIMAS resulted from the literature of children's behavior problems (Stiffman, Orme, Evans, Feldman, & Keeney, 1984), other measures of children's functioning (Meier, 1998), and suggestions from mental health professionals. Identified categories included hiding thoughts from others, deviancy, internalizing behaviors (e.g., anxiety, depression), externalizing behaviors (e.g., fighting), and problems in cognitive, social, and academic functioning (Stiffman et al., 1984). This review resulted in a 32-item scale (labeled as the Original scale), and items were worded in both a positive (labeled the Strengths scale) and negative (Distress/Problems scale) direction to avoid acquiescence and criticalness biases.

Paired *t* tests examined change in item scores from intake to follow-up using an alpha level of.10 to detect statistically significant change (cf. Meier, 2000). As shown in Table 6.12, 12 of 19 items evidenced statistically significant change in one or both subsamples: *Controls temper, Pays attention to speakers, Stays out of trouble, Communicates clearly, Shares thinking, Feels depressed, Behaves differently, Acts impulsively, Fights with others, Family members fight, Lies or cheats*, and *Gets failing grades*. All 12 items that evidenced significant change in Table 6.12 improved from intake to follow-up. Although clients worsened in at least one subsample on the items *Makes friends easily, Limits set with children*, and *Helps with household tasks*, these changes did not reach statistical significance. Meier et al. (2008) also examined different combinations of items for the largest homogeneous subgroups in this dataset (i.e., for total sample, boys and girls, and Caucasian boys). They found that a scale composed of the original 32 items had a lower ES (0.15) than the mean ES (0.29) for the IISR scales across all subgroups. More homogeneous subgroups also displayed higher ESs: Boys' scales ranged from 0.30 to 0.33 and Caucasian boys' scales from 0.34 to 0.43.

SUMMARY

The short list of PMOA measures described in this chapter brings up a major problem for both clinicians and researches—that is, the proliferation of PMOA measures. New web-based PMOA measures appear regularly (e.g., http://www.outcometracker.org) and dozens of well-known measures such as the *Symptom Checklist-90*, the *Beck Anxiety Scale*, the *State-Trait Anxiety Inventory*, and the *Global Assessment of Functioning Scale* also exist. It is currently not feasible to maintain an up-to-date comprehensive list of previous and newly published measures that might be employed for PMOA purposes. And given the lack of criteria, it is unsurprising that many authors of these scales report only traditional psychometric properties (i.e., coefficient alpha, factor analytic results, and convergent validity correlations) and fail to include information relevant to PMOA purposes (e.g., change sensitivity, time to complete).

Performing the type of research needed to evaluate PMOA measures is difficult because of the inherent complexity and resources required. With traditional test construction, a single administration is often all that is necessary to produce estimates of reliability (e.g., coefficient alpha) and validity (e.g., factor analysis and correlations with other measures to estimate convergent and discriminant validity). In contrast, multiple administrations of a PMOA measure

Table 6.12. RESULTS OF CHANGE ANALYSES FOR THE PARENT ELEMENTARY
FORM OF THE BEHAVIORAL INTERVENTION MONITORING
ASSESSMENT SYSTEM (PE-BIMAS) ITEMS

Item Content	*Subsample A*			*Subsample B*		
	M Diff	*Std Err*	*t*	*M Diff*	*Std Err*	*t*
STRENGTHS						
Communicates clearly[a]	.13	0.04	3.47**	.05	0.03	1.33
Stays out of trouble[a]	.13	0.04	3.08**	.05	0.04	1.13
Controls temper[b]	.13	0.05	2.80**	.14	0.05	2.93**
Pays attention to speakers[b]	.12	0.04	2.78**	.16	0.04	4.07**
Well behaved at home	.07	0.05	1.51	.05	0.05	1.02
Shares thinking[a]	.06	0.04	1.36	.09	0.04	2.10*
Limits set with children	.05	0.04	1.12	−.03	0.04	−0.63
Starts conversations	.06	0.08	0.78	.06	0.07	0.75
Makes friends easily	.00	0.04	0.03	−.06	0.04	−1.51
Helps with household tasks	−.00	0.05	−0.02	.02	0.04	0.45
DISTRESS/PROBLEMS						
Feels depressed[b]	.22	0.05	4.69**	.14	0.05	3.17**
Behaves differently[b]	.13	0.04	2.91**	.18	0.04	4.01**
Family members fight[b]	.16	0.06	2.79**	.11	0.06	1.96*
Acts impulsively[b]	.10	0.04	2.59*	.14	0.04	3.38**
Fights with others[b]	.10	0.04	2.46*	.14	0.04	3.37**
Lies or cheats[b]	.12	0.05	2.43*	.11	0.04	2.55*
Gets failing grades[b]	.10	0.05	1.98*	.10	0.05	1.98*
Fidgets	.08	0.05	1.60	.07	0.04	1.60
Sleepy or tired	.01	0.09	0.10	.07	0.08	0.83

NOTE: Items are arranged by descending absolute *t* value of subsample A. A negative mean change score indicates that scores for this item worsened from initial to follow-up period. Source is Meier et al. (2008).

[a] Items evidence statistically significant change in either subsample A or B.
[b] Items evidence statistically significant change in both subsample A and B.

* $p < .10$.
** $p < .05$.

must occur, over the course of multiple sessions of psychotherapy, to estimate change sensitivity, usually with clinical samples. As appears to be the case with self-report PMOA measures, repeated administration itself can be reactive and leads to improvement independent of intervention effects. To create controls, multiple administrations of the PMOA with individuals who do not receive an intervention can be equally difficult, particularly if the goal is to perform this task with a clinical sample. Similarly, random assignment to treatment or control conditions in many clinical settings is often not feasible or ethical. A lack of grant funding related to the development and evaluation of PMOA measures means that researchers must perform individual studies over a period of years to accumulate the necessary information.

7

Tools for Interpreting Progress Monitoring and Outcome Assessment Data

INTRODUCTION

As described in Chapter 4, making sense of progress monitoring and outcome assessment (PMOA) test scores usually includes interpreting graphics, tables, and statistical analyses. These tools present a summary of PMOA data to aid in making judgments about the type, direction, and amount of progress made by clients. Thus, clinicians and others who employ PMOA tests and the resulting data need at least a basic understanding of commonly employed graphics, tables, and statistical analyses, which are the focus of this chapter. That understanding should also include knowledge of important limitations for PMOA usage.

VISUAL DISPLAYS AND TIME SERIES

Visual displays of quantitative and qualitative information can be particularly helpful to organize and simplify complex clinical information, recognize trends in data, and recall clinical data (Mattaini, 1993; Tufte, 1983). Visual displays should be employed first when examining PMOA quantitative data if the possibility exists that the data will display a nonlinear shape. In some progress and outcome domains (e.g., reading fluency), examination of the data's slope can provide feedback about progress as well as the effectiveness of the provided intervention (e.g., Van Norman, Christ, & Zopluoglu, 2013). In many problems areas, however, change can evidence nonlinear, cyclical, and even chaotic properties (cf. the successful therapy cases examined by Mergenthaler, 1996). These patterns may be best detected in visual displays.

Typically employed with data that show or have the potential to show substantial variability, time series displays illustrate a single variable recorded over an extended period of time (Tufte, 1983). A time series is constructed by plotting a single data point by some event, such as session number. **Multivariate**

or multiple time series can be constructed with more than one variable if the relation among variables is also of interest. Time series graphics can be applied to PMOA data for the purposes of examining progress and outcome with the same client over time. Figure 7.1, from Chapter 2, displays progress monitoring data from the *Depression/Anxiety Negative Affect* (*DANA*). The display shows a single variable, the Highest Intensity Level (HIL) score, for a female client who completed 10 sessions of therapy in a college counseling center. The time series shows that her HIL scores essentially remained stable across the first 10 sessions of therapy.

With a multivariate time series, data points for two or more measures over time can illustrate potential relations between these measures. For example, data from Abramowitz's (2002) three progress monitoring measures for a client with obsessive-compulsive disorder are displayed together in Figure 7.2. The measures are fear of intrusive thoughts, avoidance of situations associated with intrusive thoughts, and neutralizing rituals (i.e., behaviors believed to lessen anxiety). The dashed vertical line in Figure 7.2 is a **phase change line** that separates the baseline period (Sessions 1 through 3) from the intervention period (Sessions 4 through 16). After evidencing stability during a baseline period of three sessions, the multivariate time series shows that Mr. F's scores decreased steadily until Session 9, where they reached a new, low baseline. One interpretation of this figure is that the convergence of the three measures increases confidence in the effectiveness of the provided interventions.

In general, however, measures of different clinical constructs should provide different information. The use of different methods (e.g., self-reports, clinical ratings) increases confidence in the results if the data converge. In the case of Abramowitz's therapist ratings, however, the data appear highly correlated: Ratings of fear of intrusive thoughts correlated at 0.92 with avoidance of situations and at 0.95 with neutralizing rituals; avoidance and rituals correlated at 0.91 (Meier, 2008). **Correlation coefficients** describe the extent to which two variables covary and can range from –1.00 to +1.00; a value of 0 indicates that the two sets of scores have no relation. In the case of Mr. F., it appears that any one of the three measures could have been used in place of all three measures.

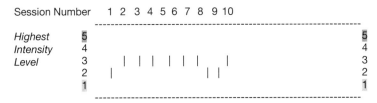

Figure 7.1 Depression/Anxiety Negative Affect (DANA) Progress Monitoring Data. *Higher ratings indicate more intense negative affect (NA). A Highest Intensity Level (HIL) score of 3 indicates that the therapist rated the client as evidencing moderately intense NA and an HIL score of 2 indicates that the client evidenced increasing NA.*

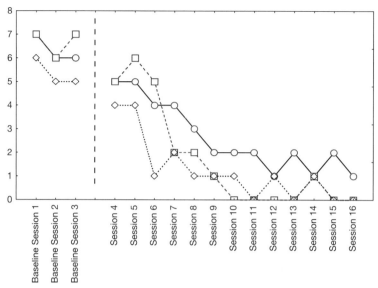

Figure 7.2 Change Over Time on Three Therapist Ratings of Mr. F. *Abramowitz (2002) rated Mr. F on three dimensions: Fear of intrusive thoughts (circles), Avoidance of situations associated with intrusive thoughts (squares), and Neutralizing rituals (diamonds), behaviors believed to lessen anxiety. Therapist ratings on the scale could range from 0 (None) to 8 (Severe). The dashed vertical line is a phase change line that separates the baseline period (Sessions 1 through 3) from the intervention period (Sessions 4 through 16). The multivariate time series shows that over the course of therapy, data from all three measures evidenced improvement, usually in close symmetry. Essentially the three measures reach a new, low baseline near Session 9. Source: Meier (2008).*

PMOA data from an undergraduate female student in therapy with a graduate student therapist in training provide another example of covarying PMOA data. Based on her case conceptualization, the therapist collected data across 10 sessions on two self-constructed, therapist-rated 9-point scales, depression and stress (with lower scores indicating more depression and stress). Essentially, the therapist believed that the client's situational stressors (including a difficult relationship with a boyfriend) influenced the client's self-reported depression. Figure 7.3 displays the resulting PMOA data. Around Session 6 the client broke up with her boyfriend, and her depression/stress levels, as rated by the therapist, evidenced considerable improvement. The client's mean depression level before Session 7 equaled 2.7 ($SD = 1.4$); after Session 6, the mean depression equaled 6.8 ($SD = 0.5$). The depression and stress data are highly correlated ($r = .81$), indicating that as with Mr. F, either measure could have been used to track progress.

These data provide some confirmation of the suggested relationships in the case conceptualization but raise the question of the usefulness of therapy since the major change occurred after the client's interpersonal situation changed. Certainly the supportive therapeutic relationship may have helped the client

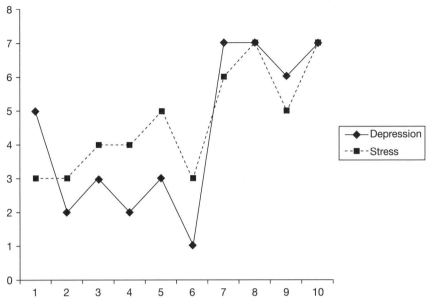

Figure 7.3 Therapist Ratings of Depression and Stress Show Improvement and Covariation in Undergraduate Client. *Lower scores indicating more depression and stress. The client's mean depression level before Session 7 equaled 2.7 (SD = 1.4); after Session 6, the mean depression equaled 6.8 (SD = 0.5). The client broke up with her boyfriend after Session 6.*

make a decision about the relationship, but the issue remains whether the client's improved mood will remain stable, particularly when the client begins a new relationship in the future.

DESCRIPTIVE STATISTICS

Descriptive statistics are numerical indices for describing, summarizing, and organizing quantitative data. These analytic methods are common to many of the procedures described in this chapter. These statistics include the **mean,** the average of a distribution or group of scores. Summing the scores in a group and dividing the number of scores produces the mean. Two other measures of central tendency are the **median** (i.e., the numerical value separating the top and bottom halves of a distribution of scores) and the **mode** (i.e., the most frequently occurring score). These measures provide a typical score that characterizes the performance of the entire distribution of scores. Finally, a **standard deviation** (SD) shows the degree to which the scores vary around the mean. The SD is the square root of the variance of a distribution of scores. The more widely spread the distribution of scores is, the larger the standard deviation.

EFFECT SIZE ESTIMATES

In the PMOA literature, effect size (ES) is a basic index of the amount of change resulting from psychotherapy. Typically employed to compare the amount of change in two groups (e.g., intervention vs. control), ES can also be used for such purposes as examining the size of change in a single group over two time points or the amount of change an individual client shows over time. ES can be calculated in any situation where mean and standard deviation statistics, whether for an individual client or a group of clients, are available from data at two time points.

Various ES formulas have been proposed in the literature (Volker, 2006). ES can be calculated, for example, based on raw scores from a PMOA measure administered at two different points in time using this formula:

$$ES = (\text{Time 2 Mean} - \text{Time 1 Mean}) / \text{Standard Deviation}$$

where *Time 1 Mean* is the mean of all scores at Time 1 (e.g., at intake) and *Time 2 Mean* is the mean of all scores at Time 2 (e.g., a follow-up assessment post-intervention). The *Standard Deviation* can be calculated in a number of ways. A **pooled SD** is calculated by adding the Time 1 SD and Time 2 SD and then dividing by the degrees of freedom (number of item responses at Time 1 + number of item responses at Time 2 minus 2).

ES has been applied in the literature for evaluating whether individuals exhibit change over time (e.g., Clement, 1999). Table 7.1 shows how ES is calculated with student A's self-reported item scores on the *Behavioral Intervention Monitoring Assessment System (BIMAS)* Conduct scale for Time 1 and Time 2:

$$ES = (\text{Time } 2M - \text{Time } 1M) / \text{Pooled } SD = (1.22 - 3.22) / 1.09 = -1.83$$

Table 7.1. STUDENT A'S SELF-REPORTED ITEM SCORES FOR BEHAVIORAL INTERVENTION MONITORING ASSESSMENT SYSTEM CONDUCT SCALE

		Time 1	Time 2
Angry		4	2
Risky behaviors		4	2
Fought (verbally/physically)		4	2
Lied/cheated		0	1
Lost temper		4	1
Aggressive		4	0
Alcohol and/or drug use		2	1
Disciplinary referral		3	1
Tobacco use		4	1
Means	3.22	1.22	
Standard deviations (SDs)	1.39	0.67	
Pooled SD =	1.09		

Clement (1999; see Table 4.1) offered an interpretive guideline for gauging the amount of change with ES, but researchers have yet to settle on the best metric for estimating ES in a single subject. No tests of statistical significance exist to suggest that a certain level of ES indicates that a definitive change has occurred.

During test development of PMOA measures, clinicians and researchers may employ ES to evaluate the change sensitivity of item and scale scores. Figure 7.4 (also displayed in Chapter 3) displays ES estimates by item for clients who completed the *Outcome Questionnaire-45* (*OQ-45*) in the Vermeersch, Lambert, and Burlingame (2000) study. The graph displays the range of ES scores by items, from 0.44 (*Feel blue*) to less than 0.15 (e.g., *Headache*). These ES values are useful for item selection in the context of a set of rules for evaluating change-sensitive items (such as the Intervention Item Selection Rules [IISRs] described in Chapter 3). For example, inspection of Figure 7.5 indicates that the ES values could be split into two groups, those with ESs greater or less than 0.25. If a brief, change-sensitive form of the *OQ* was desired, the 13 items with ES values above 0.25 could be chosen.

However, other factors could influence the selection or deletion of items based on ES values. The item content (e.g., suicide or homicidal behavior), for example, could be theoretically or clinically important (e.g., drinking problems) for the clinical population of interest, but endorsement of those items may occur so infrequently that item scores show a floor effect and subsequently low ES in a psychotherapeutic evaluation. Also, the ES values may depend on the type of

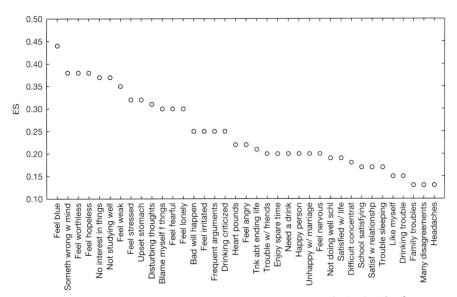

Figure 7.4 Item Effect Sizes for the Outcome Questionnaire-45 (OQ45). *This figure displays an effect size (d) for the 37 OQ items that displayed statistically significant differences in slope between treatment and controls as reported by Vermeersch et al. (2000). Abbreviated item wording is reported in the figure.*

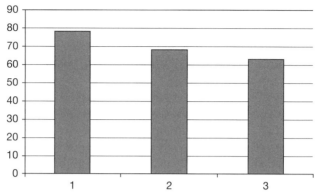

Figure 7.5 John's Behavioral Intervention Monitoring Assessment System (BIMAS) *t* Scores for Negative Affect Scale as Rated by His Teacher, Mother, and Himself. *Bar charts 1, 2, and 3 refer to John's Negative Affect (NA) t scores as rated by his teacher, mother, and self; low scores indicate lower NA. With a mean score of 50 and a standard deviation of 10, the self-report score (63) falls nearest the mean and the teacher score of 78 falls almost 3 standard deviations above the mean. These scores show relative consistency within the respective scales.*

psychotherapeutic intervention(s) employed; a study that employs an intervention targeting a specific problem (e.g., anger management, as in the development of the *BIMAS*; McDougal et al., 2012) may primarily change scores on PMOA items related to that domain. Third, characteristics of the client may influence the response to intervention; an item with a low ES in a large clinical sample may evidence different values when examined by gender, age, race/ethnicity, diagnosis, or other relevant characteristics. Thus, the choice of which items to include in or exclude from a PMOA measure, based at least partially on ES values, will depend on the criteria, creativity, and test purposes employed by the test developer.

MULTIPLE BASELINES

In behaviorally oriented approaches, clinicians and researches often employ a combination of the **AB design** (where A represents a baseline period and B an intervention period). Here a PMOA variable is assessed during the baseline (where it should show stability or no change) and then across an intervention (where it should evidence change). This design can be strengthened by the use of two or more variables that should show different periods of stability and change depending on their sensitivity to the specific intervention employed. With **multiple baseline designs** (also called the nonequivalent dependent variables design), the basic idea is that an intervention occurs that should change scores on one or more of the PMOA measures, but not all (Kazdin, 2003). Multiple baseline designs in the literature often refer to the evaluation of an intervention through the use of multiple participants, but the discussion here will focus on the use of single subjects to gauge client progress and intervention effectiveness.

With the *BIMAS* anger management intervention reported by McDougal et al. (2012), for example, the Conduct Disorder scale should evidence the largest change based on the match between the scale and the focus of the intervention on anger management. An anger management intervention should also improve scores on the Negative Affect scale because improvement in anger management skills should lead to a decrease in negative affect (NA) states such as anger, depression, and anxiety. In fact, McDougal et al. (2012) found that across forms, Conduct scale scores did evidence the most improvement. Negative Affect scores similarly improved, but scores on the Cognitive/Attention scale unexpectedly evidenced substantial change, raising questions about whether reactivity, placebo, and/or expectancy effects may also have been influencing scores.

Making sense of the multivariate display in a multiple baseline will partially depend on the interdependence of the multiple PMOA scores (Kazdin, 1980). The high correlation in Figure 7.4, for example, is problematic because the changes in the two measures (depression and stress) appear to occur simultaneously. This suggests that these scores reflect one measure; if one variable had changed first, and then the second subsequently changed, that would strengthen the argument that the two variables assess different constructs and one was causal. In addition, the magnitude and relative speed of change on the PMOA measure may also influence the interpretability of scores in a multivariate display.

The effect of therapy frequency versus number of sessions can also influence the interpretation of multiple baseline designs and other time series analyses. In Figure 7.3, for example, stress and depression scores are plotted against session number; such a plot assumes that the time between sessions is roughly equal. Before the introduction of managed care and its approach to curtailing mental health costs through minimizing sessions, the typical client participated in a weekly session. Now the norm in many mental health settings is a session every 2 weeks. From a perspective of the dose-response literature (Hansen, Lambert, & Forman, 2002), the duration or number of sessions is the key variable in that the effects of psychotherapy are assumed to be cumulative. What remains largely unknown in the research literature is whether session frequency or spacing impacts client progress and outcome.

In terms of whether to display session number or date in a multiple baseline, with data obtained at regular intervals, with no more than 2 weeks intervening, session number should be adequate to illustrate the effect of the intervention. For data obtained at irregular intervals, or that include periods of longer than 2 weeks, date may be a better indicator of the stronger influences on the examined variables. That is, if sessions occur irregularly or more than 2 weeks apart, displaying session number alone may mislead interpretations attempting to link changes on variables with the provided interventions. Displaying both session number and date may be optimal with many clients, although many data display programs lack this capacity.

NORMATIVE COMPARISONS

The basic idea here is that if psychotherapy works, a client's score on a PMOA measure should move toward the mean of the distribution of scores of a normal or nonclinical population. This is the key idea of employing **clinical significance** as a criterion for judging client progress and outcome (Hansen et al., 2002). To compare a client's PMOA score, it can be useful to transform the score so that the discussion is not about the raw scores but about a distribution of scores. For example, a **standard score** or *z* **score** is a transformation of a raw score to show how many deviations from the mean the score lies. The formula is:

$$z = (\text{Raw score} - \text{mean}) / \text{Standard deviation}$$

Thus, *z* equals the person's raw score minus the mean of the group of scores, divided by the standard deviation of the group of scores.

Frequently the best information that a test score can give us is the degree to which a person scores in the high or low portion of the distribution of scores. The *z* score is a quick summary of the person's standing: positive *z* scores indicate that the person scored above the mean, whereas negative scores indicate that the person scored below the mean.

Other types of standard scores have also been developed, including stanines, deviation IQs, sten scores, and *t* scores. *t* scores, for example, translate scores on a test to a distribution of scores of our choice. *t* scores use arbitrarily fixed means and standard deviations and eliminate decimal points and signs. The formula is:

$$t = (\text{SD} * z) + \text{X}$$

where SD is the chosen standard deviation, X is the chosen mean, and *z* is the standard score for a person's score on a test. For example, it may be simpler for a test interpreter to provide feedback about normative data using a distribution of scores whose mean is 50 and whose standard deviation is 10. If a person had a score on a test whose *z* equaled –.5, the *t* score would be:

$$(10 * (-.5)) + 50 = 45$$

Tests such as the SAT and GRE used 500 as the mean and 100 as the standard deviation. Again, the *t* score provides a convenient translation of scores so that they might be more understandable during test interpretation.

T scores are helpful for interpreting PMOA data in relation to a distribution of scores. The *BIMAS*, for example, translates the client's raw score into a *t* score for comparison with a distribution of scores by nonclients (the normative sample). Recall the example of John from Chapter 2 (as shown in Figure 7.5). John's initial *t* scores on the teacher (78), parent (68), and self-report (63) forms show consistency in assessing John's Negative Affect score as well above the mean. Treatment with John decreased his Negative Affect scores over time.

RELIABLE CHANGE INDEX

Jacobson and Truax (1991) proposed the calculation of a Reliable Change Index (RCI) to estimate whether a change in scores between test administrations for a single client is statistically significant, taking a reliability estimate of the specific PMOA measure into account. A statistically significant result means that the measured change can be attributed to reliable differences between the scores rather than random changes or measurement error. When normative data with a nonclinical sample are available, statistical methods can be used to decide whether scores have moved toward the distribution of nonclinical individuals (Jacobson & Truax, 1991; Zahra & Hedge, 2010). An RCI calculator is available at http://www.psyctc.org/stats/rcsc1.htm.

The use of a reliability estimate is both a strength and a weakness of the RCI as a change statistic. The reliability estimate employed in the formula may vary for a number of reasons, including the choice of reliability statistic (e.g., a test–retest estimate is usually lower than coefficient alpha), characteristics of the sample employed with the test (e.g., age, experience with the construct being assessed), and the construct measured (e.g., reliability, in the sense of stability over time, is typically higher for cognitive constructs such as intelligence than for constructs such as NA). Reliability estimates for many PMOA measures fall in the 0.7 to 0.9 range, leading to fairly large RCI estimates. With lower reliability estimates, RCI consequently becomes a conservative estimate of change since large Time 1 to Time 2 differences are necessary to reach a statically significant level.

The RCI statistic attempts to provide a yes/no answer to the question, Did statistically significant change occur? In many situations (e.g., Is the client ready to end treatment?), a definite answer would be very useful. But given concerns about the choice of the reliability estimate and other unexamined factors that are influencing the size of the found change (e.g., practice effects; Zahra & Hedge, 2010), making a decision solely based on the RCI (or any other single statistic) is unwise in clinical situations. The RCI has the disadvantage of **false precision**, in which a sophisticated statistical formula appears to provide a definite answer that should be taken cautiously. Given the state of the art in PMOA measurement, RCI and all indices of change should be used in clinical situations in conjunction with other sources of information (such as the clinician's and client's judgment) to make decisions.

TREND ANALYSES

Trend analyses compare one or more clusters of PMOA data points with each other in a single case. The grouping of multiple scores should decrease the effects of random error compared to the use of any single score. An outcome assessment can be computed, for example, to compare a client's first three sessions' data with the last three sessions' scores. Depending on the number of rated sessions, a variety of trend analyses are potentially available. These include the following:

1. To assess outcome, group the first three sessions (a baseline period) and then compare with scores on the last three sessions.
2. To assess progress, group scores from the first three sessions and then compare with any subsequent grouping of three sessions.
3. Compare the first, middle, and final third cluster of PMOA ratings (minimum six session ratings).

Recall the case of Mr. F, a 19-year-old Asian American who experienced intrusive thoughts such as about cursing at others during class, looking at people's genitals, and raping a particular female friend (Abramowitz, 2002). Mr. F maintained that he would never take such actions, but he was very fearful that he might do so and reported accompanying symptoms of anxiety and depression. Abramowitz (2002) collected data with three measures created specifically for Mr. F: *Fear of intrusive thoughts, Avoidance* (of situations associated with intrusive thoughts), and *Neutralizing rituals* (i.e., behaviors believed to lessen anxiety). As shown in Table 7.2, these therapist ratings were collected for a baseline period of three sessions (where no intervention occurred) and collected after each subsequent treatment session.

Table 7.2 displays the mean and standard deviations for all of Mr. F's idiographic scores as well as for three periods: (a) observations of all 16 sessions; (b) observations of the baseline period, the first three sessions; and (c) observations for the final three sessions. These groupings allow trend analyses of scores to evaluate such questions as whether data from baseline periods and final sessions differ from each other. One way to check for differences over time is to examine whether mean scores differ across comparison periods by at least 1 standard deviation (the 1SD method described in Chapter 4). For example, the *Fear of*

Table 7.2. DESCRIPTIVE STATISTICS FOR MR. F'S IDIOGRAPHIC MEASURES

	Baseline		Final Three Sessions		All Observations	
Measure	X	SD	X	SD	X	SD
Fear of intrusive thoughts	6.33	0.58	1.33	0.58	3.31	1.99
Avoidance of situations	6.67	0.58	0.33	0.58	2.63	2.83
Neutralizing rituals	5.33	0.58	0.33	0.58	2.00	2.07

NOTE: Adapted from Meier (2008).

intrusive thoughts mean score for the three baseline sessions (6.33) exceeds the mean score of the final three sessions (1.33) by greater than the standard deviation of all observations (5 > 1.99).

Descriptive statistics can also be computed from qualitative information such as that found in persistence tables. Table 7.3 displays the **frequency count** (i.e., how often an event occurs) and percentages for the five major themes displayed in the persistence table for the 20-session client (Table 7.4). These data match the visual impressions of Table 7.4. For example, much of the working through family conflict happens in the first half of therapy, with other issues emerging after the resolution of this conflict.

The effect of the frequency of data collection during the baseline and intervention periods on the quality of the subsequent analysis and interpretation has received some research attention. In general, researchers recommend the collection of multiple data points during baseline periods and suggest that in general, more data produce better analysis and interpretation (Ardoin, Christ, Morena, Cormier, & Kingbeil, 2013; Van Norman et al., 2013). If baseline data are invalid (e.g., they underestimate true scores), questions arise about subsequent interpretations regarding the need for treatment and treatment effects. In the area of reading fluency, data collection recommendations range from a minimum of 10 observations to two observations per week for 10 weeks (Van Norman et al., 2013). Similar to the idea proposed previously in trend analyses, the use of the median to summarize data values during particular periods (such as baseline or during an intervention period) tends to decrease the effects of outliers, particularly when initial or final estimates are based on single observations. What constitutes a baseline period in counseling and psychotherapy can also be problematic since the working alliance can quickly form in initial sessions before a formal intervention begins.

Table 7.3. *Descriptive Statistics for Individual Client Themes in Therapy for 20 Sessions*

		Frequency Count (% Total)	
Theme	*Total*	*Sessions 1–10*	*Sessions 11–20*
Negative affect	10 (32%)	8 (26%)	2 (6%)
Family conflict	10 (32%)	6 (19%)	4 (13%)
Partner	3 (10%)	0	3 (10%)
Positive changes	2 (06%)	0	2 (6%)
New interventions	6 (19%)	4 (13%)	2 (6%)
Total	*31 (100%)*	*18 (58%)*	*13 (42%)*

NOTE: Much of the working through of the individual client's conflict with family happened in the first half of therapy (Sessions 1 through 10), accompanied by negative affect. Therapeutic work on other issues and positive changes occurred toward the end of the 20 sessions.

Table 7.4. PERSISTENCE TABLE FOR AN INDIVIDUAL CLIENT IN THERAPY FOR 20 SESSIONS

Session Number

Themes	1	2	3	4	5	6	7	8	9	10	11	12	**13**	14	15	16	17	18	19	20
Neg Affect		■		■	■		■	■	■			■					■			
Family conflict		■		■	■		■		■		■		■					■	■	
Partner															■	■	■			
Positive changes																			■	■
New interventions		■	■				■	■				■					■			

NOTE: Boxes designate which major themes were discussed in a session. Client no-showed for Session 13.

TABLES AND QUALITATIVE ANALYSES

Tables are matrices composed of columns and rows that display quantitative and/or qualitative information by preselected categories. Tables with qualitative information based on progress and other clinical notes may be useful for tracking PMOA data over time. Notes contain qualitative data such as themes, stories, problems, and metaphors that can be a potentially important source of information about process and outcome factors (Meier, 2003). Persistence tables, for example, display the frequency with which a client discusses major clinical themes across sessions; the assumption is that as a client resolves an issue, she or he will cease to talk about that issue.

Creating a table to display key clinical data involves several steps. First, the important categories should be identified; these may be selected on the basis of theory, research, or a careful reading of progress notes with a particular client, group, family, or couple. Qualitative research methods involve rereading original material to perform careful comparisons, detect differences, note patterns, and identify trends (Miles & Huberman, 1994). **Grounded theory analysis** (Corbin & Strauss, 2007; Creswell, 2002), for example, requires a reader to make explicit identification of important concepts in field notes. These identified concepts are then subjected to a coding scheme designed to organize them conceptually to create theoretical constructs that explain the actions and processes occurring in a social setting. Rows and/or columns can be ordered so that the most important information is presented and/or displayed first (Henry, 1995). As shown in Table 2.4 in Chapter 2, important themes in progress notes, for example, can be extracted by session and then placed in a table organized by session number and containing a few summary sentences for each session.

A persistence table can be a more targeted method for tracking client progress over time. A depiction of the continuity of client topics provides a method for consideration of treatment alternatives and termination. If the client continues to cycle through discussion of therapeutic-related themes, accompanied by changes in the intensity of NA, psychotherapy is likely to be effective (cf. Mergenthaler, 1996). When such discussions persist without resolution, however, the therapist may introduce new or additional interventions to determine if they help the client. A decrease in NA intensity and the cessation of talk about the past problem, however, suggests a resolution for the client and consideration of termination.

Although the analysis of tables may match client and clinician experiences more closely than quantitative methods, subjectivity remains an issue. Simply, different therapists and coders are likely to identify different themes. For the purposes of supervision, these differences may be unremarkable, but the use of tables as PMOA data to justify third-party payment may be more problematic until the field reaches a consensus about acceptable PMOA methodologies, particularly around qualitative approaches. To the extent that two or more raters (e.g., clinician and supervisor) create similar tables or cocreate a single table, the table's reliability and validity should be strengthened.

ERRORS IN INTERPRETING PROGRESS MONITORING AND OUTCOME ASSESSMENT DATA

This section describes several categories of error that can occur when interpreting patterns of change with PMOA scores. These errors occur during the process of PMOA measurement but affect the resulting test scores.

Measurement Error

PMOA measures differ in their sensitivity to change produced by different psychotherapeutic interventions (Guyatt, Walter, & Norman, 1987; Lipsey, 1983, 1990; Meier, 2004; Saylor et al., 2007; Vermeersch et al., 2000; Vermeersch et al., 2004). As noted in Chapter 3, Lambert (1994, p. 85) observed that the "most popular... measures used to assess depression following treatment provide reliably different pictures of change." Many measures employed for PMOA purposes were not specifically developed to detect change and so are less able to detect the small to moderate effects often seen with psychosocial interventions (Meier, 2004). Thus, researchers and clinicians may conclude from PMOA data that change (of any type) has not occurred with individual or groups of clients when the PMOA measure has been insensitive to the change that did occur.

A second problem occurs when clients underreport their problematic cognitions, affect, and behaviors at some (or all) points in the measurement process. This is particularly apparent in the assessment of NA. Baker, Holloway, Thomas, Thomas, and Owens (2004), for example, reported that patients with panic disorders were more likely to suppress and constrict the experience and expression of negative affect.

As noted in Chapter 5, Meier and Schwartz (2007) found that adolescents entering treatment in community mental health centers may have been under-reporting behavioral problems *only* at intake. As shown in Figure 7.6, if the adolescent clients more validly report a greater number of problems at subsequent periods, repeated measurement (a) over a short time period will suggest that the psychotherapy *increased* the problem and (b) over a longer period will suggest that the counseling had no effect on the problem. For valid interpretation of PMOA data in such cases, the starting point for analysis of change should not be the initial data point because the PMOA report does not reflect the actual severity of the client's problem.

Instead, two alternatives can be considered when analyzing change over time in such situations. First, consider using the highest (worst) PMOA data reported in initial sessions as the starting point for interpreting subsequent changes. A second, more conservative option is to conduct a trend analysis by averaging the data points (or using the median) between the initial report and the highest NA reported in early sessions. This may better reflect the range of PMOA data the client experiences than the initial, possibly underreported, account of client problems.

Clients may be motivated to avoid valid reporting of problems because of social desirability bias, where respondents provide information that promotes a favorable impression and suppress information that promotes an unfavorable impression. For men in some Western cultures, for example, it is often embarrassing to share feelings of strong sadness; for some women, anger may be considered socially inappropriate to feel or express. Some clients may be motivated to exaggerate NA reports (e.g., suicidal thoughts) because of desired consequences (e.g., disability payments, excused absences from work or school). Clinicians may be aware of this manipulative reporting but feel compelled to report the exaggerated affect because of concerns about malpractice liability.

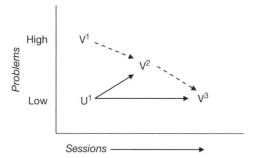

Figure 7.6 Underreporting Can Lead to Underestimation of Treatment Effects. *U^1 refers to an underreport of a client problem at intake or initial sessions. V^1 refers to a valid report of the client problem at intake or initial sessions. V^3 refers to a valid report of a client's problem at the end of counseling. Comparison of U^1 and V^3 would indicate no change, whereas an analysis of valid data from V^1/V^2 and V^3 would indicate a decrease in the problem.*

Finally, calculation of PMOA indices will be affected by measurement error. As noted earlier, the RCI (Jacobson & Truax, 1991) includes a reliability estimate in a formula designed to calculate how large a change must be to conclude that a client has experienced meaningful improvement. The size of the reliability estimate employed in the formula, however, may vary substantially for a number of reasons, including the choice of reliability statistic, characteristics of the sample employed with the test, and the construct measured. The small to modest effects of many psychosocial interventions, which may still provide useful feedback during progress monitoring, may be more apparent on times series graphs and ES calculations than with the RCI statistic.

Clinical Decision Making

The process of interpreting PMOA data and making clinical decisions on the basis of those interpretations may also produce errors. First, the simplest explanation for any pattern of PMOA scores is **randomness**. A variety of methodological factors, as described in Chapter 3, can influence PMOA scores, and the combination of these factors can produce what are essentially random, small changes over time. With the *DANA*, for example, a client whose HIL ratings fluctuate between Levels 3 and 4 over five to 10 sessions may not be experiencing or expressing substantial changes in NA. Particularly when examining small time intervals and a small number of sessions, assessors must be careful not to overinterpret small changes as evidence of treatment effectiveness.

A similar problem occurs with the **hypothesis confirmation bias** (HCB; Meier, 2008). HCB with mental health professionals occurs when the clinician prematurely decides on a diagnosis or hypothesis and then proceeds to ignore any subsequent information that disconfirms that diagnosis/hypothesis. In the case of psychotherapy, for example, clinicians and clinical raters may assume that the treatment will ultimately be successful and see improvement in instances where it does not actually occur.

Both clinical judgment and statistical decision making have well-documented problems. Ziskin (1995, p. 261) summarized the criticism about the former:

> Even if there were not a massive body of research strongly suggesting that clinicians actually have limited capacity to manage complex information and often stumble over a few variables, it should be clear that the obstacles facing the clinician who hopes to integrate all of the data are not merely difficult hurdles, but impossible ones.... Perhaps it would not be entirely unfair to say that a large percentage of clinicians do in fact evidence a shared myth about their own judgment capacities.

Problems also occur when one statistical index is employed as a threshold for clinical decisions, such as deciding when to continue or terminate psychotherapy. Different PMOA measures produce different estimates of the amount of change, as do different statistical indices (Lambert, 1994; McDougal et al., 2012).

So if clinical judgment or data alone do not suffice for decisions about altering treatment or continuing or concluding treatment, what can be done? A reasonable approach is to integrate the two methods within a theoretical basis for working with a particular client. As described in Chapter 3, incorporating data-based feedback into clinical judgment is an empirically supported method for improving outcomes, particularly for clients who do not initially progress during psychotherapy. Reviewing research on clinicians' judgment of client progress, Gray and Lambert (2001) concluded that while clinicians are not generally effective in gauging client progress, "when they are provided with feedback on poor treatment response, they develop a perspective on their patient's clinical progress that enables them to recalibrate treatment and make a substantial impact on improvement rates" (p. 26).

Evaluation of Therapists

It would seem a logical step to employ PMOA data for comparing therapists within and across organizations and programs. Although PMOA scores can be employed with individuals completing any type of psychotherapy, comparison of one therapist's performance with others should be done with extreme caution (Luchins, 2012). To make such comparisons, at least two important variables should be included in the analysis: (a) an assessment of the type and severity of client problems and (b) a sufficiently large sample size to rule out the effects of chance. Unless therapists' caseloads are roughly equivalent in terms of problem type and severity, comparisons among therapists in terms of PMOA scores may be misleading. Unfortunately, meeting both conditions is unlikely unless the analyses involve a large (relative to each therapist) and homogeneous client sample or random assignment of clients to therapists. Consider a situation where an evaluator attempts to compare PMOA scores for 10 therapists using only 30 cases per therapist. One or two unusual cases (by chance) might be sufficient to influence the aggregated score of one therapist's scores, thereby increasing the chance of an invalid interpretation. In such an instance, a subsequent collection of data and analysis is likely to lead to completely different conclusions about any therapist shown to be effective or ineffective in the first analysis.

The Importance of Theory and Research in Progress Monitoring and Outcome Assessment Interpretations

As noted previously, PMOA data primarily provide an alert function for therapists and clients. That is, they signal when a client is not making progress and consideration should be given to alternative treatment plans. However, PMOA data typically provide little information about causality, that is, the factors that influence the observed PMOA data trends. Theory and research specific to particular PMOA data and psychotherapeutic interventions are needed to fill this gap and provide a foundation for interpreting the meaning and implications of PMOA data for therapeutic decisions.

Interpretation of PMOA data across sessions may also depend on the psychotherapy theory underlying specific client interventions (Hawkins & Meier, 2012). In some theories and interventions, for example, a period of worsening may be expected when psychotherapeutic interventions are introduced. This may trigger an alert with a measure such as the *OQ45* that might be safely ignored by a psychodynamic therapist who expects an initial deterioration. Yet most clinical support tools that employ PMOA data are explicitly atheoretical (cf. Worthen & Lambert, 2007). A variety of additional factors may influence an evaluation of whether to continue therapy. Prochaska (1995; see also Prochaska & Norcross, 2006), for example, describes six **stages of change** in counseling and psychotherapy: (a) **precontemplation**, when a client has little or no awareness about the major problem; (b) **contemplation**, when a client becomes aware of the problem and begins to think about how to remedy it; (c) **preparation**, when a client intends to change and begins to take preliminary actions; (d) **action**, when a client changes behavior or the environment in an attempt to remedy the problem; (e) **maintenance**, when a client attempts to continue the changes made; and (f) **termination**, when the problem is fully resolved and the client is confident it will not reoccur. A female college student in therapy who is in the precontemplation stage about her eating disorder may not benefit from any length of therapy, for example, whereas one who has taken action to change may benefit from additional sessions at spaced intervals to help maintain therapeutic gains.

The use of progress and outcome measures derived without a theoretical basis makes interpretation of PMOA data problematic. The atheoretical *Global Assessment of Functioning (GAF)* scale, for example, is a brief one-item 100-point rating scale with which a clinician can summarize a client's functioning and symptomatology. The *GAF* is a commonly employed scale (Hatfield & Ogles, 2004) often mandated by insurance companies for continued reimbursement with psychotherapy clients. Typically completed at intake and termination, the *GAF* may also be employed throughout the course of treatment to provide information about client progress. But the reactivity or transparency of the *GAF* rating often raises questions about the meaning of change on *GAF* scores. A steady decrease in scores over a period of 4 to 6 weeks (corresponding to an increase in symptomatology) may indicate a worsening in the client, which could lead to a denial of future services or payment by an insurance company that conducts utilization reviews and concludes the treatment is ineffective.

That worsening, however, could also reflect a client who has been avoiding NA but is now experiencing a short-term increase in symptoms as she or he begins to process difficult material (cf. Mergenthaler, 1996). Similarly, very slight but steady increases in scores may reflect client improvement, but the *GAF*'s transparency presents an alternative explanation: The clinician has learned what *GAF* scores are needed to obtain and maintain reimbursement and services from insurers. Similar to what teachers face in high-stakes testing in education, clinicians may be tempted to alter *GAF* scores so that their clients continue to receive needed help.

As noted in Chapter 3, psychotherapy theories have described avoidance as a frequently occurring obstacle to therapeutic progress. Avoidance and related constructs such as resistance and suppression have historically been recognized as key theoretical and empirical constructs relevant to clients' progress and outcome in counseling and psychotherapy (Hess, Hess, & Hess, 2008; Meier, 2012). Clients clearly differ in their ability to experience and express threatening behaviors, cognitions, and NA. Clients' methods for coping with NA, for example, have significant potential to influence treatment progress and failure. Despite its theoretical importance and clinical implications, however, most PMOA measures do not explicitly assess avoidance-related constructs.

A few PMOA measures such as the *DANA* (Meier, 2012) produce data about avoidance, and therapists can also create idiographic measures related to avoidance, as was employed with Mr. F (i.e., *Avoidance of anxiety-provoking situations*; Abramowitz, 2002). Three examples are presented here to illustrate the potential uses of avoidance data. Ideally, a PMOA report would alert the clinician to client session(s) where avoidance was an issue and suggest a review of other material, such as progress notes, that could provide clinical hypotheses about the source and potential interventions for avoidance. Figure 7.7 displays *DANA Avoidance* and HIL (Meier, 2012) data for a client's first five sessions. Clinicians assess avoidance on the *DANA* with a yes or no response to the question, "Any indication that this individual is *avoiding negative affect?*" HIL refers to the highest intensity level of any NA descriptor endorsed per session, with higher levels indicating more intense NA (Meier, 2012).

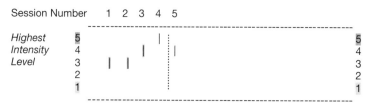

Figure 7.7 Depression/Anxiety Negative Affect (DANA) Highest Intensity Levels (HILs) and Avoidance Rating for Five Sessions, Numbers 1 Through 5. *A thicker tick mark indicates that the therapist rated the client as avoiding negative affect (NA) in that session. HIL equaled 3, 3, 4, 5, and 4 in the first five sessions, respectively. This client may have required several sessions to build a working alliance with the therapist and become comfortable enough to begin disclosing more problematic, emotionally intense material.*

As shown in the figure, the client avoided NA for the first three sessions, which likely contributed to the HIL Levels 3, 4, and 5 (*Moderate, Strong,* and *Intense Negative Affect,* respectively). One interpretation of the avoidance and HIL data is that this client needed several sessions to build a working alliance with the therapist and become comfortable enough to begin disclosing more problematic, emotionally intense material. If the client began to experience more intense NA in Sessions 4 and 5, the client could then begin to work through the emotional material and experience a lessening of emotional intensity over time. Also note in Figure 7.7 the insertion of a phase change line after Session 4; the therapist now expects the client to show decreases in NA intensity, although perhaps in a cyclical manner.

In Figure 7.8, *DANA* HIL data are displayed for five sessions (sessions 33 through 37). Therapist ratings indicated that the client avoided NA for four of the five sessions. If avoidance of NA maintains or increases NA (Hayes, Wilson, Gifford, Follette, & Strosahl, 1996; Moses & Barlow, 2006) and this client has a history of avoidance, it makes sense that HIL remains high for this client even after 30 sessions of psychotherapy. An increased focus on this client's avoidance is the first option for therapy adjustment if this has not already occurred. Although the availability of sessions will be a major consideration, a PMOA data pattern that indicates persistent difficulties (e.g., *DANA* HIL ratings of 3 or higher, over 10 or more sessions) provides concrete feedback for consideration of a referral to another therapist or program.

Finally, Figure 7.9 displays *DANA* HIL data for five sessions (Sessions 8 through 12). The therapist indicated that in Session 11, the client evidenced avoidance of NA. Although Sessions 8 through 11 show a decrease in HIL, at Session 12 the HIL rebounds to Level 4. Although this may be part of the working-through cycle of affective intensity and cognitive reflection (Mergenthaler, 1996), it may also indicate that the client's avoidance of NA in Session 11 resulted in a worsening of NA and an obstruction of therapeutic progress.

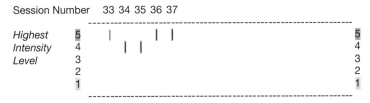

Figure 7.8 Depression/Anxiety Negative Affect (DANA) Highest Intensity Levels (HILs) and Avoidance Rating for Five Sessions, Numbers 33 Through 37. *A thicker tick mark indicates that the therapist rated the client as avoiding negative affect (NA) in the session. HIL equaled 5, 4, 4, 5, 5 in these five sessions, respectively. If this client has a history of avoidance that continues in therapy, the client is unlikely to have experienced NA sufficiently to decrease HIL even after 30 sessions of psychotherapy.*

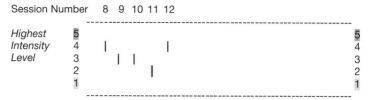

Figure 7.9 Depression/Anxiety Negative Affect (DANA) Highest Intensity Levels (HILs) and Avoidance Rating for Five Sessions, Numbers 8 Through 12. *A thicker tick mark indicates that the therapist rated the client as avoiding negative affect (NA) in the session. HIL equaled 4, 3, 3, 2, and 4 in these five sessions, respectively. The avoidance of NA in Session 11 may have led to the rebound of HIL in Session 12.*

SUMMARY

A variety of quantitative and qualitative methods exist for displaying and analyzing PMOA data across sessions and over time. Time series (individual and multiple variables), correlations, standard scores, ES estimates, descriptive statistics, RCI, progress notes, and tables all have the potential to inform interpretations of PMOA data and provide feedback about therapeutic progress and outcome. But each has its limitations, as none of these indices provides an unequivocal answer to the question of how much a client has changed.

Regarding the interpretation of PMOA test scores, perhaps the most important issue to be resolved is that the field has little consensus about methods for estimating error in change scores. When the amount of error equals or exceeds the amount of growth, providing valid interpretations of PMOA data patterns becomes problematic. Problems exist with each method and source of information, and difficulties with estimating error stem primarily from the field's lack of theoretical knowledge about what influences change scores. A number of potential methods were described for handling error, including the use of RCI, which takes a PMOA measure's reliability estimate into account when evaluating the amount of change. At the level of an individual client, a therapist may develop a sense of what scores mean, including variability and sources of error, but therapists are likely to differ substantially in their ability to make such judgments. Developing simple methods of estimating error for PMOA data relevant to individuals and groups of clients remains a priority for the field.

Exercise 4 *Using the 1 Standard Deviation Method to Estimate Client Progress*

The following list contains a teacher's ratings of a student's (John) thoughts about self-harm for 9 different weeks, in the order presented: 3, 2, 1, 1, 1, 0, 0, 0, 0.

Calculate the mean and standard deviation for this set of scores. Then compare the first two values with the last two values—is the difference greater than 1 standard deviation? On this basis, what would you conclude about John's progress on this score?

See the appendix for answers.

Exercise 5 *Trend Analyses of Mr. F's Therapist Ratings*

In the text describing the case of Mr. F, a trend analysis was computed comparing the first three baseline sessions with the final three treatment sessions on the therapist ratings of *Fear of intrusive thoughts.* Using the data in Table 2.5, answer the following questions:

1. Using the two therapist ratings, *Avoidance of situations* and *Neutralizing rituals,* compare the three baseline sessions with the final four treatment sessions.
2. To assess progress, group scores from the three baseline sessions on *Avoidance of situations* and then compare with any subsequent grouping of three sessions (e.g., Sessions 7, 8, and 9). What would you conclude about Mr. F's progress based on this analysis?

See the appendix for answers.

Table 2.5. IDIOGRAPHIC THERAPIST RATINGS FOR MR. F's FEAR OF THOUGHTS, AVOIDANCE, AND RITUALS

Session	Fear of Thoughts	Avoidance	Rituals
	BASELINE SESSIONS		
1	7	7	6
2	6	6	5
3	6	7	5
	THERAPY SESSIONS		
1	5	5	4
2	5	6	4
3	4	5	1
4	4	2	2
5	3	2	1
6	2	1	1
7	2	0	1
8	2	0	0
9	1	0	1
10	2	0	0
11	1	1	1
12	2	0	0
13	1	0	0

NOTE: Therapist ratings on the scale could range from 0 (None) to 8 (Severe).

Exercise 6 *Using Progress Notes as Progress Monitoring and Outcome Assessment Data*

Table 2.4 displays a list of clinically relevant themes extracted from 20 sessions with an individual client. Use a method such as highlighting or underlining to identify process and outcome information in these summary sentences. The appendix has an example of a completed table with which to compare your work.

Table 2.4. QUALITATIVE ANALYSIS OF PROGRESS NOTES WITH A DEPRESSED/ANXIOUS CLIENT

Session Number	Key Issues
1	Presenting problem centers on **depression and anxiety**; agrees to referral for possible medication; reports history of conflicted family relationships, particularly with long-deceased alcoholic father
2	Has started medication and will continue counseling; reports difficulty at work with "crazy" customers; we establish a schedule of activities designed to increase positive reinforcement for him
3	Reports *a history of trying to re-create a family life*, but with people other than immediate family of origin; for example, becomes a physical, emotional caretaker for distant relatives, older neighbors; reports no effect from reinforcement activities
4	**Reports that he is very angry** with *many past incidents with family of origin*, particularly father, and some current events with mother
5	**Is much less anxious, moderately less depressed, but seems almost manic**; very strong emotional reactions to many current events
6	Agrees to start a journal where he writes thoughts, feelings, and related events
7	Reports that he has come to the conclusion that **he hates himself**; reading books about identity development; **now frequent, angry arguments with partner**
8	Reports becoming **easily angry with coworkers**, even when their behavior does not affect him directly, as well as with partner and family members
9	Reads for 30 minutes from a journal about *past family incidents* that provoked **anger, rage, and sadness in him**; question arises whether he should pursue family therapy with mother and siblings
10	Notes that **he is angry with his mother** *but cannot express those feelings to her or even explore much in session; family culture indicates that being angry with parents is equivalent to disobeying them*
11	Despite father's death 15 years ago, reports that he still **wishes there was some way he could be emotionally close to father**; I confronted about this unrealistic idea; he later cancels next session

(continued)

Table 2.4. (Continued)

Session Number	Key Issues
12	Some processing in session of *how he experiences emotion*; relates stories that provide evidence (to him) that his role was to function as *emotional caretaker in his family; tried to protect mother from abusive, alcoholic father*
13	No-show; later reported that he forgot about the session
14	*Wondering whether to stay in current relationship*; debating financial security versus partner's treatment of him as a child
15	Considering whether to leave town, start a new life elsewhere; now spending much time considering therapy issues between sessions
16	Same issues as Session 15
17	Ran into his brother's friend who had no idea that client's father was alcoholic; *confirmed for client that mother and siblings denied family difficulties*; I noted that in the past he had denied such problems as well
18	Clearly has changed locus of responsibility for family conflict away from himself; **anger and rumination about family has decreased**; more focus on work, other people
19	*Discusses buying a house with partner; one brother is now contacting him for social interactions*
20	Termination; **client reports greater self-confidence, emotional independence from family**, stable work performance; describes himself as "better integrated"

NOTE: Bold text indicates material conceptualized as relevant to outcome, whereas italicized content relates to process. Sources are Meier (1999, 2003), reprinted by permission.

Exercise 7 *Create a Persistence Table to Track Themes Discussed Across Sessions*

Use the information in Table 2.4 to create a persistence table of the topics discussed in Sessions 1 through 20. See the appendix and Table 7.3 for an example of a completed table.

8

Rater Training

INTRODUCTION

Although some general guidelines exist about how to enhance observational skills (Meier, 1994), clinical training in the use of contemporary progress monitoring and outcome assessment (PMOA) measures seldom occurs. Typically PMOA measures are assumed to be face valid; the assumption is that the rater, whether client (self), clinician, or other, can produce valid ratings with little or no preparation. As described later with the *Global Assessment of Functioning* scale (*GAF*; Endicott, Spitzer, Fleiss, & Cohen, 1976), training procedures are occasionally produced for a particular measure, and these procedures may be provided online. This chapter presents two examples of rater training for PMOA measures. The first example focuses on the *GAF*; because of its brevity and face validity, the *GAF* is a frequently employed scale for PMOA purposes. The second, more elaborate example describes training in the use of the *Depression/Anxiety Negative Affect* scale (*DANA*; Meier, 2012).

The considerable research literature on assessment training generally supports the hypothesis that rater training improves psychometric estimates (Meier, 2008; Wagner, Helmreich, Lieb, & Tadic, 2011). Wagner et al. (2011), for example, reported that a standardized 1-day training that included videotapes of patients with major depressive disorder established satisfactory interrater reliability estimates with the *Hamilton Rating Scale for Depression*. In contrast, Paul et al. (1986) observed that "The schema employed by untrained or minimally trained observers are generally loose, with fuzzy category boundaries based on prototypes" (p. 50); consequently, untrained raters tend to produce data with lower reliability and validity estimates (Meier, 2008). Test developers have focused on rater training as a method of decreasing rater error (Gronlund, 1988; Hartman, 1984; Hill, 1982; Paul, 1986), with observers learning how to record specific behaviors in particular settings. With behavioral assessment, for example, observers record overt behavior in staff and clients (Paul, 1986). These assessors learn how to record specific behaviors and are then assigned to make observations in specific clinical settings. Hartman (1984) proposed that rater training should include (a) a general orientation, (b) memorization of coding procedures and examples, (c) training to predetermined standards, (d) practice in the actual clinical setting, and (e) periodic evaluation and retraining. The last two components appear particularly relevant for maintaining the reliability of behavioral observers because research indicates that reliability estimates (i.e., interobserver agreement) drop from a 0.70 to 0.80 range in evaluation conditions to 0.30 to 0.40 in nonevaluated conditions (Nay, 1979). Laboratory studies in which actual performance is videotaped indicate that valid ratings are related to a variety of factors, including motivation to rate validly, variability of performance, memory aids, and the social context in which rating occurs (Murphy & Davidshofer, 2005).

LEARNING THE GLOBAL ASSESSMENT OF FUNCTIONING SCALE

The *GAF* is a 100-point rating measure, with 10-point intervals, that allows raters to assess an individual's symptoms and functioning in the psychological, social, and occupational domains. High scores (100) indicate a lack of symptoms and good functioning; middle scores (50) reflect serious symptoms, such as suicidal ideation; the lowest scores (0) indicate severe symptoms and dysfunction, such as a serious suicidal act. An Internet search will produce a copy of the scale. Given its brevity and ease of use, the *GAF* is likely to continue to be a widely used measure despite the fact that the *Diagnostic and Statistical Manual of Mental Disorders*, fifth edition (DSM-V; American Psychiatric Association, 2013) no longer supports its use.

The *GAF* itself includes little instruction about its proper use, and few studies have been conducted to evaluate rater training for the *GAF* (Aas, 2011). However, some online training procedures are available (http://www.esocialworker.com/gaf.htm; http://www.annals-general-psychiatry.com/content/10/1/2). For example, the Washington Institute and the Washington State Mental Health Division created a series of 20 brief case descriptions (http://depts.washington.edu/washinst/Resources/CGAS/Index.htm) that allow the rater to provide a *GAF* rating for each case and then receive brief feedback. Here is one example:

> Kim is a 31 year old Caucasian female with Major Depression. She has a history of heavy alcohol abuse and has been in inpatient chemical dependency treatment programs. Her family of origin has a long history of mental illness and chemical dependency on both sides. She is currently in a co-dependent relationship with an abusive boyfriend. Kim's mother tries to support her, but is regularly involved in heavy alcohol use. Kim is on the verge of losing another job and is expressing suicidal ideation, but has agreed to a "no harm" contract.

Upon submitting a *GAF* score for a particular individual, the program provides immediate feedback in terms of the proximity of the rater's answer to the expected answer. The program provides a mean score, along with a range, for the expected *GAF* value. What *GAF* score would you assign for Kim? To check against the program, go to the website.

LEARNING THE DEPRESSION/ANXIETY NEGATIVE AFFECT SCALE

The goal of rater training is to help the rater learn how to employ a particular PMOA instrument or type of instrument. The remainder of this chapter provides information about how to perform clinical ratings with the *Depression/Anxiety Negative Affect* (*DANA*) scale, a measure of negative affect (NA; Meier, 2012). All rater training assumes that the rater knows and understands the conceptual information presented in this book about tests (e.g., administration, scoring, and interpretation), specific information about the PMOA measure itself (including test development procedures), and aspects of the individual providing the data (e.g., clinician, client, or other) that might introduce error.

By learning the standard method for producing *DANA* ratings, ratings will become more consistent. This consistency translates into increased reliability and validity estimates for *DANA* scores. Watch the online video, a brief student role-play about Jeremy, a social phobic, and identify the affect the client shares with the therapist. The link is displayed in the section Getting Started—Part 2—Preparing to Watch the Clinical Vignette.

After reading the instructions in the next section, watch the video and complete *DANA* ratings twice. For the first viewing, complete your *DANA* ratings at the *end* of the video. Take no notes during the video, but simply try to remember the NA Jeremy expresses during the 6 minutes of counseling. After watching the video, complete the *DANA* form. For the second rating, complete the *DANA as you watch* Jeremy. If possible, write the time period down in the space next to the NA term when you hear or observe Jeremy's NA.

When finished, compare your ratings to the completed *DANA* form in Table 8.2. If differences exist, use the time period information in the table to review differences on the endorsed NA terms.

Getting Started—Part 1—Reviewing Depression/Anxiety Negative Affect Intensity Levels

In Chapter 4, *DANA* NA intensity levels were introduced. If you read that material and know it well, proceed to the next section, Getting Started—Part 2. If not, or you would benefit from a review, continue reading this section.

A key characteristic of an NA measure intended for use in measuring change in psychotherapy is the differing intensity levels of its items. Intensity refers to

Table 8.1. *Depression/Anxiety Negative Affect Scale's Five Negative Affect (NA) Intensity Levels*

Level	Label	Brief Description	Example Descriptors
1	*Transient NA*	Common NA states, usually of short duration, infrequently experienced	*Bored, uncomfortable*
2	*Increasing NA*	NA accompanying an emerging or recurring problem(s)	*Tense, concerned*
3	*Moderate NA*	NA accompanying problem(s) experienced as more persistent, severe, accompanied by frequent problem-related thoughts, behaviors	*Worried, depressed*
4	*Intense NA*	NA accompanying problem(s) experienced as highly significant, often accompanied by attempts at avoidance of feelings, thoughts, behaviors	*Overwhelmed, hopeless*
5	*Extreme NA*	NA with severe problem(s), person may be in crisis	*Traumatized, panicked*

"the strength of a particular affective state" (Diener, Larsen, Levine, & Emmons, 1985, p. 1263). The *DANA* describes NA in five item clusters representing increasing intensities, consisting of *Transient NA* (Level 1), *Increasing NA* (2), *Moderate NA* (3), *Intense NA* (4), and *Extreme NA* (5). Levels 1 and 5 represent the extremes of affective experiencing. The affective states in Level 1, *Transient NA*, such as *Bored* and *Deflated* may be considered part of usual human experiencing. Izard (2007, p. 264) noted that basic NA states typically "have a low base rate and a short duration." Table 8.1 presents the *DANA's* five intensity levels with a label for each level, a brief description, and two example NA descriptors from that level.

DANA items at Levels 2, 3, and 4 will be the most frequently endorsed for persons presenting for counseling and psychotherapy in outpatient settings such as counseling centers, outpatient clinics in hospitals and other medical settings, community mental health centers, and private practices. Persons with NA at Levels 3 and 4 (e.g., *Anxious, Moderately sad*, and *Depressed, Overwhelmed*) are likely to be experiencing more severe and persistent problems in their environments. The emotions at Level 5, *Extreme NA*, such as *Enraged* and *Actively Suicidal*, may be experienced and/or expressed as if there is no upper limit to their intensity.

Getting Started—Part 2—Preparing to Watch the Clinical Vignette

Go to http://www.youtube.com/watch?v=7O45nSwxDJ8&feature=fvw. Advance the slider at the bottom of the page to get to the time period 2:44. Pause the video

Table 8.2. DEPRESSION/ANXIETY NEGATIVE AFFECT (DANA) TERMS
ENDORSED FOR JEREMY

Author's NA Terms	Author's Source (Time)	Students' NA Terms
	LEVEL 1	
Unrelaxed	Frequent nonverbals	
Uncomfortable	Frequent nonverbals	
	LEVEL 2	
On edge	Frequent nonverbals	
Tense	Frequent nonverbals	
Difficulty relaxing	Frequent nonverbals	
	LEVEL 3	
Pressured	5:00, 7:15	Embarrassed
Anxious	Frequent nonverbals	Moderately angry
<u>Worried</u>	2:50	Agitated
Moderately angry/"hostile"	8:15	
	LEVEL 4	
<u>Overwhelmed</u>	3:40, 6:00	Demoralized
<u>(Very) pressured</u>	5:20	Ashamed
		Worthless
		Helpless
	LEVEL 5	
	No endorsed items	

NOTE: Nonverbal cues were employed to endorse items in *italics*, while underlined items were rated on the basis of information reported by individuals other than the client. Numbers in *Author's Source* indicate the time period where Jeremy expressed NA. Thanks to Bianca Jones and Shannon McClain at the University of Texas for permission to use their video.

if it starts. Before starting the video and the rating process, have two blank paper copies of the *DANA* ready (from Appendix 10). Play the time period 2:44 to about 8:44 (6 minutes).

Although you will be reviewing only a 6-minute segment, most of the *DANA* instructions apply. First, be familiar with the five levels of the *DANA*. Note that Level 1 (*Transient NA*) is the least intense and Level 5 (*Extreme NA*) is the most intense. Ideally, you will also understand all of the NA terms and have a good idea of their placement by level. If you are unfamiliar with the *DANA* levels and items, please look them over now.

The process of rating the *DANA* consists of listening to client reports about NA and endorsing the appropriate terms. If you find an NA term that is similar but not identical to the listed term, choose the similar term that already exists on the *DANA*, particularly if the similar term is equivalent in intensity to the client's observed NA state. Sometimes completing the *DANA* ratings can involve more complex judgments. In this practice exercise, decisions are made about (a) endorsing an NA term at a *different level* than shown on the rating form, (b) endorsing an NA term on the basis of client *nonverbals* (compared to a client self-report), and (c) endorsing an NA term on the basis of a report by *someone other than the client*. Each of these possibilities is described next.

Regarding items at different intensity levels (a), you can employ an NA term at a different level than it is listed on the *DANA* form. *Moderately angry*, for example, is an NA term listed on Level 3 (*Moderate NA*). If a client expresses intense anger, however, you can write "anger" on Level 4 (*Intense NA*) or simply endorse a similar item on Level 4.

Regarding nonverbal expression of NA (b), you can check a *DANA* term on the basis of the client's nonverbal behaviors. As indicated in the author's scoring (Table 8.2), Jeremy expresses several NA states nonverbally. Assessing NA in terms of nonverbals is particularly important for clients who are unexpressive or avoidant of NA. Many clients try to avoid experiencing and expressing feelings of NA, such as sadness and fear. As reviewed in Chapter 3, research indicates that avoidance of affect can sustain and/or increase the intensity of the affective state. Therapists are often in the best position to assess this avoidance, and attention to client nonverbals is one method for doing so.

Other sources of information (c) can be utilized if the clinical raters believe the information is valid. A client might report, for example, that a significant other indicated that the client experienced worry. Thus, the rater could endorse *Worried* for this client even though the client did not directly report experiencing worry. Similarly, the therapist might sense that the client is experiencing a particular NA state and directly ask the client about the state ("Did you feel overwhelmed?"). The client's report, as elicited by the therapist, can then be employed for the *DANA* rating.

This discussion brings up the issue of **questionable instances**, that is, aspects of the client's behavior that may or may not be appropriate to include in *DANA* ratings. In general, nonverbal expressions of NA are appropriate, but there may also be aspects of nonverbal communication that are unrelated to the client's therapeutic work and therefore excluded from *DANA* endorsement. Similarly, the therapist may judge a significant other's report of the client's NA states as untrustworthy and therefore decide to exclude that information from the *DANA* ratings. More problematic may be idiographic expressions of particular clients related to NA expression. For example, when asked how a client is feeling, she may typically respond, "I don't know." Is this an indication of avoidance of NA? The answer may not be immediately apparent to the therapist, who may need repeated interactions with the client to gain an understanding of what "I don't know" means in terms of the client's NA experiencing. Once the therapist has a sense of the meaning of "I don't know" for affective avoidance, the therapist can retroactively edit previous *DANA* entries if necessary.

Evaluating Your Depression/Anxiety Negative Affect Ratings

Table 8.2 displays the author's list of the endorsed *DANA* items for Jeremy along with endorsed items from graduate students who completed this training as part

Table 8.3. Jeremy Transcript

Therapist: Hi, Jeremy. Whatever you'd like to talk about today to help me to get to know you better I'd love to hear.

Client: OK. Um, where do you want me to start?

Therapist: Wherever you'd like to start is fine.

Client: Well, my roommate is the one that wanted me to come here today.

Therapist: Mmhmm. Your roommate wanted you to come in?

Client: I guess she's been worried about me; I probably wouldn't be here if she hadn't wanted me to come here.

Therapist: So am I getting this right, that you didn't really want to come in here today?

Client: Uh, yeah, but… I guess I've been having problems.

Therapist: Mmhmm. There are some things you've been struggling with?

Client: Yeah, it's… I don't know. I've tried talking about this to someone about this before, but I … I just couldn't.

Therapist: Mmhmm. It seems like you feel overwhelmed when you think about these things that you've been struggling with. Like, I know there's something wrong but I can't quite put it into words. Is that right?

Client: Yeah, I … I just don't know. I don't really like to think about it so that's part of the reason why I didn't want to come here today, but my roommate insisted.

Therapist: Mmhmm. It's really difficult talking about these things.

Client: Yeah.

Therapist: Well, I was wondering if you might try something with me. Um, all you have to do first is just sit there and really try to relax, and then pay attention to what's going on in your body internally, any feelings that come up in certain parts of your body. Do you think you'd like to do that?

Client: Yeah, I could try.

Therapist: And then maybe you could ask yourself the question: What's going on in my life right now? And consider one problem in particular and just think about that problem. And really pay attention to what's going on internally, and really pay attention to any sort of sensations that you're having inside your body.

Client: OK. Well, I guess the problem I have right now is that I didn't really want to be here, and I guess what I'm feeling right now is… this intense pressure in my chest. Like, um, this heavy weight that is making it kind of difficult for me to breathe sometimes.

Therapist: Mmhmm. So, when you think about the problem of how you didn't want to come in here today but your roommate insisted, it feels like there's pressure on your chest?

Client: Yeah, like, um… I guess bricks maybe, like pressure from that, almost like a burden, even.

Therapist: Mmhmm. It feels like there are bricks weighing down on your chest, and you feel burdened? Does that fit with what you're feeling?

(continued)

Table 8.3. (Continued)

Client: Yeah, I guess I do. I felt this heaviness and burden before, like, when I leave my room, it's... it's too much going on at once.

Therapist: It seems like it would be overwhelming to feel that.

Client: Yeah, yeah it is. My mom wants me to be more outgoing and to do more things, I guess like my brother. He's always been sociable and popular and... I don't know, it's just hard to compete with that or to think that I need to show the same personality. But I mean... I don't know, it's hard for me to do that sort of thing. I just want to tell my mom I'm not Jason, you know, I'm not going... I probably can't be like that.

Therapist: It sounds like you don't like when your mom puts pressure on you. And I want to be open and transparent in our relationship here. When you said that, I sort of had an image come up in my mind of a small boy in the corner who is really afraid to go out and experience different things because of this pressure you feel from others.

Client: Yeah. I guess that's interesting; I want to try to be more sociable, but I do enjoy spending time by myself. But there's still... I still feel pressure that. I guess, I need to try to be more outgoing and, I guess, try to make more friends, but, I mean, maybe my mom is right. What kind of loser hardly has any friends and never leaves his dorm room?

Therapist: Mmhmm. It seems like if you don't have any friends then maybe you're a loser, but just in our interactions here, you seem very personable, very friendly, and it seems like you'd make someone a really good friend.

Client: Maybe, but, my mom's just always telling me that you need to go out and do more, and it feels like a lot of pressure.

Therapist: From what we've been talking about, it seems like you may feel a little hostile toward your mother.

Client: Yeah, I guess I am. How horrible is that? I mean, my own mother.

Therapist: It feels horrible to have these negative emotions toward your mother, but here I am trying to do my best, and, you know, my mother's putting all this pressure on me. Is that right?

Client: Yeah, I'm trying to do my best. I mean, I do want more friends, but it's just too much pressure. I don't know, I guess my problem seems to make a little bit more sense now.

Therapist: Mmhmm. Good.

of a class exercise. Table 8.3 presents a transcript of Jeremy's conversation with the therapist. You can evaluate your ratings by comparing them to the author's and graduate students' ratings.

The author's ratings indicate that only two endorsed items (*Pressured* and *Moderately angry*) are directly based on Jeremy's self-reports. Jeremy reported feeling "pressure" (5:00, 7:15) at several points during the session; he also reported feeling "hostile" (8:15) toward his mother, which resulted in the endorsement of the *Moderately angry* item. Relatedly, Jeremy's obvious discomfort with expressing his feelings led to an answer of "yes" to the question, "Any indication that this client is avoiding negative affect?"

In contrast to the two endorsements based on self-reports, six NA terms (italicized in Table 8.2) were endorsed on the basis of Jeremy's body movements and tone of voice. During the session, he could be described as conveying a sense of being tense, on edge, uncomfortable, anxious, and having difficulty relaxing.

The therapist twice inquired about whether Jeremy felt "overwhelmed" (3:40, 6:00) and he agreed. *Overwhelmed* at Level 4 (*Intense NA*) is one of the two most intense endorsed terms. The other, *Pressured*, is normally a Level 3 term that was moved to Level 4 by the author in this rating because of the intensity Jeremy expressed about feeling pressured by his mother.

The ratings on the basis of nonverbals and the decision to move one NA term up a level of intensity are a matter of the rater's judgment. A useful rule of thumb is to endorse an item if some evidence exists that the client is experiencing that NA state (e.g., self-report, nonverbals, reports by others). Most important, however, is that the rater consistently employs the same standard across sessions for each client. For example, if a rater endorses items on the basis of nonverbals, as is appropriate with Jeremy, the rater should continue to do so with all of Jeremy's sessions and ratings.

Score the Depression/Anxiety Negative Affect for This Session

Based on the author's *DANA* ratings in Table 8.2, three of Jeremy's major NA scores are as follows:

DANA Score	Author	Your Score
Highest Intensity Level (HIL)	4	—
Total number of endorsed items (TOT)	11	—
Did client evidence NA avoidance?	Yes	—

The author's scores form a baseline from which to compare Jeremy's NA states after additional information gathering and intervention(s). For example, determine your HIL for Jeremy's ratings (i.e., report the HIL for your endorsed *DANA* items). As shown in Table 8.4, 1 standard deviation (SD) for HIL at both the first and last session equals 1 intensity level. So if your HIL was 3, 4, or 5, your ratings are roughly equivalent to the standard rating. Similarly, sum the total number of items you endorsed. One SD for the TOT is approximately 5, so if your total number of items endorsed ranged from 6 to 17, your ratings are within 1 standard deviation of the author's rating.

Table 8.4. DEPRESSION/ANXIETY NEGATIVE AFFECT DESCRIPTIVE STATISTICS FOR
FIRST AND LAST SESSIONS

	First Session			Last Session		
	Total	*Males*	*Females*	*Total*	*Males*	*Females*
	M (SD)	*M (SD)*	*M (SD)*	*M (SD)*	*M (SD)*	*M (SD)*
HIL	3.79 (0.7)	3.67 (0.8)	3.87 (0.7)	3.2 (0.8)	3.13 (0.9)	3.22 (0.8)
AIL	2.56 (0.5)	2.33 (0.6)	2.67 (0.4)	2.3 (0.6)	2.19 (0.5)	2.34 (0.6)
TOT	7.22 (4.4)	7.25 (5.4)	7.25 (4.0)	4.64 (4.6)	4.13 (5.5)	4.76 (4.2)

NOTE: HIL refers to Highest Intensity Level, AIL to Average Intensity Level, and TOT
to Total Number of Endorsed Negative Affect Items. Data are from Meier (2012).

Finally, if you answered "yes" to whether Jeremy evidenced avoidance of NA,
your answer matched the author's. Jeremy repeatedly said that he did not want
to be talking to the counselor and also answered "I don't know" to several of the
counselor's inquiries.

If your *DANA* scores do not fall within the ranges suggested previously,
repeat the Jeremy ratings exercise at least one more time. To develop consistency across sessions, you should be aware of decay and drift errors. Recall from
Chapter 3 that decay refers to random changes in an observer's reliability, while
drift occurs when the observer makes systematic changes to the definition or
interpretation of coding categories (Paul et al., 1986). Finally, use the information here to develop a strong understanding of what constitutes NA intensity at all five levels. If you perform the Jeremy ratings exercise twice and still
experience difficulty, go to the last section, Additional Practice to Increase and
Maintain Proficiency.

The reader can also compare ratings with graduate students in counseling
psychology who also completed this task. The students' ratings evidenced agreement for HIL: All four students had HIL equal to 4, the same as the author's HIL
value. But the students exhibited considerable variability in the total number of
endorsed *DANA* items: 15, 12, 8, and 5; recall that the authors' TOT was 11.

Thus, if your HIL rating did not equal 4, repeat the exercise. For TOT, use 10
as a threshold: If your total number of NA endorsements was nine or less, repeat
the exercise.

Interpreting and Understanding Jeremy's Negative Affect

The PMOA data alone cannot inform the clinician about what alternative conceptualizations and intervention(s) may be useful for a particular client. Instead, data
and theory that explain PMOA patterns must be found in other sources. Overall,
the themes listed in Table 8.5, typical of the type of information that might be
found in a session's progress notes, provide a context for understanding the *DANA*

Table 8.5. JEREMY'S MAJOR THEMES

Avoidance

    Tried to talk with someone before, "but I just couldn't"

    I don't like to think about it, that's why I didn't want to come here today

    "Horrible" that he feels "hostile" toward mother

Affect

    Overwhelmed, burden, pressure

    "Horrible" that he feels "hostile" toward mother

    Smiles briefly after compliment

Relationships

    Roommate wants him to come, worried about him

    Pressure from mom to be "outgoing" like brother

            Wants to tell mom, "I'm not Jason!"

            "There's too much pressure"

Self-image

    "Loser" who has no friends and seldom leaves dorm room

Counselor

  themes

    Nondirective

    Reflection of feelings, content

    Compliments him about his potential to be a friend

    Relaxation exercise

            Awkward: "Do you think you'd like to do that?"

    Too much explaining?

ratings for Jeremy and for developing a case conceptualization and associated interventions.

First, Jeremy appears avoidant of experiencing and expressing NA. Jeremy states, "I don't want to think about it," a good indication of avoidance (3:55). Similarly, he states that it is "horrible" that he feels "hostile" (the counselor's choice of a word) toward his mother. Much of the "pressure" Jeremy experiences appears to result from his ideas about his mother's expectations for his social interactions. Also, Jeremy communicates more NA through nonverbals than verbally, as evidenced by the number of *DANA* terms endorsed through nonverbals (five) than through self-report (two).

This discomfort with affect suggests that building a working alliance with Jeremy will be difficult but important to keep him engaged in therapy. Relationships, particularly with his family of origin, appear critical to understanding Jeremy and developing a case conceptualization and intervention(s). And from the perspective of narrative therapy, noteworthy aspects of this session include Jeremy's **metaphors** (i.e., a figure of speech that compares one thing to another). These include the following:

1. "Intense pressure in my chest" (5:00)
2. "Like bricks" (5:32)
3. "Almost like a burden even" (5:32)
4. "Heaviness… it's too much going on at once" (6:00)
5. Self-described "loser" (7:30)
6. "Pressure" from mom (7:30)

The student counselor does an overall skillful job of tracking Jeremy and offering reflections based on Jeremy's language and descriptions. The counselor provides a useful response to Jeremy's initial description of his situation by saying, "It seems like it would be overwhelming to feel that." Jeremy laughs in agreement and then explores experiences with his mother and brother. The counselor also provides a useful metaphor: "I had an image of a small boy in the corner who's afraid to go out" (6:50). However, the counselor also missed some potentially important information. For example, Jeremy initially says his roommate wants him to see a counselor and is "worried about me" (3:08). The counselor ignores this statement. It might have been useful to ask, "What is your roommate worried about?" If the roommate is worried, one possibility is that Jeremy has been discussing or hinting at suicide.

Treatment Planning

Based on these initial *DANA* scores and themes, what might we expect from Jeremy's subsequent psychotherapy sessions? First, Jeremy's description of his mother's expectations for him as the source of his feelings of pressure suggests this is a long-standing issue. Jeremy's moderate anxiety and accompanying nonverbal expressions of discomfort are likely to continue at least through initial sessions. Useful questions include, Will Jeremy's nonverbals become more relaxed as he builds a working alliance with the therapist? How difficult will it be for the therapist to build a working alliance with Jeremy?

If Jeremy's anxiety persists in initial sessions, Jeremy's *DANA* scores are likely to be stable and high during that period. Figure 8.1 displays another case where

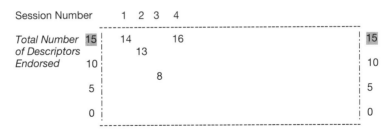

Figure 8.1 Example of Large Number of Total Number of Endorsed Item Responses per Session.

Figure 8.2 Case Conceptualization for Jeremy. *This figure depicts one possible set of process outcome elements for Jeremy, namely, that his mother's high expectations for his social performance have led to feelings of anxiety and pressure. Potential interventions, such as exploration of feelings, exposure to threatening social situations, and group counseling, follow from this conceptualization.*

TOT scores were initially high and relatively stable; this client is expressing a variety of NA states. Jeremy's initial TOT of 11 suggests he is also likely to continue to evidence a high number of NA states, particularly if he continues to express them nonverbally.

HIL scores, the highest intensity level of any endorsed item, might also remain elevated (Levels 3, 4, and perhaps 5) for initial sessions. Recall that two NA terms at Level 4 (*Intense NA*), *Pressured* and *Overwhelmed*, were endorsed for Jeremy. If Jeremy felt suicidal at times, for example, he might be more willing to disclose this information as the therapeutic alliance strengthened. Jeremy's NA levels could also remain high or increase if the therapist pursued in-depth discussion of Jeremy's relationship with his mother or placed Jeremy in social situations that he felt were threatening, including group counseling. Jeremy might be one of those individuals who initially felt worse in therapy before he felt better.

Jeremy's avoidance of NA is likely to be a useful therapeutic issue. Jeremy's nonverbal expressions of anxiety and discomfort might change with a therapist who helped Jeremy to focus on and process his bodily sensations. Jeremy's use of metaphors about pressure also provides an opportunity for the therapist to introduce therapeutic metaphors and actions. For example, the therapist might ask, "What could we do to take those bricks off your chest?" or "Let's place those bricks on this chair and talk about how you feel with them removed." This processing and related assertiveness training, where Jeremy learns to express feelings appropriately to the therapist and then to others, would likely result in a decrease in HIL and TOT.

Family therapy might allow Jeremy to talk with his mother and brother, and group counseling could provide a medium for Jeremy to develop social skills and learn to be appropriately assertive in his feelings and interactions with others. As mentioned, developing a working alliance with Jeremy by itself may provide a corrective emotional experience to his family interpersonal history (Teyber & McClure, 2011).

These factors are displayed in a graphic case conceptualization in Figure 8.2.

ADDITIONAL PRACTICE TO INCREASE AND MAINTAIN PROFICIENCY

This section will help the reader gain additional practice in creating *DANA* ratings as well as maintaining rating proficiency over time. Because of delay and drift errors, raters may alter their ideas about what constitutes an NA state and become inconsistent over time in *DANA* ratings. This is particularly problematic when a rater becomes inconsistent with the same client over time because it becomes difficult to attribute changes on *DANA* scores to the intervention and not to rater error.

Exercise 9 contains transcripts for three videos. Review the instructions in the section Getting Started—Part 2 before you complete practice *DANA* ratings with these videos. To rate the videos, use the version of the *DANA* in Appendix 10. Other rating scales (e.g., the *GAF*) may be employed with these materials for additional PMOA practice.

SUMMARY

This chapter provided an introduction and initial training for performing *GAF* and *DANA* ratings. This includes learning about rater errors such as decay and drift, which can cause inconsistent clinical ratings over time, as well as recall errors, which can occur when ratings take place too long after a client session. With the *DANA* and *GAF*, raters should view multiple clinical examples for practice and training. Practicing the *DANA* rating with Jeremy and other cases helps raters learn how to provide reliable and valid PMOA data; raters should continue to practice clinical ratings with clients specific to their practice settings. Feedback from supervisors or other sources about clinical ratings is also useful to maintain proficiency. As noted previously, continued practice and feedback are important for maintaining the reliability of clinical observers (Nay, 1979). When observers know their work will be evaluated, they provide reliable observations; in other conditions, some may not (Meier, 2008).

An important component of rater training is becoming aware of potential problems with PMOA instruments and including these limitations as part of the interpretative report of PMOA data. For example, the **reactivity** of the *GAF*'s global score means that clinicians can easily manipulate this transparent scale, leaving open the question of how much change actually occurred versus how much change the clinician reported to maintain funding for therapy from insurance companies or other sources. The *DANA* is a newer measure with relatively little psychometric information; clinicians who use it should interpret its scores with caution and treat it as an experimental scale until additional research can support its usefulness as a PMOA measure.

Although this chapter focused on training for clinical raters, it is also possible that training clients could improve the psychometric properties of self-report PMOA scales. Theoretical explanations for poor rater performance (Meier, 2008; Paul et al., 1986), such as fuzzy schemas and memory errors, should also apply to client self-report. Although psychotherapy itself may improve clients' ability to self-report relevant psychological states (e.g., increased awareness of NA), structured training, strong rationales, and enhanced instructions may increase PMOA scores' reliability and validity estimates in self-reports. The driving forces for widespread self-report use are low cost and ease of use; certain psychological states (such as quality of the working alliance) may be more accessible via self-report. But implied in the training of both raters and clients is the allocation of additional resources (i.e., time and money) than may be currently available in some mental health settings.

Exercise 8 *Learning the GAF*

Complete at least 10 of the examples provided by the Washington State Mental Health Division at depts.washington.edu/washinst/Resources/CGAS/Index.htm. Continue until your *GAF* scores match the expected range 80% to 90% of the time. Write the name of each client below, along with your score and the range of acceptable scores.

Client	*Your GAF Rating*	*Acceptable Range*
1. _Kim_____	___	*20–40*
2. _____	___	__ – __
3. _____	___	__ – __
4. _____	___	__ – __
5. _____	___	__ – __
6. _____	___	__ – __
7. _____	___	__ – __
8. _____	___	__ – __
9. _____	___	__ – __
10. _____	___	__ – __
11. _____	___	__ – __
12. _____	___	__ – __
13. _____	___	__ – __
14. _____	___	__ – __
15. _____	___	__ – __

Exercise 9 *Additional Brief Practice in DANA Ratings*

Below are links to three YouTube videos (and transcripts) that show clients displaying a variety of NA states. Copy the *DANA* scale in the Appendix and complete it for each video; also note whether the client appeared to avoid NA in the video segment. When finished, the Appendix has corresponding *DANA* ratings as completed by the author.

1. **General Hospital—Robin's Therapy** http://www.youtube.com/watch?v=0fDdXDb2Y_c

Watch time period 3:30–5:00:

Client: This isn't the way things were supposed to be; I had it all figured out.
Counselor: You talk a lot about how things should be, but I don't hear a lot about how you feel.
Client: Um, I feel stretched too thin, that's how I feel. I feel irritated, and bitchy, I snap at Patrick, I don't want to eat, I feel angry, I feel a lot, but not when it comes to Emma; I feel nothing.
Counselor: How about your husband? How's that relationship?
Client: I've lost interest in sex, which makes me feel guilty, incompetent. Of course, I blame him for it and get angry then start to feel guilty all over again, and then that becomes a whirlwind of all these impulses.

2. **Perls with Gloria** https://www.youtube.com/watch?v=it0j6FIxIog

Watch time period 4:10–9:00:

Perls: We are going to interview for half an hour.
Gloria: Right away I'm scared.
Perls: You say you're scared but you're smiling. I don't understand how one can be scared and smile at the same time.
Gloria: And I'm also suspicious of you; I think you understand very well. I think you know that when I get scared I laugh or I kid to cover up.
Perls: You do have stage fright.
Gloria: Um, I don't know. I'm mostly aware of you, I'm afraid that—I'm afraid you'll have such a direct attack that you're going to get me in the corner and I'm afraid of it. I want you to be more on my side.
Perls: You say get me in your corner and you put your hand on your chest. Is this your corner?
Gloria: Well, it's like—Yeah, it's like I'm afraid, you know.
Perls: Where would you like to go? Can you describe the corner you'd like to go to?
Gloria: Yeah, it's back in a corner, where I'm completely protected.
Perls: And there you would be safer from me.

Gloria: Well, I know I wouldn't really.... But, it feels safer, yes.

Perls: You made your way to this corner, you're perfectly safe now. What would you do in this corner?

Gloria: I'd just sit.

Perls: You'd just sit.

Gloria: Yes.

Perls: Now, how long would you sit?

Gloria: I don't know, but this is so funny that you're saying this. This reminds me of when I was a little girl, every time when I was afraid, I'd feel better sitting in a corner.

Perls: OK. Well, are you a little girl?

Gloria: Well, no—but it's the same feeling.

Perls: Are you a little girl?

Gloria: This feeling reminds me of it—

Perls: Are you a little girl?

Gloria: No. No. No.

Perls: At last. How old are you?

Gloria: 30.

Perls: So you are not a little girl.

Gloria: No.

Perls: Ok. So, you are a 30-year-old girl who is afraid of a guy like me.

Gloria: Well, don't even know if—well, yeah, I do know I'll be afraid of you, I get real defensive with you!

Perls: Now, what can I do to you?

Gloria: You can't do anything but I can sure feel dumb and I can feel stupid for not having the right answers.

Perls: What would it do for you to feel dumb and stupid?

Gloria: I hate it when I'm stupid.

Perls: What would it do for you to be dumb and stupid? Let's put it like this: What would it do to me for you to feel dumb and stupid?

Gloria: It makes you all the smarter and all the higher above me then I really have to look up to you because you're so smart.

Perls: Ah, yeah, butter me up right and left.

Gloria: No, I think you can do that all by yourself.

Perls: Uh huh. I think the other way around. If you play dumb and stupid, you force me to be more explicit.

Gloria: That's been said to me before, but I don't buy it. I don't really—

Perls: What are you doing with your feet now?

Gloria: Wiggling them. [Laughing]

Perls: So it's a joke now?

Gloria: No! I'm afraid you're going to notice everything I do! Gee!

Perls: Don't you want me to—

Gloria: Yeah, I want you to help me become more relaxed, yes. I don't want to be so defensive with you. I don't like to feel so defensive. Uh... you're acting like—You're treating me as if I'm stronger than I am and I want you to protect me more and be nicer to me!

Perls: Are you aware of your smile? You don't believe a word you are saying.

Gloria: I do too and I know you're gonna pick on me for it!

Perls: Sure, you're bluffing, you're a phony.

Gloria: Do you believe—You're meaning that seriously?

Perls: Yeah, you say you're afraid and you laugh and you giggle and you squirm; it's phony. You put on a good performance for me.

Gloria: Oh, I resent that very much.

Perls: Can you express this?

Gloria: Yes sir, I most certainly am not being phony. I will admit this: It's hard for me to show my embarrassment and I hate to be embarrassed, but boy I resent you calling me a phony. Just because I smile and when I'm embarrassed or I'm being put in a corner doesn't mean I'm being a phony.

Perls: Wonderful. Thank you. You did this well for the last minute.

Gloria: Well, I'm mad at you. I—

Perls: That's great. You didn't have to cover up your anger with your smile. In that moment, in that minute, you were not a phony.

3.   **Behavior Therapy**

www.youtube.com/watch?v=MCyfMFXR-n0&feature=related

Watch time Period 1:15–2:26.

Client: They're naughty boys, you know this. And they're everywhere. They're all over school, they're getting in trouble, then I'm late home, preparing dinner for my husband, and then he gets annoyed, and on it goes. It's all getting to too much—

Counselor: OK. Uh… OK. You're supposed to finish at 3:30; those are the hours you're reporting. So, why do you think you're not finishing at 3:30, Kathleen?

Client: Oh, I have too much work—

Counselor: Who's giving you too much work? What's happening?

Client: Oh, I work in a doctor's surgery; I don't know if I told you that. One doctor employed me, but there are four within the practice, and I'm doing work for all of them, when I should really be doing work for one.

Counselor: So that's the problem. There are four people giving you work and there's no way you can fit it into the times that you report to work.

Client: No. And I just can't say no to them. They put the work in my in-tray, and, and then… and then—

Counselor: OK.

Client: And it's not getting to my out-tray, and—

Counselor: Right.

Client: And, and the day goes by and it's there the next day, and it's—

Counselor: All right.

Client: And it's, it's… it's all too much for me—

Counselor: Yes. Yes. All right. I can see that. And I can see that you're getting quite stressed about it.

9

Using Progress Monitoring and Outcome Assessment Data in Supervision

INTRODUCTION

Clinical supervision typically involves interventions designed to enhance a student's or mental health provider's professional functioning (Bernard & Goodyear, 2008). Providing supervision constitutes a significant proportion of experienced clinicians' time in many mental health settings where supervisees deliver services. Supervisory skills include establishing a working relationship with supervisees, conceptualizing supervisee issues, giving appropriate feedback and support to supervisees, and most importantly, helping supervisees learn to implement these skills with their clients. Although many supervision approaches simply translate particular psychotherapy theories into use in the supervision process, other theories focus on developmental aspects of supervisees (Stoltenberg & Delworth, 1987) and social role aspects (Bernard & Goodyear, 2008).

Clinical supervision should provide trainees with the skills and abilities necessary to provide effective counseling and psychotherapy. Supervision includes an extended evaluation of the interventions' effectiveness, particularly regarding the quality of the professional services provided to clients (Lambert & Hawkins, 2001; Worthen & Lambert, 2007). Ellis and Ladany (1997, p. 485) described client outcomes as the "acid test" for the effectiveness of supervision; that is, supervision should increase positive outcomes and decrease negative effects in clients. Callahan, Almstrom, Swift, Borja, and Heath (2009) reviewed research, however, that found that premature termination can be as high as 75% in training clinics (compared to 40% to 60% in other outpatient settings) and that successful improvement happens more slowly with clients of trainees. Improving the training of psychotherapists should be a high priority for the mental health professions.

RESEARCH ON SUPERVISION AND OUTCOMES

Currently, little evidence exists to demonstrate that clinical supervision improves client outcomes (Saptya, Riemer, & Bickman, 2005). Because of the practical and theoretical complexities of the undertaking, however, the literature contains relatively few studies that attempt to examine this relation directly (Freitas, 2002; Lambert & Hawkins, 2001; Reese et al., 2009; Sapyta et al., 2005). Given that client outcomes are influenced by a potentially large set of causal factors, both internal and external to therapy, the impact of most supervision may be too small to be detected in many individual psychotherapy cases and by traditional research designs employed in quantitative research (Ellis & Ladany, 1997; Ronnestad & Ladany, 2006). Several recent studies have shown modest positive effects of supervision on client outcomes (Callahan et al., 2009; Reese et al., 2009) but have also illustrated the difficulties involved with such research.

Callahan et al. (2009) analyzed archival records for 76 adult clients who received mental health services from 40 doctoral clinical psychology trainees in a training clinic. These clients completed at least three sessions and had a mean age of 18 years; the nine supervisors were program faculty who also conducted research and taught courses with these students. The preinternship trainees received 1 hour of individual supervision and 2 hours of group supervision weekly. Clients completed the *Beck Depression Inventory-II (BDI-II)* at intake and termination, and each client's outcome status was coded using the Reliable Change Index (Jacobson & Truax, 1991) into one of four categories (i.e., no reliable change, reliably deteriorated, reliably improved, recovered). Results indicated that Supervisor as a variable approached statistical significance on *BDI* outcome ($p = .08$) and accounted for 16% of outcome variance.

Callahan et al. (2009) found considerable differences in outcomes among supervisors. The five cases associated with one supervisor, for example, all evidenced recovery (i.e., movement on *BDI-II* scores from the clinical range at intake to the normal range at termination), whereas clients associated with another supervisor experienced no reliable change in 12 of 16 cases. Primary among the methodological problems found in this study was the small sample size of the supervisor by client matrix and the use of the *BDI* as the sole outcome measure. Six of the nine supervisors had only four or five cases associated with them, raising the possibility that their diverging outcomes were due to chance. As noted in Chapter 6, the *BDI* can be problematic because repeated administrations of such self-reports have been found to result in score changes indicating improvement (Persons & Fresco, 2008) and *BDI* scores can evidence sudden changes independent of any intervention (Kelly, Roberts, & Ciesla, 2005; Tang & DeRubeis, 1999).

INCORPORATING STRUCTURED FEEDBACK INTO SUPERVISION

In most graduate programs and mental health settings, supervision consists of a relatively informal discussion about one to a few of the therapist's clients. Feedback about therapist performance typically is delivered informally during supervision and then by an evaluative checklist at the completion of the supervision period. The informal or unstructured feedback may include listening to audio and/or videotape recordings of the supervisee's actual work, enabling the supervisor to provide feedback about particular therapist actions and strategies in the context of client–therapist interactions. But therapists typically receive little feedback about client progress and outcomes, instead working "in the absence of information about client treatment response from objective sources" (Sapyta et al., 2005, p. 147).

Because trainees often have significant problems with premature termination and slow client progress (Callahan et al., 2009), incorporating progress monitoring and outcome assessment (PMOA) feedback into supervision may require different procedures (Cross & Angelo, 1988) and greater tact on the part of the supervisor. In a semester-length counseling process course where students were taught case conceptualization and PMOA assessment, Meier (1999) noted that some students resisted close supervision of a data-based approach, fearing the negative feedback about the absence of client change. Supervisees may understandably view negative trends in client data as critical of their work, and beginning therapists are often very concerned about appearing credible to self, other students, faculty, and supervisors (Meier, 2001). Consequently, supervisors may wish to provide new trainees with realistic expectations about rates of premature termination and client growth, particularly with client groups who evidence more severe, chronic issues. Educating students about the 75% premature termination rate and that half of their clients may not show appreciable progress (particularly over relatively short periods of time) may provide more realistic expectations about the difficulty of learning and doing psychotherapy well. These data may also increase students' perceived need for quality training and supervision: The goal is to move the trainee's focus from "let me show you how well I am doing" to "let's discuss what I can learn to improve as a therapist."

Instead of reviewing all clients, supervision may be most effective when progress monitoring data are employed to identify the trainee's clients who are failing to improve (Reese et al., 2009). Supervisors may scan PMOA data in time series, for example, to identify supervisee clients who are worsening or failing to improve. Evidence of treatment failure appears particularly important to recognize because research suggests that many clinicians assume that if they implement generally accepted approaches, success must follow (Kendall, Kipnis, & Otto-Salaj, 1992).

Supervisors can also help supervisees to develop a few alternative methods for working with failing clients so that supervisees possess a clear, easily remembered idea about how to alter their treatment. Supervisors can also model flexibility for generating alternative conceptualizations and treatment approaches; it is important to teach students how to develop multiple hypotheses about client processes and outcomes. Again, progress notes may be a key source of such hypotheses, but knowledge about client history, relevant research, psychotherapy theories, and additional assessment methods can also help.

Finally, PMOA data should be discussed during most, if not all, supervisory sessions. Progress monitoring data can change rapidly for many clients, and regular discussion of data patterns for clients who are not improving is important for tracking progress and considering alternative interventions. A long lag time between feedback from PMOA data and its application with the client essentially defeats the purpose of employing PMOA data as feedback. Timely supervision that includes regular discussion of progress monitoring data enhances the likelihood that the trainee will continue to monitor client progress and actually implement alternative interventions.

WEAKNESSES OF CURRENT FEEDBACK-ENHANCED APPROACHES

Researchers who describe feedback-enhanced therapies typically focus on the **alert function** of PMOA data. That is, the primary purpose of PMOA data is to signal to a clinician that a client is not making expected progress or meeting a standard (Lambert, Harmon, Slade, Whipple, & Hawkins, 2005; Lambert et al., 2001; Saptya et al., 2005). Lambert and Hawkins (2001), for example, described the case of a young bipolar patient who received medication and experienced a decrease in symptoms but stopped taking the medication after the symptom decrease. The symptoms then returned and were evident in the PMOA data. In this case, the appropriate action was to persuade the client to resume taking the medications, the original intervention.

Clinical tools that employ PMOA data can provide generic, research-based suggestions for altering interventions. Worthen and Lambert (2007, p. 50) reported the suggestions provided by the interpretative component of the *OQ45* when a client shows a negative response:

> Steps should be taken to carefully review this case and identify reasons for poor progress. It is recommended that you be alert to the possible need to improve the therapeutic alliance, reconsider the client's readiness for change and the need to renegotiate the therapeutic contract, intervene to strengthen social supports, or possibly alter your treatment plan by intensifying treatment, shifting intervention strategies, or decide upon a new course of action, such as referral for medication. Continuous monitoring of future progress is highly recommended.

PMOA data alone, however, cannot inform the clinician about specific alternative intervention(s) that may be useful for a particular client. Interpreting PMOA data without an understanding of possible causes establishes a black box design that cannot provide information needed for developing hypotheses related to improving interventions (Posavac, 2011). The black box design involves examining the output of a system or intervention without understanding what produces those outcomes. Using another research metaphor, PMOA data are the **dependent variables** in the design of the individual case study, whereas the therapeutic interventions are one of the known **independent variables**. Other casual factors and explanations for the PMOA data patterns must be identified elsewhere.

Interpretation of PMOA data over time partially also depends on the psychotherapy theory and related research underlying the interventions and case conceptualization (Hawkins & Meier, 2013). In some theories and interventions, for example, a period of worsening may be expected when psychotherapeutic interventions are introduced (Mergenthaler, 1996). This may trigger an alert with some PMOA measures that might be safely ignored by a therapist who expects an initial deterioration. Yet most clinical support tools that employ PMOA data are explicitly atheoretical (Worthen & Lambert, 2007).

EMPLOYING AND INTERPRETING PROGRESS MONITORING AND OUTCOME ASSESSMENT DATA IN SUPERVISION

Both quantitative data and qualitative information may be useful as structured feedback in supervision. PMOA data from a quantitative progress monitoring measure can provide an alert to indicate that a particular client is not improving and should be a focus in the limited time of supervision. The search for clinical hypotheses about why the client is failing to improve, however, can begin in the qualitative progress notes of trainees and supervisors. As described in previous chapters, progress notes may be a key source of information about why particular patterns of PMOA scores appear with a specific client. Easily accessible and routinely completed in most mental health settings (Sommers-Flanagan & Sommers-Flanagan, 2002), progress notes can provide context about how situations and history influenced the client in the past and are influencing the client during current sessions. Both qualitative and quantitative methods are described later.

As previously described, the *Depression/Anxiety Negative Affect (DANA)* scale provides PMOA data based on clinician ratings of negative affect (NA). NA is theoretically and empirically related to the initiation, persistence, and response to psychotherapy of many client problems (Moses & Barlow, 2006). *DANA* scores have evidenced adequate internal consistency, evidence of convergent and discriminant validity, and sensitivity to change over the course of psychotherapy (Meier, 2012). Effect sizes (ESs) of *DANA* scores consistently equaled or exceeded the average ES of 0.68 found for scales assessing the outcomes of counseling and psychotherapy in meta-analytic studies (Smith & Glass, 1977). ESs greater than 1 were found on *DANA* variables for clients whose therapists rated them as experiencing, rather than avoiding, NA. Since a higher *DANA* rating indicates more intense NA, improvement in therapy should be indicated by eventual decreases in NA intensity level.

Figure 9.1 displays ratings for the Highest Intensity Level (HIL) of NA experienced by an adult college student client who completed eight sessions in an outpatient mental health clinic. Although *DANA* ratings are typically completed by the therapist, these ratings were completed by the trainee's supervisor, based on supervisee reports and audiotapes of client sessions.

The *DANA* ratings of the HIL reported for the client over the past week range from 5 (Sessions 3, 4, and 7) to 1 (Session 8). These ratings indicate that the client experienced periods of intense and moderate NA until the final session. Without Session 8 (a termination session where the client reported little therapeutically relevant information), the overall pattern suggests a client who is cycling through processing and reflecting on emotional material (Mergenthaler, 1996). Mergenthaler's (1996) research suggests that successful clients alternate phases of high and low emotion and reflection. Based on this research, one interpretation of this pattern is that the client experienced two periods of intense emotion (i.e., Sessions 1 through 4 and another around Session 7); those periods were likely interspersed by a single interval (around Sessions 5 to 6) of high reflection where the client considered emotional material. Thus, the NA data suggest that one cycle of abstraction–emotion was completed. The question becomes, Was this processing sufficient for the client to resolve the presenting problem(s)?

The *DANA* ratings alone cannot answer this question. One alternative is to conduct a systematic examination of trainee and supervisor progress notes. Although the content of such notes may vary by therapeutic setting and associated requirements, most therapists conclude each session with a summary of key issues related to treatment progress and planning. Using those notes, one strategy is to track the consistency of client themes over time. Major themes or issues should have persistent relevance (Beutler & Hamblin, 1986); that is, the topic should appear repeatedly across sessions. Emotional reactions to an event increase the likelihood that an event will be remembered (Payne & Kensinger, 2010); as problems resolve and NA diminishes, clients should stop discussing

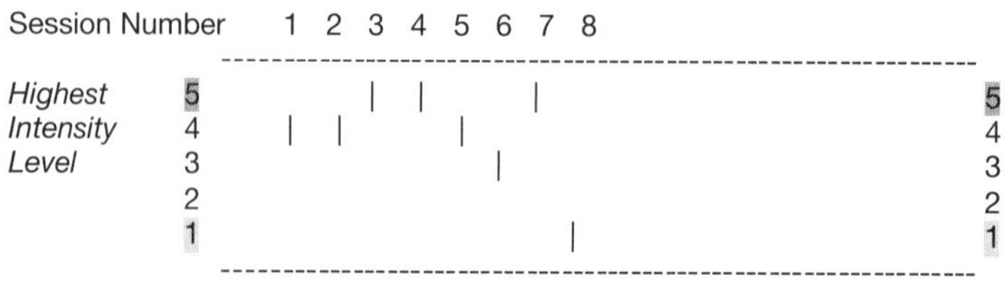

Figure 9.1 *Depression/Anxiety Negative Affect (DANA)* **Ratings for an Adult Client Over Eight Sessions.** *Tick marks indicate DANA Highest Intensity Level endorsed for that session.*

the themes that they talked about earlier in therapy. With effective therapy, what may have been a pressing topic when a client began therapy will lose its sense of urgency. Other topics may replace the presenting problem, but if the presenting problem has been resolved, the client should be less interested in talking about it. In general, a decrease in the presentation and length of discussion of a clinically relevant theme, as well as a decrease in NA around that theme, suggests that the client is ready for closure on these topics.

Table 9.1 displays a persistence table constructed by a supervisor using audio-tapes and supervisee reports of the same adult client with the *DANA* ratings. Seven themes related to client problems are listed, including *avoidance of affect, affect expressed, self-injurious behaviors, in crisis, academic problems, relation-ships,* and *coping skills exhibited* by the client. The client appears to avoid experi-encing or expressing affect across all sessions; what affect the client did express was primarily anger and hostility (all sessions except Session 8). Given this client's diagnosis of Borderline Personality Disorder, it follows that self-injurious behav-iors and relationship issues were frequent topics of the therapeutic conversations.

Both *avoidance of affect* and *affect expressed* are topics of therapeutic discus-sion across almost all sessions. Similarly, *relationship* issues are discussed in seven of eight sessions. These themes suggest that the client continues to strug-gle with experiencing, moderating, and expressing affect, particularly in rela-tionships with others. In turn, this hypothesis indicates that the client should continue therapy and that relationship issues and experiencing of affect around those relationships should be the major foci. Helping this client to learn emo-tional experiencing and regulation, perhaps as part of mindfulness, assertive-ness, and coping skills training, might be one useful approach (Linehan, 1993).

Themes in this or any persistence table may be rearranged to display infor-mation in a way that enhances conclusions. Themes in Figure 9.1, for example, could be related to *DANA* HIL scores. For example, are any unique themes in the persistence table associated with the highest *HIL* scores (i.e., Levels 4 and 5)? The themes of *avoidance of affect* and *affect expressed* can be eliminated because they are present in almost every session. *Relationship* issues, however, are present in Sessions 3, 4, and 7 when HIL equals 5; similarly, *self-injurious*

Table 9.1. PERSISTENT THEMES FOR ADULT CLIENT ACROSS EIGHT SESSIONS

Themes	1	2	3	4	5	6	7	8
Avoid affect	▦	▦	▦	▦	▦	▦	▦	▦
Affect expressed	▦	▦	▦	▦	▦	▦	▦	
Self-inj beh	▦	▦	▦		▦		▦	
In crisis	▦	▦	▦			▦		
Acad problem		▦				▦		
Relation issues	▦	▦	▦	▦		▦	▦	▦
Coping skills		▦		▦		▦		

Session Number

behaviors are present in Sessions 1, 2, and 5 when HIL equals 4. These two issues appear to be associated with the client's most intense NA.

SUMMARY

Traditionally, psychotherapists and supervisors have primarily relied on clinical judgment, instead of objective data, to gauge progress. Surveys examining clinical practices in mental health indicate that only about 20% to 30% of mental health professionals employ PMOA measures (Clement, 1999; Hatfield & Ogles, 2004). One explanation is that few practitioners receive formal training regarding how to apply PMOA data as clinical feedback. Supervision appears to be a particularly appropriate professional setting where applied training about and practice with PMOA data can occur.

Supervisors currently employ their best judgment about how to assist their students in the learning process. One empirically based complement is to teach trainees to employ PMOA data in their practices (Reese et al., 2009). Research indicates that routine use of progress monitoring data serves as an alert function that signals therapists to pay increased attention to clients who might prematurely terminate or otherwise fail to improve. New measures such as the *OQ45* and the *DANA* have been developed explicitly for the purpose of functioning as change-sensitive measures of psychotherapy progress and outcome.

One of the major limitations of PMOA measures, however, is their general inability to provide information that explains the patterns of observed scores over time and across sessions. As a result, most PMOA tools do not provide client-specific information about alternative interventions or conceptualizations. Qualitative methods such as persistence tables based on therapist and supervisor progress notes supply a relatively low-cost, easily accessible option for exploring clinical hypotheses that might explain PMOA data patterns. Incorporating psychotherapy theory into the development of a persistence table further strengthens the resulting clinical hypotheses and explanations (Hawkins & Meier, 2012). Clinical examples presented earlier in this chapter demonstrated how PMOA scores can track progress over time, and themes summarized in the persistence table illustrated the ongoing severity of the client's problems, the likely need for continued treatment, and possible interventions.

Many supervisors will benefit from additional training to learn the rationale for using PMOA data and how to find and evaluate the increasingly diverse measures that have recently been created. Evaluation of PMOA measures is a complicated task given that the field has yet to settle on criteria for assessing such tests (cf. National Center for Intensive Intervention, http://www.intensiveintervention.org). Relatively few tests have been explicitly designed for the purposes of PMOA (Meier, 2000; Vermeersch et al., 2004), and use of traditional psychological tests for PMOA purposes is often problematic. Froyd, Lambert, and Froyd's (1996) review of the *Minnesota Multiphasic Personality Inventory*, for example, found that it was one of the 10 most frequently used outcome measures "despite the fact that it is excessively long, very expensive, and contains many items that are not sensitive to change" (p. 38). Similarly, the review of the *Outcome Rating Scale* in Chapter 6 suggested that it may be a relatively insensitive measure for detecting change in therapy. Although the use of available PMOA measures for clinical feedback is likely to decrease overall treatment failure, the variability in tests' change sensitivity means that different measures will produce different estimates of change, complicating decisions about which clients are making progress. Supervisors who are well informed about the current status of PMOA tests will be in a better position to guide their supervisees through the process of PMOA use and clinical feedback.

10

Controversies and Opportunities

INTRODUCTION

Contemporary progress monitoring and outcome assessment (PMOA) efforts stand on the voluminous work of many researchers and clinicians who have provided the field with a solid foundation of theory, methodologies, and findings. Whereas the research findings on clinical feedback and progress monitoring provide the empirical foundation for this book, the chapters have primarily described applications of and procedures related to PMOA use in counseling and psychotherapy. For professionals who conduct research and practice in this area, however, a number of basic questions remain unanswered. More research, thought, and discussion are needed in these areas, and this chapter addresses seven of these key topics. Other sources for state-of-the-art discussions related to research, policy, and clinical applications include Boswell, Kraus, Miller, and Lambert (2013) and Lambert (2013).

OPTIMAL METHODS FOR PROGRESS MONITORING AND OUTCOME ASSESSMENT TEST CONSTRUCTION

One of the most important and largely unrecognized questions in the PMOA domain concerns the best method(s) for constructing change- and treatment-sensitive tests. Essentially, can PMOA test developers use traditional test development procedures and then assume the resulting test is optimally sensitive to change? For example, Stinchfield, Winters, Botzet, Jerstad, and Breyer (2007) described the development of the *Gambling Treatment Outcome Monitoring System* (*GAMTOMS*). Using gambling treatment clients, Stinchfield et al. provided evidence for the *GAMTOMS*'s internal consistency, 1-week test–retest reliability, content validity, convergent validity, discriminant validity, predictive validity, and construct validity—but no data indicating that *GAMTOMS*'s items or scores could detect change over time. Goodman, McKay, and DePhilippis (2013) suggested that test developers typically investigate tests' traditional psychometric properties but fail to evaluate their use in practice, with one of the most important questions being whether test scores can detect change resulting from interventions.

Although test users are interested in test score interpretation (i.e., the meaning of a particular test score), interpretation depends on all of the preceding steps, including test construction, administration, and scoring. In other words, the procedures employed to construct, administer, and score tests all influence the meaning of the subsequent uses of test scores. As described earlier, contemporary educational and psychological testing standards indicate that test validity depends on empirical evidence supporting test use *for particular purposes.* Traditional test development procedures, which historically were designed to measure psychological traits (Meier, 2008), will likely be less sensitive to measuring the psychological states that are the focus of most psychosocial interventions. Different tests vary in their ability to detect change, which has been empirically demonstrated with a number of PMOA measures (e.g., Lambert, Hatch, Kingston, & Edwards, 1986; Meier, 2004; Weinstock & Meier, 2003). Is this a result of different test construction procedures? Although many reviews conclude that contemporary PMOA measures have adequate psychometric properties (Boswell et al., 2013), additional investigations should be conducted to examine the change and treatment sensitivity of PMOA measures.

Traditional test procedures often include the development of norms, typically at a great expense because of the number and types of individuals needed for a representative sample. Comparing clients' scores to normative data is currently one way of determining whether clients have made progress (e.g., movement toward mean scores on a relevant dimension) and whether treatment can be terminated (e.g., once scores are within 1 standard deviation of the mean). At present, this is only one among numerous comparisons that can be made with PMOA data to address client progress and outcome. Other criteria may be equally or more valuable, such as estimates of the amount of progress made by an individual client or other criteria against which PMOA scores may be compared. While generating normative data as part of the PMOA test construction process is a valuable option, PMOA tests can be created and usefully employed without such information.

EFFECT OF SOURCE ON PROGRESS MONITORING AND OUTCOME ASSESSMENT DATA

Developers of all types of psychological tests tend to default to self-report for reasons including efficiency and low cost (Meier, 2008). But for many constructs with a social desirability component, such as avoidance of negative affect or addiction problems, self-report is problematic. Future research should contrast the effects of data source on the validity of PMOA scores. Relatedly, future research should also investigate methods for motivating clinicians to provide valid PMOA data (Boswell et al., 2013). This could be as simple as paying clinicians for more thorough outcome assessments and progress monitoring data. Such reimburse-ment, however, should not be linked to the PMOA scores themselves. Past efforts by managed care companies that connected therapist reimbursement to client improvement or fewer sessions often led therapists to game the system by report-ing small improvements whose absolute levels still indicated a need for therapy; the transparent *Global Assessment of Functioning (GAF)* was an ideal measure for such a use (Davis & Meier, 2001; Meier, 2008). If reimbursement and the provision of PMOA data cannot be uncoupled, then PMOA data may need to be collected by external assessors in settings similar to work assessment centers (Murphy & Davidshofer, 2005).

Researchers should also examine the feasibility and practicality of PMOA measures and methods. In general, the more complex and time consuming the PMOA procedure is, the less likely the resulting data will be regularly employed in clinical settings. PMOA procedures include test construction, administration, score, and interpretation, all of which can be technically complex. For research-ers and test developers, how can these procedures be made transparent and understandable for clinicians? Also, brevity appears to play an important role regarding clients' and clinicians' willingness to complete PMOA measures. But what is the range of time and items that increases the chances of providing valid data?

UNDERSTANDING THE PROCESS OF CLINICAL FEEDBACK

Researchers should continue to probe the intricacies of feedback methods employed with PMOA data. Cross and Angelo (1988) proposed four principles of effective feedback, suggesting that feedback should be timely (i.e., given as soon as possible after relevant events), focused (i.e., cover only a few topics/domains), forward looking (i.e., linked to potential future actions), and linked to consequences (e.g., connecting clinician pay or promotion to PMOA scores). Regarding the focus aspect, for example, should clinicians and clients who receive feedback about the *Outcome Questionnaire-45 (OQ45)* receive data only about the total score, or should information about the *OQ*'s subscales also be included? Similarly, regarding linkage to consequences, use of the *GAF* scale has often led clinicians to report slight improvements in *GAF* scores so that clients can receive additional sessions (with no information about whether those ses-sions are actually needed or not). In both education and mental health, many examples exist of how high-stakes testing motivates professionals to cheat. To what extent do PMOA scores need to be independent of funding for therapy so that clinicians and clients provide reliable and valid data?

At this early stage of theory building, research, and practice, more work needs to be done to ascertain which components of the clinical feedback process are key for client improvement (cf. Boswell et al., 2013). The specific tests employed to assess client progress, and the tests' change sensitivity and treatment sensitivity, may be important. To what extent, for example, do the strengths of a PMOA measure's psychometric properties relate to its usefulness for clinical feedback? Theoretically, even a measure that has little or no sensitivity to change could still be useful as feedback if regular discussion of test scores focused a clinician's or client's attention on therapeutic progress. All PMOA measures, if employed consistently, should direct clinical attention to client progress, thereby increasing the chance that failure to improve will be noticed and adjustments to therapy made. Without such attention, the clinician may continue therapy without reflection, particularly if the therapeutic relationship appears to be positive. If PMOA test scores significantly under- or overestimate a client's progress, however, those scores are likely to hinder valid decision making about the implemented treatment(s). Use of a psychometrically stronger instrument brings the benefit of structured focus, increased validity and precision to therapeutic considerations of progress, and some predictive ability about the client's future movement.

Finally, PMOA measures can be created to provide more information about what may be influencing clinical progress in individual clients. The *Session Rating Scale* provides data about the therapeutic alliance and the *Depression/Anxiety Negative Affect* about client avoidance of negative affect, for example, but PMOA measures generally offer little theoretical explanation in terms of what is influencing client progress or treatment failure. Such hypotheses are important when considering how to adjust therapy with clients who are failing to improve. Other factors relevant to the utility of feedback include the communicability of the PMOA data (e.g., qualitative and quantitative data, visual displays), the timeliness of the feedback (in supervision, and to individual clinicians), to whom feedback is provided (e.g., client, clinician, and/or supervisor), motivation to use a feedback system, and the amount of training and education users receive for clinical feedback.

ON WHAT BASIS SHOULD THERAPY-RELATED DECISIONS BE MADE?

Currently decisions about whether to start, alter, or stop therapy are based on clinical judgment and client input. The increasing availability of PMOA data provides a means to make those decisions empirically based. If PMOA data from the *OQ45* can forecast which clients are likely to fail treatment, for example, those data could be a major factor in deciding when treatment should be altered for at-risk clients. But the field need not simply choose between the two extreme positions. The problem with relying on clinical judgment alone is that considerable evidence exists to suggest that some clinicians are poor prognosticators of client failure (Gray & Lambert, 2001). And the problem with relying on PMOA data alone is the tests' imprecision: Current measures are first-generation PMOA tests and evidence considerable variability in their estimates of the amount of client change.

Psychological assessors typically do not make clinical decisions solely on the basis of test scores, nor will therapists in the future when they employ PMOA data to make therapy-related decisions. But some situations may be more amenable to a greater focus on empirical data. For example, clinicians with heavy caseloads may rely on PMOA data that signal problems about possible treatment failure to decide which clients should (a) be discussed in limited supervision time, (b) receive more time for treatment planning and case conceptualization, (c) receive additional sessions, and (d) be referred for more appropriate treatment.

A related issue is whether the field should systematically include qualitative data in the clinical decision-making process. Progress notes are often employed for the process of documentation, that is, providing a record of what problems the client discussed and what interventions and services were subsequently provided. Such notes are typically too unstructured to be used as progress monitoring data, particularly when compared to PMOA measures that have been psychometrically evaluated. Whether the qualitative information in progress notes can provide or augment valid progress monitoring data is an empirical question that remains to be investigated.

The qualitative information in progress notes, however, can already fulfill an important role. That is, progress notes can provide hypotheses to explain the patterns observed in repeated PMOA measurements. A time series showing depression scores across sessions, for example, can evidence improvement, stability, cycles, or worsening, but the explanation for the observed pattern is usually not evident in the data alone. Progress notes can offer causal explanations necessary to interpret PMOA data and thus inform the clinician and supervisor about potential alterations in the case conceptualization, treatment plan, and provided interventions.

WHO SHOULD PAY FOR PROGRESS MONITORING AND OUTCOME ASSESSMENT?

As noted earlier in this chapter, more thought is needed about how to fund PMOA measurement. When asked to provide PMOA data now, clinicians and their clients typically do so without additional reimbursement or resources (e.g., time). This situation is akin to asking physicians to perform x-rays, blood work, or other sophisticated measurements as part of a regular visit without additional time or reimbursement (Boswell et al., 2013). Current school systems that introduce Response To Intervention (RTI) systems for teachers also provide an on-the-ground example of the problems that can arise without sufficient resources. Many teachers who were not trained in RTI approaches have little understanding of its rationale; many also struggle to find the time and motivation to perform data collection when those duties must be wedged into an already packed teaching, class preparation, and grading schedule. Similarly, simply adding PMOA assessments to mental health professionals' overwhelming schedules is a recipe for failure. Lack of funding and resources may be a significant part of the explanation for why so few clinicians historically have invested the time necessary to administer, score, and interpret PMOA measures (Clement, 1999).

Funding could include direct payments to clinicians, particularly for more thorough outcome assessments at the beginning and end of therapy as well as for repeated progress measures. The task of completing PMOA measurement may also become more efficient as a result of technology: As computer software and hardware become increasingly adept with transcribing and analyzing human speech, it may become feasible to record and transfer video and audio recordings of therapy conversations for subsequent PMOA analysis by external assessors trained specifically for this task.

PROGRESS MONITORING AND OUTCOME ASSESSMENT USE AND STANDARDS OF CARE

Particularly if Obamacare does result in an influx of new psychotherapy clients in the United States, mental health professionals should strive to improve treatment failure rates, which can be as high as 50% (Persons & Mikami, 2002). In addition, providers of talk therapies can do a better job of explaining what they do and how such therapies are effective. Olfson and Marcus (2010) examined surveys of the US population and found that the percentage of individuals utilizing psychotherapy dropped from 3.37% in 1998 to 3.18% in 2007. In contrast, the use of psychotropic medication alone increased from 44.1% to 57.4% over the same period.

Among the steps that could be taken are the following:

1. Upgrading professional standards so that PMOA data collection, particularly with clients who fail to improve, becomes a common practice (Clement, 1999). One approach would be to incorporate PMOA data into case notes. All case notes would include some form of or reference to PMOA data; even if PMOA data were not collected at or during a particular session, that would be referenced in the notes. The expectation that PMOA data are routinely included in case notes changes the perception that "PMOA data are an extra burden" to "PMOA data are a routine part of client care." In addition, the juxtaposition of qualitative notes and quantitative data should increase the likelihood that each component can inform the other: The qualitative notes should provide potential explanations for observed patterns of PMOA data, and the quantitative data should help focus the clinician's attention on important topics and trends in the client. Such a procedural change might involve rewriting the practice guidelines of relevant professional organizations. Other methods could include the widespread adoption of PMOA measures by funding organizations and the adoption of PMOA content in graduate school curricula. That content could be taught as part of didactic material in

psychotherapy practicums, assessment, supervision, and stand-alone courses. Infusion in supervision may be particularly powerful in that routine measurement of client progress and outcomes should provide students with a clearer picture of what is and is not helpful (Miller, Hubble, Chow, & Seidel, 2013).

2. Changing the professional culture so that treatment failure and discussion of failing cases is considered routine. Therapists who seek out critical feedback from supervisors and others can improve their self-awareness and skills. Seeking to improve the provision of mental health care should be considered the norm for professional therapists.

3. Convening one or more professional working groups to propose a consensual set of methods for evaluating PMOA measures. The criteria employed in this book to evaluate PMOA measures are provisional; clearly, the field needs additional research and discussion to develop a common set of criteria for evaluating PMOA measures as they become more widely adopted. Given the complexity involved in measuring change resulting from psychosocial interventions (e.g., Cook & Campbell, 1979), large doses of humility, cooperation, and tentativeness will be necessary to reach a consensus on PMOA evaluation criteria.

Currently, many PMOA test developers select and report differing criteria for evaluating change-sensitive measures (cf. Erbes et al., 2004). The National Center on Intensive Intervention (http://www.intensiveintervention.org), for example, evaluates measures on criteria related to reliability and validity estimates. Their reliability criteria include estimates such as coefficient alpha, test–retest reliability, and reliability of the slope of change on a PMOA measure. Validity criteria include evidence that a PMOA measure represents the underlying construct and the validity of the slope of change. Other proposed rules include empirical decision rules for changing the intervention and changing goals. Difficulties remain, however, with evaluating data related to these rules. For example, what evidence is there that a particular threshold value for coefficient alpha or test–retest reliability can be employed to rate a PMOA measure as useful or not? This question also applies to the evaluation guidelines described earlier in this book.

FOCUS ON PROGRESS MONITORING AND OUTCOME ASSESSMENT USE IN EDUCATION AND TRAINING

In current practice, the mental health professions focus more on the craft than the science of counseling and psychotherapy. Deciding whether to continue, alter, refer, or terminate treatment remains a subjective decision on the part of the client and/or therapist. The American Psychological Association's (http://www.apa.org/ethics/code/index.aspx) Ethical Principles, for example, state that "Psychologists terminate therapy when it becomes *reasonably clear* that the client/patient no longer needs the service, is not likely to benefit, or is being harmed by continued service" (italics added). "Reasonably clear" is a judgment that could be aided by PMOA data. As described in Chapter 3, PMOA data can be employed to complement clinical judgment for such tasks as deciding whether to continue or alter treatment.

But choosing, evaluating, administering, scoring, and interpreting PMOA measures require a different set of skills than the primarily interpersonal, relationship competencies of much psychotherapy. Although PMOA assessment has long been either an implicit or explicit requirement of ethical and practice guidelines in some mental health professions, seldom has this requirement been translated into specific course or training materials in required courses for mental health professionals in master's or doctoral programs. Thus, it is not surprising that in most contemporary clinical practices, PMOA assessment is still the exception, not the norm (Clement, 1999).

Clinicians and students can receive the necessary training through graduate-level courses, either as stand-alone offerings or as modules in beginning and advanced practicum courses. Such courses should be incremental and start with basic knowledge about clinical feedback and PMOA measures. Teaching methods should include case examples appropriate to the student and the clinician's caseload and opportunities for repeated practice and application, whether in supervision or classroom discussions. Continuing education and workshops are another option for practicing clinicians. The International Center for Clinical Excellence (http://www.centerforclinicalexcellence.com), for example, offers PMOA-related online forums and training, workshop instruction, and networking with peers interested in mental health issues.

SUMMARY

Observers of the history of psychotherapy often employ a wave metaphor to describe when a new type of therapy arrives and is widely adopted. The first wave was psychodynamic theory, followed over the decades by behavioral, humanistic, and feminist/multicultural waves (cf. Carlson & Englar-Carlson, 2011). Although the notion of waves implies a sweeping away of previous approaches, adding structured feedback through PMOA data has the potential to improve the outcomes of all theoretical approaches. From a research perspective, psychotherapies that incorporate a feedback loop using PMOA data can substantially increase their observed effect sizes (e.g., sometimes doubling effect size). For individual clinicians, a lack of therapeutic success is often the most stressful aspect of their work (Norcross & Guy, 2007). Incorporating PMOA feedback into the clinical process should translate into a noticeable decrease in treatment failures and an increase in job satisfaction for mental health professionals. The tasks now are to disseminate these feedback results and procedures through publication and teaching and to investigate further how to improve the PMOA data collection and feedback process.

APPENDIX EXERCISES

Exercise 1 *Identifying a Client's Negative Affect*

Using the therapist–patient dialogue below, search for *negative affect (NA) states* expressed by the client. Write what you find on the lines below, and see answers below:

1. _____   2. _____

3. _____   4. _____

COUNSELOR: And how are you feeling about being in session and talking about the stuff you've been talking [about].... How are you feeling about how things are going here?

PATIENT: I think it... I mean I feel good. When I came in, I was feeling really hopeless about my relationship and feeling like I was doing everything wrong and here I think we've been able to identify what are the causes of the things that are making me upset. Maybe not necessarily as much what role I play in it, but at least targeting the incidences and why I'm feeling the way I'm feeling [and]instead of just feeling like nothing's working, I can say, "Well I feel upset because these things are happening." And it kind of helps me put a handle on it. I think I've seen myself become a little bit more assertive with him and stop... you know, if he says something to me, stop overreacting and assuming... like if he says something to me and it's very curt, I wouldn't (ph) generally start arguing back and been a little bit better about sitting back and thinking about how I'm feeling and expressing how I'm feeling. At least I can say what's on my mind. [0:06:38]

COUNSELOR: What would happen if you said you don't know?

PATIENT: Well he's telling me that it's okay with him if I'm just saying, "I don't know," or "No, I didn't do this." Most of the time, I think he would be frustrated that I didn't... what was it... I had to get a credit card from Lowe's because [we're going to get some of our] (ph) things on there, you know, the no finance charges whatever. I didn't do it, and he asked me and I was like, "Well, I was going to do it but blah-blah-blah-blah." And he's like, "You could have just said you didn't do it and left it at that." He was like, "I don't need a whole story about why it wasn't done."

COUNSELOR: So when you talk about this, do you have any sense of what it is for you, like what is it that happens for you that you feel kind of this need to say, "Yes I did do it" even though you haven't done it? [0:08:03]

PATIENT: I haven't but I do that at work too. If my boss says, "Well what about this?" and I'll come up with an answer and generally (inaudible) while I'm talking, I'll remember what's going on, but I don't think I need to do that and I don't know why.... It's almost like being like panicked, you know, like, whatever. I say it and then I'm like…[well at least I'm making like] (ph) that's kind of tough.

SOURCE: Alexander Street Press (2009).

Answers

Here is one interpretation of NA terms found in this dialogue: *hopeless, upset, panicked. The phrase* "whatever" *and the surrounding statements imply shame or embarrassment. See the words and phrases in bold below.*

COUNSELOR: And how are you feeling about being in session and talking about the stuff you've been talking [about]. . . . How are you feeling about how things are going here?

PATIENT: I think it…I mean I feel good. When I came in, I was feeling really **hopeless** about my relationship and feeling like I was doing everything wrong and here I think we've been able to identify what are the causes of the things that are making me **upset**. Maybe not necessarily as much what role I play in it, but at least targeting the incidences and why I'm feeling the way I'm feeling [and] instead of just feeling like nothing's working, I can say, "Well I feel upset because these things are happening." And it kind of helps me put a handle on it. I think I've seen myself become a little bit more assertive with him and stop…you know, if he says something to me, stop overreacting and assuming…like if he says something to me and it's very curt, I wouldn't (ph) generally start arguing back and been a little bit better about sitting back and thinking about how I'm feeling and expressing how I'm feeling. At least I can say what's on my mind. [0:06:38]

COUNSELOR: What would happen if you said you don't know?

PATIENT: Well he's telling me that it's okay with him if I'm just saying, "I don't know," or "No, I didn't do this." Most of the time, I think he would be frustrated that I didn't…what was it…I had to get a credit card from Lowe's because [we're going to get some of our] (ph) things on there, you know, the no finance charges whatever. I didn't do it, and he asked me and I was like, "Well, I was going to do it but blah-blah-blah-blah." And he's like, "You could have just said you didn't do it and left it at that." He was like, "I don't need a whole story about why it wasn't done."

COUNSELOR: So when you talk about this, do you have any sense of what it is for you, like what is it that happens for you that you feel kind of this need to say, "Yes I did do it" even though you haven't done it? [0:08:03]

PATIENT: I haven't but I do that at work too. If my boss says, "Well what about this?" and I'll come up with an answer and generally (inaudible) while I'm talking, I'll remember what's going on, but I don't think I need to do that and I don't know why. . . . It's almost like being like **panicked**, you know, like, **whatever**. I say it and then I'm like…[well at least I'm making like] (ph) that's kind of tough.

Exercise 2 *Using Qualitative Data for Clinical Feedback*

Table A1 (reproduced below) displays one list of qualitative themes extracted from a brief student role-play of "Jeremy," a social phobic (play 2:49 to about 8:00). Review the table and then answer the questions below.

Table A1. MAJOR CLIENT THEMES FOR JEREMY

Avoidance

    Tried to talk with someone before, "but I just couldn't" (3:30)

    "I don't like to think about it, that's why I didn't want to come here today" (3:55)

    "Horrible" that he feels "hostile" toward mother

Affect

    Overwhelmed, burden, pressure

    "Horrible" that he feels "hostile" toward mother

    Smiles briefly after compliment

Relationships

    Roommate wants him to come, worried about him

    Pressure from mom to be "outgoing" like brother

        Wants to tell mom, "I'm not Jason!"

        "There's too much pressure"

Self-image

    "Loser" who has no friends and seldom leaves dorm room

Counselor themes

    Nondirective

    Reflection of feelings, content

    Compliments him about his potential to be a friend

    Relaxation exercise

        Awkward: "Do you think you'd like to do that?"

    Too much explaining?

1. Interpret these themes in terms of a theoretical orientation. (The provided answer focuses on narrative therapy and Jeremy's use of language.)

    From the perspective of a *narrative therapy* orientation, for example, it would be useful to focus on the client's and counselor's use of language, particularly metaphors. Noteworthy language aspects of this session include the following:

    a. Jeremy provides useful metaphors when he describes how his problem feels to him:

      i. "Intense pressure in my chest" (time 5:00)

      ii. "Like bricks" (5:32)

      iii. "Almost like a burden even" (5:32)

      iv. "Heaviness…it's too much going on at once" (6:00)
      v. Self-described "loser" (7:30)
      vi."Pressure" from mom, (7:30)

These metaphors about pressure provide an opportunity for the therapist to introduce therapeutic metaphors and actions. For example, the therapist might ask, "What could we do to take those bricks off your chest?" or "Let's place those bricks on this chair and talk about how you feel with them removed."

    b. Jeremy states, "I don't want to think about it," a good indication of *avoidance* of cognitions (3:55). Similarly, he states that it is "horrible" that he feels "hostile" (the counselor's choice of a word) toward his mother, an indication of avoidance of negative affect.

2. Including the qualitative data from Table A1 and your theoretical interpretation of it, what feedback and suggestions could a supervisor provide the student therapist?

From a language perspective, the student counselor does an overall nice job of tracking Jeremy and offering reflections based on Jeremy's language and descriptions. Examples include the following:

    a. The student counselor provides a good response to Jeremy's initial description of his situation: "It seems like that would be overwhelming to feel that." Jeremy laughs in agreement and then goes into exploration of experiences with his mother and brother.
    b. The counselor provides a useful metaphor: "I had an image of a small boy in the corner who's afraid to go out" (6:50).
    c. However, the counselor also missed some potentially important information. For example, Jeremy initially says his roommate wants him to see a counselor and is "worried about me" (3:08). The counselor ignores this statement. It might have been useful to ask, "What is your roommate worried about?" If the roommate is worried, one possibility is that Jeremy has been discussing or hinting at suicide or homicide, topics that can be intimidating to the counselor in training.
    d. At times the counselor seems too active and/or awkward in terms of explaining therapeutic concepts. Part of this may be the videotape situation, and part of it may be that counselors in training sometimes want to explain topics to clients that the counselors do not confidently understand.

Exercise 3 *Assessing Client Nonverbals*

Psychotherapists and other clinical raters may have access to information sources, such as client nonverbals, that provide more unbiased information about client traits and states (Shedler, Mayman, & Manis, 1993). Clinical observations can be made on the basis of both verbal reports and nonverbal expressions of affect during the session. Many clinicians, however, trust nonverbal indicators of affect because of clients' ability to censor verbal reports (Meier & Davis, 2011). Many clients who are avoidant of NA, for example, may express more affect nonverbally than through verbal reports (e.g., see the Jeremy video employed for *Depression/ Anxiety Negative Affect* [*DANA*] training in Chapter 8).

If a client is unable or unwilling to report valid information about sensitive topic(s) in therapy, it is important to be able to identify client nonverbals. Nonverbals offer another window into process and outcome constructs.

For this brief exercise, watch time period 4:11–6:20, *Perls working with Gloria* (http://www.youtube.com/watch?v=8y5tuJ3Sojc). Fritz Perls was a well-known Gestalt therapist, highly skilled in working with client nonverbals. Answer the following questions:

1. What are some nonverbal indicators of Gloria's affect?

   a. Smoking, at the start of the session
   b. Smiling (4:30)
   c. Pauses in speaking (4:45)
   d. Hand on chest (4:55)
   e. Furrowed eyes (6:16)

2. What are some of Gloria's likely feelings?
   At least in terms of therapeutically relevant affect, Gloria expresses, both verbally and nonverbally, fear, social anxiety, vulnerability (need to protect herself), defensiveness, and confusion. Verbally, Gloria expresses fear, feeling dumb and stupid, anger, and resentment. Thus, feelings of anxiety, vulnerability, and defensiveness were more apparent nonverbally.

3. If Gloria made progress in therapy, how might these feelings change? How might her avoidance of these feelings change?
   Insight-oriented and cognitive-behavioral approaches would aim to help Gloria become aware of her feelings and be able to express them to others as appropriate.

Exercise 4 *Using the 1 Standard Deviation Method to Estimate Client Progress*

The following list contains a teacher's ratings of a student's (John) thoughts about self-harm for 9 different weeks, in the order presented: 3, 2, 1, 1, 1, 0, 0, 0, 0.

Calculate the mean and standard deviation for this set of scores. Then compare the first two values with the last two values—is the difference greater than 1 standard deviation (1SD)? What would you conclude about John's progress on this score?

The mean for these nine scores equals 0.89 and the standard deviation is 1.05. The sum of the first two values is 5, and the sum of the last two values is 0. The difference is 5, greater than 1SD of 1.05. As shown in Figure A1, in agreement with the 1SD analysis, John's thoughts about self-harm appear to decrease steadily until they are no longer occurring.

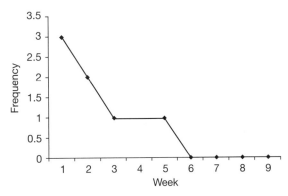

Figure A1 Teacher Ratings of John's Thoughts of Self-Harm by Week.

Exercise 5 *Trend Analyses of Mr. F's Therapist Ratings*

Read the following case description and data table to understand this client, and then answer the questions to demonstrate your ability to calculate and interpret basic statistics about progress monitoring data.

Mr. F is a 19-year-old Asian American who experienced intrusive thoughts such as about cursing at others during class, looking at people's genitals, and raping a particular female friend (Abramowitz, 2002). Mr. F maintained that he would never take such actions, but he was very fearful that he might do so and reported accompanying symptoms of anxiety and depression. Abramowitz (2002) collected data using three measures specific to Mr. F: *Fear of intrusive thoughts, Avoidance* (of situations associated with intrusive thoughts), and *Neutralizing rituals* (i.e., behaviors believed to lessen anxiety). As shown in Table A2, these therapist ratings were collected for a baseline period of three sessions (where no intervention occurred) and collected after each of 13 subsequent treatment sessions.

Using the data in Table A2, answer the following questions:

Table A2. THERAPIST IDIOGRAPHIC RATINGS FOR MR. F ON THREE VARIABLES

Session	Fear of Thoughts	Avoidance	Rituals
	BASELINE SESSIONS		
1	7	7	6
2	6	6	5
3	6	7	5
	THERAPY SESSIONS		
1	5	5	4
2	5	6	4
3	4	5	1
4	4	2	2
5	3	2	1
6	2	1	1
7	2	0	1
8	2	0	0
9	1	0	1
10	2	0	0
11	1	1	1
12	2	0	0
13	1	0	0

NOTE: Therapist ratings on the scale could range from 0 (None) to 8 (Severe).

1. Using the other two therapist ratings, *Avoidance of situations* and *Neutralizing rituals*, compare the three baseline sessions with the final four treatment sessions to see if changes occurred..

Below are the means and standard deviations for Mr. F, comparing the baseline period to the final four sessions.

	Baseline		Final Four Sessions	
	M	SD	M	SD
Avoidance of situations	6.67	0.58	0.25	0.50
Neutralizing rituals	5.33	0.58	0.25	0.50

The difference between the means is obvious. For the sake of practice, now compute the effect size (ES) for both measures, using the baseline SD in the denominator.

6.67 – 0.25 / 0.58 = 11.07 for *Avoidance of situations*

5.33 – 0.25 / 0.58 = 8.76 for *Neutralizing rituals*

Clement (1999) suggested that an ES greater than 1.50 indicates very large improvement in clinical settings. Thus, these are very large ESs for both therapist ratings, indicating substantial change over the course of therapy.

2. To assess progress, group scores from the three baseline sessions on *Avoidance of situations* and then compare with any subsequent grouping of three sessions (e.g., Sessions 7, 8, and 9). What would you conclude about Mr. F's progress based on this analysis?

	Baseline		Sessions 7, 8, 9	
	M	SD	M	SD
Avoidance of situations	6.67	0.58	0.00	0.00

Inspection of Table A2 and the descriptive statistics above suggests that this problem, along with *Neutralizing rituals,* essentially ceased by Session 7. As seen in Table A2, *Fear of intrusive thoughts* also shows a similar pattern, suggesting that the therapy's effectiveness with Mr. F was maximized by Session 7.

Exercise 6 *Using Progress Notes as Progress Monitoring and Outcome Assessment Data*

Table A3 displays a list of clinically relevant themes extracted from 20 sessions with an individual client. **Bold** text indicates material relevant to outcome, whereas *italicized* content relates to process.

Table A3. QUALITATIVE ANALYSIS OF PROGRESS NOTES WITH AN INDIVIDUAL CLIENT

Session Number	Key Issues
1	Presenting problem centers on **depression and anxiety**; agrees to referral for possible medication; reports history of conflicted family relationships, particularly with long-deceased alcoholic father
2	Has started medication and will continue counseling; reports difficulty at work with "crazy" customers; we establish a schedule of activities designed to increase positive reinforcement for him
3	Reports *a history of trying to re-create a family life*, but with people other than immediate family of origin; for example, becomes a physical, emotional caretaker for distant relatives, older neighbors; reports no effect from reinforcement activities
4	**Reports that he is very angry** with *many past incidents with family of origin*, particularly father, and some current events with mother
5	**Is much less anxious, moderately less depressed, but seems almost manic**; very strong emotional reactions to many current events
6	Agrees to start a journal where he writes thoughts, feelings, and related events
7	Reports that he has come to the conclusion that **he hates himself**; reading books about identity development; **now frequent, angry arguments with partner**
8	Reports becoming **easily angry with coworkers**, even when their behavior does not affect him directly, as well as with partner and family members
9	Reads for 30 minutes from a journal about *past family incidents* that provoked **anger, rage, and sadness in him**; question arises whether he should pursue family therapy with mother and siblings
10	Notes that **he is angry with his mother** *but cannot express those feelings to her or even explore much in session; family culture indicates that being angry with parents is equivalent to disobeying them*
11	Despite father's death 15 years ago, reports that he still **wishes there was some way he could be emotionally close to father**; I confronted about this unrealistic idea; he later cancels next session

(continued)

Table A3. (Continued)

Session Number	Key Issues
12	Some processing in session of *how he experiences emotion*; relates stories that provide evidence (to him) that his role was to function as *emotional caretaker in his family; tried to protect mother from abusive, alcoholic father*
13	No-show; later reported that he forgot about the session
14	*Wondering whether to stay in current relationship*; debating financial security versus partner's treatment of him as a child
15	Considering whether to leave town, start a new life elsewhere; now spending much time considering therapy issues between sessions
16	Same issues as Session 15
17	Ran into his brother's friend who had no idea that client's father was alcoholic; *confirmed for client that mother and siblings denied family difficulties*; I noted that in the past he had denied such problems as well
18	Clearly has changed locus of responsibility for family conflict away from himself; **anger and rumination about family has decreased**; more focus on work, other people
19	*Discusses buying a house with partner; one brother is now contacting him for social interactions*
20	Termination; **client reports greater self-confidence, emotional independence from family**, stable work performance; describes himself as "better integrated"

SOURCES: Meier (1999, 2003), reprinted by permission.

Exercise 7 *Create a Persistence Table to Track Themes Discussed Across Sessions*

Use the information in Table A3 (Exercise 6) to create a persistence table of the topics discussed in Sessions 1 through 20. With a persistence table, the key questions are as follows:

1. What topics and processes persist across sessions?
2. What topics and processes are sparse or missing, and when?

The distribution of topics discussed in Table A3 is clearly not random. First, NA and family conflict are key topics of the first 10 sessions. This client was expressing a range of intense NA related to family issues, including depression, anxiety, anger, mania, self-hate, and rage. The therapist introduced several interventions during those first 10 sessions, including medication, journaling, processing emotions, and discussing denial of family problems; during Session 12, however, the client and therapist began explicitly discussing how he experienced and processed NA. The client no-showed for the next session, perhaps indicating that it was too soon to discuss this topic or the topic was too intense and that the client needed additional time to adjust to this discussion. After Session 13, however, the client's topics shifted, including a discussion in Session 17 of how the client and his family had denied family problems. This explicit processing of avoidance of the topic and explicit recognition of his difficulty experiencing NA appeared to help the client resolve the past conflicts with family. As shown in Table A3, after Session 12, discussion of family conflict topics essentially ceased, with new discussion about issues with the client's partner and a noticeable decrease in the intensity of NA. The client soon terminated, describing positive increases in self-confidence as well as social interactions with his partner.

Table A4. PERSISTENCE TABLE FOR AN INDIVIDUAL CLIENT IN THERAPY FOR 20 SESSIONS

Session Number

Themes	1	2	3	4	5	6	7	8	9	10	11	12	*13*	14	15	16	17	18	19	20
Neg affect		■		■	■	■		■	■	■	■		■				■			
Family conflict		■		■	■			■		■	■	■	■					■	■	
Partner														■	■	■				
Positive changes																			■	■
New interventions			■	■		■	■				■					■				

NOTE: Boxes designate which major themes were discussed in a session. Client no-showed for Session 13.

Exercise 8 *Learning the GAF*

Complete at least 10 of the examples provided by the Washington State Mental Health Division at http://depts.washington.edu/washinst/Resources/CGAS/Index.htm. Continue until your Global Assessment of Functioning (*GAF*) scale scores match the expected range 80% to 90% of the time. Write the name of each client below, along with your score and the range of acceptable scores.

Client	Your GAF Rating	Acceptable Range
1. __Kim_____	___	*20–40*
2. _____	___	__ ‐ __
3. _____	___	__ ‐ __
4. _____	___	__ ‐ __
5. _____	___	__ ‐ __
6. _____	___	__ ‐ __
7. _____	___	__ ‐ __
8. _____	___	__ ‐ __
9. _____	___	__ ‐ __
10. _____	___	__ ‐ __
11. _____	___	__ ‐ __
12. _____	___	__ ‐ __
13. _____	___	__ ‐ __
14. _____	___	__ ‐ __
15. _____	___	__ ‐ __

Exercise 9 *Additional Brief Practice in DANA Ratings*

Here are the author's completed DANA ratings for the three videos in Exercise 9. To the left of the endorsed NA term (*underlined*) is the time period where the individual displayed the NA state.

1. **General Hospital—Robin's Therapy** http://www.youtube.com/watch?v=0fDdXDb2Y_c

This rating focuses on time period 3:30–5:00. Note that the raters indicated that Robin also evidences avoidance of NA. Two NA terms were added to Level 1 (*Disappointed*) and Level 2 (*Guilty*).

Level 1 TRANSIENT NEGATIVE
AFFECT

__ Bored	__ Unrelaxed
__ Preoccupied	4:18 Uncomfortable
__ Blue	3:34 Deflated
3:40 Disappointed __	

Level 2 INCREASING NEGATIVE
AFFECT

__ On edge	__ Difficulty relaxing
__ Animated	__ Gloomy
4:00 Irritable	__ Teary
__ Tense	__ Upset
4:39 Discouraged	4:10 Concerned
4:35 Guity ____	

Level 3 MODERATE NEGATIVE AFFECT

__ Embarrassed	__ Worried
__ Pressured	4:08 Moderately angry
__ Anxious	__ Frustrated
__ Ruminating	__ Moderately sad
__ Scared	__ Agitated
__ Depressed	__ Distressed
__ Vulnerable	__ _____

Level 4 INTENSE NEGATIVE
AFFECT

__ Demoralized	__ Weeping
__ Disinterested	4:48 Over-whelmed
4:37 Ashamed	__ Burned out
__ Fearful	__ Worthless
__ Hopeless	__ Helpless
__ _____	

2. **Perls with Gloria** http://www.youtube.com/watch?v=8y5tuJ3Sojc

This rating focuses on time period 4:10–9:00. This is a small segment of Gestalt therapist Fritz Perls working with the client Gloria, part of the Shostrum (1966) presentation of three types of psychotherapy. Much of Gloria's NA is in the here and now and results from her interaction with Fritz Perls. Note that the raters indicated that Gloria also evidences avoidance of NA.

Level 1 <u>TRANSIENT NEGATIVE AFFECT</u>
___ Bored   ___ Unrelaxed
___ Preoccupied 4:40 <u>Uncomfortable</u>
___ Blue   ___ Deflated

___ _____

Level 2 <u>INCREASING NEGATIVE AFFECT</u>
4:51 <u>On edge</u>   ___ Difficulty relaxing
___ Animated   ___ Gloomy
8:00 <u>Irritable</u> ___ Teary
___ Tense   ___ Upset
___ Discouraged ___ Concerned

___ _____

Level 3 <u>MODERATE NEGATIVE AFFECT</u>
8:25 <u>Embarrassed</u> ___ Worried
___ Pressured   8:30 <u>Moderately angry</u>
7:15 Anxious   ___ Frustrated
___ Ruminating   ___ Moderately sad
4:18 <u>Scared</u>   ___ Agitated
___ Depressed   ___ Distressed
5:20 <u>Vulnerable</u> _____

3. **Behavior Therapy** www.youtube.com/watch?v=MCyfMFXR-n0&featu
   re=related

This rating focuses on time period 1:15–2:26. During this brief period, the client's pace of speech provides a nonverbal indication of her NA levels.

```
┌─────────────────────────────────────────────────────┐
│ Level 2 INCREASING NEGATIVE AFFECT                    │
│ __ On edge        __ Difficulty relaxing              │
│ 1:15+ Animated   __ Gloomy                            │
│ __ Irritable      __ Teary                            │
│ __ Tense          __ Upset                            │
│ __ Discouraged  __ Concerned                          │
│ __ _____                   │
└─────────────────────────────────────────────────────┘
```

```
┌─────────────────────────────────────────────────────┐
│ Level 3 MODERATE NEGATIVE AFFECT                      │
│ __ Embarrassed   __ Worried                           │
│ 1:30 Pressured   __ Moderately angry                  │
│ __ Anxious        __ Frustrated                       │
│ __ Ruminating     __ Moderately sad                   │
│ __ Scared         1:30+ Agitated                      │
│ __ Depressed      __ Distressed                       │
│ __ Vulnerable    __ _____                  │
└─────────────────────────────────────────────────────┘
```

```
┌─────────────────────────────────────────────────────┐
│ Level 4 INTENSE NEGATIVE AFFECT                       │
│ __ Demoralized      __ Weeping                        │
│ __ Disinterested 1:24+ Overwhelmed                    │
│ __ Ashamed          __ Burned out                     │
│ __ Fearful          __ Worthless                      │
│ __ Hopeless         __ Helpless                       │
│ __ _____                   │
└─────────────────────────────────────────────────────┘
```

Exercise 10 *Experimental Depression/Anxiety Negative Affect Scale*

Depression/Anxiety Negative Affect (DANA) Experimental Version

This is an experimental version of a progress monitoring and outcome assessment (PMOA) measure intended for use in counseling and psychotherapy. Its purpose is to provide clinical feedback about an individual client's progress in therapy. DANA scores should be employed only in conjunction with other sources of information, and ultimately it is the clinician's responsibility to make therapeutic decisions. Test users can contact the author at stmeier@buffalo.edu for the latest version and scoring instructions.

DEPRESSION/ANXIETY NEGATIVE AFFECT (DANA) SCALE
Copyright, 2007–2014, Scott T. Meier, PhD
University at Buffalo

Instructions

On the next page you will find descriptive terms for five levels of negative affective states of increasing intensity and/or severity. Descriptors within each set are of approximately equal intensity and/or severity.

For each level, check one or more terms that were most salient for your patient *during the past week*. If a different term of roughly equal intensity applies, write in that term on the blank line.

For the term(s) checked at the most intense/severe level, please estimate how often your client expressed or experienced the negative affective state during the past week. For term(s) that are difficult to estimate, provide your best guess.

Note that your ratings can be made on the basis of both verbal and nonverbal expressions of affect. Also, improvement for different clients may be evidenced by a variety of patterns, including an initial increase in negative affect, maintenance of negative affect, or a decrease in negative affect.

Finally, please indicate whether the individual appears to be avoiding expressing or experiencing negative affect (e.g., denial).

Please complete your rating as soon as possible after the session ends.

1

For each of the affective terms on the right, **check any that were salient** for this individual **over the past week**. If another term applies, please write it in the blank space.

2

At the **highest level checked, rate the frequency of the most frequently occurring term**.

How often experienced in past week?

1–2   *3 or more*
days   *days*

Ever experienced more than 1× a day?

    Yes   No

3

Any indication that this individual is **avoiding negative affect?**

    Yes   No

Level 1 <u>TRANSIENT NEGATIVE AFFECT</u>
__ Bored   __ Unrelaxed
__ Preoccupied   __ Uncomfortable
__ Blue   __ Deflated
__ _____

Level 2 <u>INCREASING NEGATIVE AFFECT</u>
__ On edge   __ Difficulty
                            relaxing
__ Animated   __ Gloomy
__ Irritable   __ Teary
__ Tense   __ Upset
__ Discouraged   __ Concerned
__ _____

Level 3 <u>MODERATE NEGATIVE AFFECT</u>
__ Embarrassed   __ Worried
__ Pressured   __ Moderately angry
__ Anxious   __ Frustrated
__ Ruminating   __ Moderately sad
__ Scared   __ Agitated
__ Depressed   __ Distressed
__ Vulnerable   __ _____

Level 4 <u>INTENSE NEGATIVE AFFECT</u>
__ Demoralized   __ Weeping
__ Disinterested   __ Overwhelmed
__ Ashamed   __ Burned out
__ Fearful   __ Worthless
__ Hopeless   __ Helpless
__ _____

Level 5 <u>EXTREME NEGATIVE AFFECT</u>
__ Actively homicidal __ Enraged
__ Actively suicidal   __ Despair
__ Bewildered   __ Panicked
__ Terrified   __ Traumatized
__ Intense guilt   __ Sobbing
__ _____

GLOSSARY

1 standard deviation (1SD Method) A change criterion for progress monitoring and outcome assessment (PMOA) data that indicates that substantial change has occurred when scores differ by 1 standard deviation over two time periods (e.g., preintervention to postintervention).

AB design *A* represents a baseline period and *B* an intervention period. In this study design, a PMOA variable is assessed during the baseline (where it should show stability or no change) and then across an intervention (where it should evidence change).

Action A stage of change in psychotherapy when a client changes behavior or the environment in an attempt to remedy the problem.

Aggregated score A sum of scores on all test items. The principle is that summing or aggregating item and test responses within an individual decreases random errors that might influence a few items.

Alert function PMOA data are used primarily to signal to a clinician that a client is not making expected progress or meeting a standard.

Alexithymia Personality characteristic associated with difficulties in the identification and verbalization of emotional experiences.

Anxiety Apprehension and worry about potential future negative events and outcomes.

Attachment issues Degree to which an individual can form secure emotional bonds with others.

Avoidance Client efforts, often unconscious, to avoid awareness of negative affect or thoughts or evade certain situations or behaviors.

Baseline Collection of PMOA data in the absence of an intervention; this typically occurs before the start of an intervention.

Black box design Research design that involves examining the output of a system or intervention without an understanding of what transpired to produce those outcomes. Casual factors and explanations for the data patterns must be identified elsewhere.

Brevity Length of time needed to complete a PMOA measure.

Case conceptualization Organization of process and outcome elements to describe the key elements of a client. Process (cause) and outcome (effect) can be described on multiple levels, such as how a client's psychosocial history has influenced current symptoms and how a psychosocial intervention is expected to influence those symptoms.

Ceiling and floor effects In a ceiling effect, all ratings cluster near the top of the scale; with a floor effect, they cluster at the bottom. When an intervention is implemented, ceiling and floor effects can hinder the detection of the intervention's impact. For example, suppose a researcher designs a pretest/posttest study examining the effects of a stress reduction program. If an observer's judgments of participants' stress significantly underestimate those levels at the pretest, how could a decrease resulting from the intervention be detected at posttest? In fact, if the observer underestimated stress at pretest, even an effective intervention might be found to have no effect or a negative effect.

Change sensitivity Ability of a PMOA measure to assess changes that occur as a result of psychosocial intervention; also referred to as sensitivity to change.

Client characteristics Participant characteristics such as race/ethnicity, age, and gender that may influence the type and amount of change resulting from an intervention and evidenced on the scale.

Clinical ratings Data collection that occurs in the context of a counseling or psychotherapy session where the clinician has an opportunity to observe and interact with the client for an extended period of time.

Clinical significance The idea that client change has reached a meaningful criterion. Often this criterion is a range of normal functioning.

Common outcome elements Some alleviation of depression and anxiety may be present as a ubiquitous effect of all counseling interventions; thus, all interventions may produce improvement on outcome measures that contain depression- and anxiety-related content.

Common process factors The presence of universal therapeutic factors such as the presence of a therapeutic relationship and the establishment of hope.

Complex case Clients with multiple problems or diagnoses.

Confidentiality Rules about who will have access to client information, how the information will be shared, and with whom the information will be shared. Clients should also be informed about the limits to confidentiality involved with assessment data.

Confirmation bias (Hypothesis confirmation bias) The tendency to pay attention to information that confirms initial expectations and beliefs and to ignore other, disconfirming information; observers hold a belief or impression that causes them to ignore the full range of the phenomenon in question.

Construct validity Two meanings: First, construct validity historically has referred to whether a test measures what it is supposed to measure. Second, a test can also be said to have construct validity if evidence exists that it can be employed for a particular purpose. Basically identical to the idea of validity.

Contemplation A stage of change in psychotherapy when a client becomes aware of the problem and begins to think about how to remedy it.

Content validity Criterion that assesses whether a test assesses all relevant domains.

Control or comparison group In a psychotherapy experiment, a group that differs from the intervention group on some aspect. For example, a comparison group may receive another treatment (e.g., one that is the standard) or the group may be a control that receives no treatment.

Convergent validity Correlation or covariation with another test of a similar construct.

Correlation coefficients The extent to which two variables covary and can range from –1.00 to +1.00; a value of 0 indicates that no relationship exists between the two sets of scores. Thus, a correlation can provide useful information about the relatedness of scores on two or more measures.

Critical incident An event that functions as impetus for client change.

Cross-situational consistency Issue of whether personality characteristics remain stable across situations and time.

Cross-validation At its most basic, replicating psychometric properties of a test by administering the test to a second sample.

Cycling A pattern of change on client progress monitoring data that shows variability in terms of periods of improvement and periods of worsening.

Debriefing Explaining to clients about test data and uses of that data (e.g., sharing with insurance companies). Explaining and interpreting such information with a client is essentially an intervention and its effect on the client should be considered before the information is shared.

Decay Random changes in coding definitions lead to more error in clinical ratings. Decay may result from delays in the time period between when an event occurs and its observation or recording.

Defensive deniers Individuals who deny their own personal psychological difficulties.

Dependent variables In an experiment, the effects that result from causes (i.e., independent variables). In a treatment context, the independent variable might be the presence or absence of psychotherapy (i.e., treatment vs. control) and the dependent variable the variable expected to change as a result of the psychotherapy (i.e., client depression).

Depression Refers to feelings of sadness typically triggered by past events such as a significant loss. In contrast, anxiety is future focused.

Depressive rumination Repetitive thoughts that focus on depressive symptoms and their implications; rumination has been found to be related to the development of depression and to increase the length of depressive episodes and intensity of depressive moods.

Descriptive statistics Numerical indices for describing, summarizing, and organizing quantitative data.

Direct Observational Coding Paul's system for observing and recording clinical data in inpatient settings.

Discriminant validity Lack of correlation or covariation with another test of a similar construct.

Drift Rater drift occurs when the rater makes systematic changes in definition or interpretation of a construct over time. Compare to decay.

Effect size (ES) In a PMOA context, refers to a statistic that estimates the size or amount of change over time, evidenced in an individual or a group of individuals who receive psychotherapy.

Effectiveness research Outcome research conducted in applied settings. Contrast with efficacy research.

Efficacy research Studies conducted in laboratories or clinics with more controlled conditions than studies conducted in field or applied settings such as clinics, university counseling centers, or private practices.

Electronic medical records (EMRs) Computer-based systems for storage, recall, and analysis of client health information, including PMOA data.

Emotion schemas Individuals think idiosyncratically about their emotions as well as the situations that elicited those emotions

Emotional experiencing Client's awareness of and understanding of affect associated with difficult life events.

Empirically supported treatments (ESTs) Psychosocial treatments shown to be effective in research studies; also known as empirically validated treatments.

Endpoint A criterion for determining when the client has reached a predetermined goal.

Error Factors that influence test scores in ways unintended by the test developer and test user.

Error of standards Inconsistencies among raters who all employ different standards when assessing individuals' behaviors.

Exposure Treatment in which client experiences fear stimulus repeatedly to habituate and/or be able to act despite the presence of negative affect such as anxiety or fear.

False precision Situation in an analysis in which a sophisticated statistical formula appears to provide a definite answer that should, instead, be taken with several large grains of salt.

Feedback Data that provide information about client progress in psychotherapy. Feedback can be considered *structured* when some system is employed to use it.

Feedback loop Use of PMOA data to provide information about client's progress so that therapeutic interventions and/or case conceptualizations can be continued or altered; data are collected, analyzed, and interpreted in an effort to improve functioning of some system (e.g., the provision of psychotherapy).

Feedback-enhanced therapies (FETs) Interventions that employ PMOA data to provide information about the client's status during therapy. In these approaches, clinical data become an integral part of the decision-making process regarding whether to continue therapy or alter therapeutic procedures.

Frequency count A descriptive statistic technique where the number of occurrences of an event are added up

Grounded theory analysis Qualitative research method in which qualitative data (text) are collected and then key concepts are identified in that information at different levels of abstraction.

Halo These errors occur when a rater's overall impressions about the ratee influence ratings about specific aspects of the person; a rater holds a stereotype about a ratee, and that global impression hinders a more precise or valid rating in specific domains.

Heterogeneous sample Individuals who differ on a number of characteristics (e.g., intelligence, gender) of interest.

Hypothesis confirmation bias The tendency to pay attention to information that confirms initial expectations and beliefs and to ignore other, disconfirming information; observers hold a belief or impression that causes them to ignore the full range of the phenomenon in question. Also known as confirmation bias.

Idiographic Measurement assessing relatively unique aspects of an individual rather than general characteristics shared by all people.

Imprecision Measurement data that contains considerable amounts of noise or error, often because scores include unintended information. For example, imprecise data can result from a mismatch of test purpose and test construction procedures.

Improvement probability This statistic estimates the likelihood that a client will either (a) improve or (b) stay the same or worsen from an initial progress monitoring measurement to a second progress monitoring measurement over the course of a short period of psychotherapy.

Independent variables Causal factors that affect change in other (dependent) variables.

Informed consent Helping clients and research participants understand the types and effects of the procedures, including treatment, employed in the provision of care.

Intensive single-case design Where data are collected repeatedly with a single individual over time.

Intermediate outcomes Aspects of symptoms and functioning that may change after a moderate amount of psychotherapy (e.g., several months). Interpersonal functioning is one example.

Interval-level properties of measurement Measurement procedures that produce data with equal intervals between units. This typically does not occur in social science research, including psychotherapy studies.

Intervention characteristics Those aspects of an intervention that influence the capacity of a measure to detect change resulting from an intervention.

Intervention Item Selection Rules Guidelines designed to identify intervention-sensitive items during either test construction or item evaluation. The major assumptions of this approach are that (a) test items and tasks differ along a trait–state continuum and (b) different test construction and item analysis procedures are necessary to select items with a high state loading that reflect the results of interventions.

Intrusive thoughts Cognitions that come into an individual's consciousness involuntarily.

Leniency With leniency and criticalness errors, the rater is either under- or overestimating the performance of the ratee.

Long-term outcomes Aspects of symptoms and functioning that may change after a lengthy amount of psychotherapy (e.g., 1 or more years). Personality characteristics are one example.

Maintenance A stage of change in psychotherapy when a client attempts to continue the changes made.

Mean The average of a distribution or group of scores. Summing the scores in a group and dividing the number of scores produces the mean.

Median The numerical value separating the top and bottom halves of a distribution of scores

Metaphor A figure of speech that compares one thing to another.

Modality In counseling and psychotherapy, the manner in which therapy is provided, including individual, group, couples/marital, or family counseling and psychotherapy.

Mode The most frequently occurring score.

Multiple baselines Collecting data before an intervention on multiple variables. For example, some variables may be designed to be sensitive to intervention effects, but others should not.

Multivariate or multiple time series Graphic displays that illustrate change in multiple variables recorded over an extended period of time.

Negative affect Emotion experienced as aversive or unpleasant, such as depression and anxiety.

Nomothetic Comparing a client's scores to others on constructs that apply to everyone (e.g., intelligence, vocational interests). This can be contrasted with idiographic measures, which examine relatively unique aspects of the client (such as language usage).

Nonverbal communication Signals other than speech (e.g., tone of voice) that may provide more unbiased information about client traits and states.

Normal distribution The bell-shaped curve apparent in many distributions of data.

Normative comparison Comparing an individual's scores on a test to a distribution of others' scores.

Normative data Data in a distribution of test scores, used to compare an individual's test score to those of others in a particular population; the information contained in a normal distribution.

No-treatment control groups Participants in these groups receive no intervention so as to serve as a comparison for groups that do.

Observation period The length of time in which a person is observed. For example, a therapy session is presumed to be roughly 45 minutes to 1 hour, but the period could be for a shorter or longer length of time.

Outcome assessment Use of measures to produce clinical data about the amount and type of change clients experience from the start to end of therapy.

Outcome expectations Beliefs about the connections (or lack thereof) between one's behaviors and desirable outcomes

Outlier A data value that differs substantially from others in a dataset. An outlier can be problematic when computing an index of central tendencies such as the mean.

Patient Protection and Affordable Care Act Also known as Obamacare, this is a national US plan to provide healthcare insurance for US citizens. Mental health coverage is now part of all health insurance plans.

Persistence table A text display that shows the major clinical themes discussed by session.

Persistent relevance Whether clients' key problems at the beginning of therapy remain the chief issues throughout the course of therapy.

Phase change line A vertical line in a time series intended to demarcate two distinct periods of intervention. Typically the periods are baseline and intervention, but other periods could be designated as well.

Phase Model The expected direction of therapeutic improvement across sessions is remoralization (i.e., removal of distress) followed by symptom reduction and then improved life functioning.

Phase/time effects Intervention effects that may vary by time (short term, intermediate, long term) and should be detected by appropriate PMOA measures.

PMOA measure A test employed for the purpose of progress monitoring and/or outcome assessment. Progress monitoring measures tend to be used for short-term feedback, whereas outcome assessments typically provide data about pre-/postintervention change.

Pooled standard deviation A statistic calculated by adding the Time 1 *SD* and Time 2 *SD* and then dividing by the degrees of freedom.

Posttraumatic stress disorder (PTSD) Symptoms, such as anxiety and depression, that appear after an individual experiences a terrifying event or series of events.

Power analysis A method for determining whether a statistical analysis has a sufficient chance of finding statistically significant effects if they occur. This analysis is often employed to determine the necessary sample size needed to detect an effect.

Precontemplation A stage of change in psychotherapy when a client has little or no awareness about the major problem.

Preparation A stage of change in psychotherapy when a client intends to change and begins to take preliminary actions.

Progress monitoring Use of change-sensitive measures that produce clinical data to monitor client change (or lack thereof) during therapy.

Progress notes Qualitative information found in a clinician's notes about the client and therapy sessions.

Publication bias The tendency of journals to only publish studies with statistically significant results.

Qualitative data In a clinical context, this is textual material from sources such as progress notes that can provide useful clinical feedback for children, adolescents, and adult clients receiving psychosocial interventions. This information may be particularly useful for generating hypotheses to explain trends in PMOA data.

Quantitative data These are numerical data that can be collected and interpreted with PMOA measures.

Questionable instances Rating situations where some ambiguity exists about how to rate or score.

Random assignment Assignment of participants to different groups (e.g., treatment and controls) where individuals have equal chance of being selected for any group.

Randomness Nonsystematic factors that influence test scores. A variety of methodological factors can influence PMOA scores, and the combination of these factors can produce what are essentially random, often small changes over time.

Range restriction errors Tendency to employ only parts of a scale for rating. Raters do not use all available quantitative options available for assessment. For example, an employee might exhibit, over a period of time, poor performance (a rating of "1") to excellent performance ("5"), but an employer might only rate the individual's performance as "3" or "4" (good, average).

Reactivity The transparency of a measurement procedure. That is, the individual is aware that data are being collected or reported about her- or himself and this process may change the data reported. Use of reactive methods typically changes the monitored behavior in the same direction as an intervention.

Rebound effect An increase in the occurrence of negative thoughts that results from attempts to suppress them.

Recall errors These errors occur when information reporting or ratings take place too long after a client session. In general, as the length of time grows between observation of client behavior and the actual rating, recall errors may occur (Meier, 2008).

Reliability The consistency and stability of test scores. Scores on PMOA measures should evidence stability over time in the absence of an intervention.

Reliable Change Index (RCI) This statistical index estimates whether a change in scores between test administrations for a single client is statistically significant.

Resistance Tendency for a client to engage in or avoid actions necessary for improvement in therapy.

Response to intervention (RTI) Consists of two major components: (a) screening of all individuals in a school system to identify students with problems and (b) increasingly intense (as needed) psychosocial interventions accompanied by progress monitoring to determine the interventions' effectiveness with groups or specific individuals.

Sample size The number of cases employed in a statistical analysis.

Sampling error Error in a statistical measure that results from measuring only part of a sample instead of the entire sample or a representative portion of the sample.

Screening Testing whose purpose is to identify individuals at risk for developing a psychological/behavioral problem (e.g., depression).

Selection One purpose of testing, to detect individual differences on a construct of interest. The purpose of selection testing is to classify individuals for such decisions as school admission and work hiring.

Self-beliefs Appraisals and thoughts related to self and a variety of events, from how one expects to be treated in the world to estimates of self-competencies.

Self-efficacy expectations Beliefs about whether one possesses the competencies and skills necessary to perform behaviors required to obtain desired outcomes.

Self-monitoring An individual collects and/or reports data about some aspect of her or his feelings, thoughts, or behaviors. Self-monitoring is often reactive; that is, use of the method typically changes the monitored behavior in the same direction as an intervention. Repeated administration of any psychotherapy-related self-report measure may be reactive; that is, the data collection procedures change the amount or nature of data collected, typically in the same direction as an intervention.

Self-reports Client reports information about her- or himself.

Sensitivity to change The ability of a PMOA measure to assess changes that occur as a result of psychosocial intervention.

Short-term outcomes Aspects of symptoms and functioning that may change relatively quickly during psychotherapy. Distress is one example.

Social desirability A source of error in that an individual may report only information that presents her- or himself in a favorable manner.

Sources of information The person(s) who provide information about a client, such as the client, clinicians, parents, teachers, and others.

Stages of change Six stages that indicate a client's ability and willingness to take steps to change personal behavior.

Standard deviation (SD) Statistic that shows the degree to which the scores vary around the mean. The SD is the square root of the variance of a distribution of scores. The more widely spread the distribution of scores is, the larger the standard deviation.

Standard score A transformation of a raw score to show how many deviations from the mean that score lies.

Standard time period Length of time self-report or clinical rating is applicable. When ratings are completed repeatedly for a specified time period, the resulting comparisons of multiple ratings over time, for a standard time period, allow the detection of change. Traditionally, 1 week is the length of time between sessions for many psychotherapies.

Standardization A process that involves providing approximately equivalent conditions under which an individual reports information.

States Transitory phenomena that change over time in response to situational, internal, and developmental influences.

Statistical power The ability to find an effect when one actually exists (e.g., to detect the effectiveness of a treatment when it does occur). Power may be influenced by a number of factors in clinical analyses, including the same size and the change sensitivity of the employed measures.

Supervision Process of oversight of the work of a therapist.

Suppression Efforts to hide one's feelings from oneself and/or others; suppression has been associated with increased physiological arousal and impaired memory performance.

Systematic error Errors that influence PMOA data that display a repeated pattern.

T scores A statistic to translate raw scores on a test to a distribution of scores of choice.

Termination A stage of change in psychotherapy when the problem is fully resolved and the client is confident it will not reoccur.

Therapeutic cycles Process of shifting between degrees of high and low emotion and high and low abstraction/reflection during psychotherapy.

Time series Graphic displays that illustrate change in a single variable recorded over an extended period of time or number of data points. Time series graphics can be applied to PMOA data for the purposes of examining progress and outcome with the same individual and within groups over time. They are best employed with larger sets of data that show or have the potential to show substantial variability.

Trait selection approach Standard paradigm for psychological testing that (a) assumes measures of psychological traits believed to be present in all individuals, (b) is as brief as possible, (c) is administered to large groups, and (d) is evaluated primarily by the ability to predict future criteria (often related to school or work performance).

Traits Enduring, stable characteristics that remain largely stable over time, such as intelligence.

Treatment failure Instance when a client fails to improve or worsens after starting psychotherapy.

Treatment plan Method for describing interventions aimed at particular process outcome relationships.

Treatment sensitivity Whether a PMOA test can demonstrate change on variables affected to be influenced by a particular intervention. For example, a measure of anger management should show change in individuals completing an anger management program. Those individuals, however, may not show change on measures of shame or anxiety. Contrast treatment sensitivity with change sensitivity.

Treatment utility Question of whether use of psychological tests has an effect on treatment outcome. In a clinical feedback system, the test is just one of a set of components that can influence client improvement.

Trend analyses Grouping of session data to evaluate such questions as whether data from baseline periods and final sessions differ from each other.

Universal basic emotions Types of feelings experienced by everyone, such as positive and negative affect.

Vacation session This occurs when a client shows or reports substantial improvement during a therapy session but then regresses at the next session to previous functioning levels.

Validity The extent to which a test measures what it claims to measure; the purposes for which a test can be employed. Similar to construct validity.

Verbal reports Data from client speech, self-reports.

Visual display Refers to a graphic that shows multiple observations of quantitative or qualitative information. In PMOA analyses these observations may be shown over time and sessions in time series graphics and tables.

Working alliance Development of a therapeutic relationship between client and counselor in which both experience a bond toward common goals.

Z score A standard score where z equals the person's raw score minus the mean of the group of scores, divided by the standard deviation of the group of scores. Frequently the most useful information that a test score can provide is the degree to which a person scores in the high or low portion of the distribution of scores. The z score is a quick summary of the person's standing: positive z scores indicate that the person was above the mean, whereas negative scores indicate that the person scored below the mean.

REFERENCES

Aas, I. M. (2011). Guidelines for rating Global Assessment of Functioning (GAF). *Annals of General Psychiatry, 10*, 2. doi:10.1186/1744-859X-10-2

Abramowitz, J. S. (2002). Treatment of obsessive thoughts and cognitive rituals using exposure and response prevention: A case study. *Clinical Case Studies, 1*(1), 6–24. doi:10.1177/1534650102001001002

Abramowitz, J. S., Tolin, D. F., & Street, G. P. (2001). Paradoxical effects of thought suppression: A meta-analysis of controlled studies. *Clinical Psychology Review, 21*, 683–703. doi:10.1016/S0272-7358(00)00057-X

Ackerman, S. J., Benjamin, L. S., Beutler, L. E., Gelso, C. J., Goldfried, M. R., Hill, C.,… Rainer, J. (2001). Empirically supported therapy relationships: Conclusions and recommendations of the Division 29 Task Force. *Psychotherapy: Theory, Research, Practice, Training, 38*, 495–497. doi:10.1037/0033-3204.38.4.495

Alexander Street Press. (2009). *Counseling and psychotherapy transcripts, client narratives, and reference works.* Thousand Oaks, CA: Sage.

American Psychiatric Association. (2013). *Diagnostic and statistical manual of mental disorders* (5th ed.). Arlington, VA: American Psychiatric Publishing.

American Psychological Association Presidential Task Force on Evidence-Based Practice. (2006). Evidence-based practice in psychology. *American Psychologist, 61*, 271–285. doi:10.1037/0003-066X.61.4.271

Ardoin, S. P., Christ, T. J., Morena, L. S., Cormier, D. C., & Kingbeil, D. A. (2013). A systematic review and summarization of the recommendations and research surrounding Curriculum-Based Measurement of oral reading fluency (CBM-R) decision rules. *Journal of School Psychology, 51*, 1–18. doi:10.1016/j.jsp.2012.09.004

Auerbach, S. M., & Kilmann, P. R. (1977). Crisis intervention: A review of outcome research. *Psychological Bulletin, 84*, 1189–1217. doi:10.1037/0033-2909.84.6.1189

Baker, R., Holloway, J., Thomas, P. W., Thomas, S., & Owens, M. (2004). Emotional processing and panic. *Behaviour Research and Therapy, 42*, 1271–1287.

Bandura, A. (1977). Self-efficacy: Toward a unifying theory of behavioral change. *Psychological Review, 84*, 191–215. doi:10.1037/0033-295X.84.2.191

Bardeen, J. R., Fergus, T. A., & Orcutt, H. (2013). Experiential avoidance as a moderator of the relationship between anxiety sensitivity and perceived stress. *Behavior Therapy, 44*, 459–469. doi:10.1016/j.beth.2013.04.001

Barlow, D. (2010). Negative effects from psychological treatments. *American Psychologist, 65*, 13–20. doi:10.1037/a0015643

Barrett, L. F. (2006). Are emotions natural kinds? *Perspectives on Psychological Science*, *1*, 28–58. doi:10.1111/j.1745-6916.2006.00003.x

Beck, A., Steer, R. A., & Brown, G. (1996). *Manual for the revised Beck Depression Inventory-II*. San Antonio, TX: Psychological Corporation.

Beck, A. T., & Steer, R. A. (1987). *Manual for the revised Beck Depression Inventory*. San Antonio, TX: Psychological Corporation.

Berman, P. (1997). *Case conceptualization and treatment planning*. Thousand Oaks, CA: Sage.

Berman, W. H., Rosen, C. S., Hurt, S. W., & Kolarz, C. M. (1998). Toto, we're not in Kansas anymore: Measuring and using outcomes in behavioral health. *Clinical Psychology: Science and Practice*, *5*, 115–133. doi:10.1111/j.1468-2850.1998.tb00139.x

Bernard, J. M., & Goodyear, R. K. (2008). *Fundamentals of clinical supervision* (4th ed.). New York, NY: Pearson.

Berntsen, D. (2010). The unbidden past: Involuntary autobiographical memories as a basic mode of remembering. *Current Directions in Psychological Science*, *19*, 138–142. doi:10.1177/0963721410370301

Beutler, L. E., & Hamblin, D. L. (1986). Individualized outcome measures of internal change: Methodological considerations. *Journal of Consulting and Clinical Psychology*, *54*, 48–53. doi:10.1037/0022-006X.54.1.48

Beutler, L. E., & Harwood, T. M. (2000). *Prescriptive psychotherapy: A practical guide to systematic treatment selection*. Oxford: Oxford University Press.

Bickman, L., Rosof-Williams, J., Salzer, M., Summerfelt, W. T., Noser, K., Wilson, S. J.,…Karver, M. (2000). What information do clinicians value for monitoring adolescent client progress and outcomes? *Professional Psychology: Research and Practice*, *31*, 70–74. doi:10.1037/0735-7028.31.1.70

Bliese, P. D., Wright, K. M., Adler, A. B., Thomas, J. L., & Hoge, C. W. (2007). Timing of postcombat mental health assessments. *Psychological Services*, *4*, 141–148. doi:10.1037/1541-1559.4.3.141

Boswell, J. F., Kraus, D. R., Miller, S. D., & Lambert, M. J. (2013). Implementing routine outcome monitoring in clinical practice: Benefits, challenges, and solutions. *Psychotherapy Research*, *23*, 1–14. doi:10.1080/10503307.2013.817696

Botcheva, L., White, C. R., & Huffman, L. C. (2002). Learning culture and outcomes measurement practices in community agencies. *American Journal of Evaluation*, *23*, 421–434. doi:10.1177/109821400202300404

Bringhurst, D. L., Watson, C. W., Miller, S. D., & Duncan, B. L. (2006). The reliability and validity of the Outcome Rating Scale: A replication study of a brief clinical measure. *Journal of Brief Therapy*, *5*, 23–30.

Brown, G. S., & Jones, E. R. (2005). Implementation of a feedback system in a managed care environment: What are patients teaching us? *Journal of Clinical Psychology*, *61*, 187–198. doi:10.1002/jclp.20110

Burisch, M. (1984). Approaches to personality inventory construction. *American Psychologist*, *39*, 214–227. doi:10.1037/0003-066X.39.3.214

Callahan, J. L., Almstrom, C. M., Swift, J. K., Borja, S. E., & Heath, C. J. (2009). Exploring the contribution of supervisors to intervention outcomes. *Training and Education in Professional Psychology*, *3*, 72–77. doi:10.1037/a0014294

Campbell, A., & Hemsley, S. (2009). Outcome Rating Scale and Session Rating Scale in psychological practice: Clinical utility of ultra-brief measures. *Clinical Psychologist*, *13*, 1–9. doi:10.1080/13284200802676391

Campbell-Sills, L., & Barlow, D. H. (2007). Incorporating emotion regulation into conceptualizations and treatments of anxiety and mood disorders. In J. J. Gross (Ed.), *Handbook of emotion regulation* (pp. 542–559). New York, NY: Guilford.

Carlier, I., Meuldijk, D., Van Vliet, I., Van Fenema, E., Van der Wee, N., & Zitman, F. (2012). ROM and feedback on physical or mental health status: Evidence and theory. *Journal of Evaluation in Clinical Practice, 18*, 104–110. doi:10.1111/j.1365-2753.2010.01543.x

Carlson, J., & Englar-Carlson, M. (2011). Series preface. In S. Madigan (Ed.), *Narrative therapy* (pp. ix–xii). Washington, DC: American Psychological Association.

Carter, R. T. (2007). Racism and psychological emotional injury: Recognizing and assessing race-based traumatic stress. *Counseling Psychologist, 35*, 13–105. doi:10.1177/0011000006292033

Castonguay, L. G. (2011). Psychotherapy, psychopathology, research, and practice: Pathways of connections and integration. *Psychotherapy Research, 21*(2), 125–140. doi:10.1080/10503307.2011.563250

Cattell, R. B., & Scheier, I. H. (1961). *The meaning and measurement of neuroticism.* New York, NY: Ronald Press.

Christensen, A., Margolin, G., & Sullaway, M. (1992). Interparental agreement on child behavior problems. *Psychological Assessment, 4*, 419–425. doi:10.1037/1040-3590.4.4.419

Clement, P. W. (1999). *Outcomes and incomes.* New York, NY: Guilford.

Clifft, M. A. (1986). Writing about psychiatric patients: Guidelines for disguising case material. *Bulletin of the Menninger Clinic, 50*, 1–13.

Collins, L. M. (1991). Measurement in longitudinal research. In L. M. Collins & J. L. Horn, *Best methods for the analysis of change* (pp. 137–148). Washington, DC: American Psychological Association.

Cook, T., & Campbell, D. (1979). *Quasi-experimentation.* Chicago: Rand McNally.

Corbin, J., & Strauss, A. (2007). *Basics of qualitative research* (3rd ed.). Thousand Oaks, CA: Sage.

Coyne, J. C. (1990). Interpersonal processes in depression. In G. I. Keitner (Ed.), *Depression and families: Impact and treatment* (pp. 33–53). Washington, DC: American Psychiatric Press.

Coyne, J. C. (1994). Self-reported distress: Analog or ersatz depression? *Psychological Bulletin, 116*, 29–45. doi:10.1037/0033-2909.116.1.29

Craske, M. G., & Tsao, J. C. (1999). Self-monitoring with panic and anxiety disorders. *Psychological Assessment, 11*, 466–479. doi:10.1037/1040-3590.11.4.466

Crawley, S. A., Beidas, R. S., Benjamin, C. L., Martin, E. D., & Kendall, P. C. (2007). *SUDS ratings in the treatment of anxiety-disordered youth.* Presentation at the 41st Annual ABCT Convention, Philadelphia, PA.

Creswell, J. W. (2002). *Educational research.* Upper Saddle River, NJ: Merrill Prentice Hall.

Cronbach, L. J. (1957). The two disciplines of scientific psychology. *American Psychologist, 12*, 671–684. doi:10.1037/h0043943

Cronbach, L. J., Ambron, S. R., Dornbursch, S. M., Hess, R. D., Hornik, R. C., Phillips, D. C., ... Weiner, S. S. (1980). *Toward reform of program evaluation.* San Francisco, CA: Jossey-Bass.

Cronbach, L. J., & Snow, R. E. (1977). *Aptitudes and instructional methods.* New York, NY: Wiley.

Cross, K. P., & Angelo, T. A. (1988). *Classroom assessment techniques.* Ann Arbor, MI: National Center for Research to Improve Postsecondary Teaching and Learning.

Cyr, J. J., McKenna-Foley, J. M., & Peacock, E. (1985). Factor structure of the SCL-90-R: Is there one? *Journal of Personality Assessment, 49*, 571–578. doi:10.1207/s15327752jpa4906_2

Dadds, M. R., Perrin, S., & Yule, W. (1998). Social desirability and self-reported anxiety in children: An analysis of the RCMAS lie scale. *Journal of Abnormal Child Psychology, 26*, 311–317. doi:10.1023/A:1022610702439

Dawis, R. V. (1992). The individual differences tradition in counseling psychology. *Journal of Counseling Psychology, 39*, 7–19. doi:10.1037/0022-0167.39.1.7

Davis, S., & Meier, S. T. (2001). *The elements of managed care.* Belmont, CA: Cengage.

Derogatis, L. R. (1983). *SCL-90-R: Administration, scoring, and procedural manual—II.* Baltimore, MD: Clinical Psychometric Research.

Diener, E., Larsen, R. J., Levine, S., & Emmons, R. A. (1985). Intensity and frequency: Dimensions underlying positive and negative affect. *Journal of Personality and Social Psychology, 48*, 1253–1265. doi:10.1037/0022-3514.48.5.1253

Dohrenwend, B. P. (2006). Inventorying stressful life events as risk factors for psychopathology: Toward resolution of intracategory variability. *Psychological Bulletin, 132*, 477–495. doi:10.1037/0033-2909.132.3.477

Doleys, D. M., Meredith, R. L., Poire, R., Campbell, L. M., & Cook, M. (1977). Preliminary examination of assessment of assertive behavior in retarded persons. *Psychological Reports, 41*, 855–859. doi:10.2466/pr0.1977.41.3.855

Eells, T. D. (2013). In support of evidence-based case formulation in psychotherapy (from the perspective of a clinician). *Pragmatic Case Studies in Psychotherapy, 9*, 457–467.

Ellis, M. V., & Ladany, N. (1997). Inferences concerning supervisees and clients in clinical supervision: An integrative review. In C. E. Watkins, Jr. (Ed.), *Handbook of psychotherapy supervision* (pp. 447–507). New York, NY: Wiley.

Endicott, J., Spitzer, R. L., Fleiss, J. L., & Cohen, J. (1976). The global assessment scale: A procedure for measuring overall severity of psychiatric disturbance. *Archives of General Psychiatry, 33*, 766–771. doi:10.1001/archpsyc.1976.01770060086012

Epstein, S. (1979). The stability of behavior: I. On predicting most of the people much of the time. *Journal of Personality and Social Psychology, 37*, 1097–1126. doi:10.1037/0022-3514.37.7.1097

Epstein, S. (1980). The stability of behavior II. Implications for psychological research. *American Psychologist, 35*, 790–806. doi:10.1037/0003-066X.35.9.790

Erbes, C., Polusny, M., Billig, J., Mylan, M., McGuire, K., Isenhart, C., & Olson, D. (2004). Developing and applying a systematic process for evaluation of clinical outcome assessment instruments. *Psychological Services, 1*, 31–39. doi:10.1037/1541-1559.1.1.31

Faust, D. (1986). Research on human judgment and its application to clinical practice. *Professional Psychology: Research and Practice, 17*, 420–430. doi:10.1037/0735-7028.17.5.420

Finn, S. E., Fischer, C. T., & Handler, L. (2012). *Collaborative / therapeutic assessment: A casebook and guide.* New York, NY: Wiley.

Fishman, D. B. (2013). The pragmatic case study method for creating rigorous and systematic, practitioner-friendly research. *Pragmatic Case Studies in Psychotherapy, 9*, 403–425.

Forand, N. R., & DeRubeis, R. J. (2012). Antidepressant controversy: A cause for concern and an opportunity for progress. *Behavior Therapist, 36*, 4–11.

Freitas, G. J. (2002). The impact of psychotherapy supervision on client outcome: A critical examination of 2 decades of research. *Psychotherapy: Theory/Research/Practice/ Training, 39*, 354–367. doi:10.1037/00333204.39.4.354

Froyd, J. E., Lambert, M. J., & Froyd, J. D. (1996). A survey and critique of psychotherapy outcome measurement. *Journal of Mental Health, 5*, 11–15. doi:10.1080/09638239650037144

Gibbs, D., Napp, D., Jolly, D., Westover, B., & Uhl, G. (2002). Increasing evaluation capacity within community-based HIV prevention programs. *Evaluation and Program Planning, 25*, 216–269. doi:10.1016/S0149-7189(02)00020-4

Goodman, J. D., McKay, J. R., & DePhilippis, D. (2013). Progress monitoring in mental health and addiction treatment: A means of improving care. *Professional Psychology: Research and Practice, 44*, 231–246. doi:10.1037/a0032605

Gottman, J. M., & Leiblum, S. R. (1974). *How to do psychotherapy and how to evaluate it.* New York, NY: Holt, Rinehart and Winston.

Gracely, R. H., & Naliboff, B. D. (1996). Measurement of pain sensation. In L. Kruger (Ed.), *Pain and touch* (pp. 243–313). San Diego, CA: Academic Press.

Gray, G. V., & Lambert, M. J. (2001). Feedback: A key to improving therapy outcomes. *Behavioral Healthcare Tomorrow, 10*, 25–45.

Gresham, F. M., Cook, C. R., Collins, T., Dart, E., Rasetshwane, K., Truelson, E., & Grant, S. (2010). Developing a change-sensitive brief behavior rating scale as a progress monitoring tool for social behavior: An example using the Social Skills Rating System-Teacher Form. *School Psychology Review, 39*, 364–379.

Gronlund, N. E. (1988). *How to construct achievement tests* (4th ed.). Englewood Cliffs, NJ: Prentice Hall.

Grove, W. M., & Andreasen, N. C. (1992). Concepts, diagnosis, and classification. In E. S. Paykel (Ed.), *Handbook of affective disorders* (pp. 25–41). New York, NY: Guilford.

Guyatt, G., Walter, S., & Norman, G. (1987). Measuring change over time: Assessing the usefulness of evaluative instruments. *Journal of Chronic Disease, 40*, 171–178. doi:10.1016/0021-9681(87)90069-5

Hafkenscheid, A., Duncan, B. L., & Miller, S.D. (2010). The Outcome and Session Rating Scales: A cross-cultural examination of the psychometric properties of the Dutch translation. *Journal of Brief Therapy, 7*, 1–12.

Hansen, N. B., Lambert, M. J., & Forman, E. M. (2002). The psychotherapy dose-response effect and its implications for treatment delivery services. *Clinical Psychology: Science and Practice, 9*, 329–343. doi:10.1093/clipsy.9.3.329

Hatfield, D. R., McCullough, L., Frantz, S. H., & Krieger, K. (2010). Do we know when our clients get worse? An investigation of therapists' ability to detect negative client change. *Clinical Psychology & Psychotherapy, 17*, 25–32. doi:10.1002/cpp.656

Hatfield, D. R., & Ogles, B. M. (2004). The use of outcome measures by psychologists in clinical practice. *Professional Psychology: Research and Practice, 35*, 485–491. doi:10.1037/0735-7028.35.5.485

Hartman, D. P. (1984). Assessment strategies. In D. H. Barlow & M. Hersen (Eds.), *Single case experimental designs* (pp. 107–139). New York, NY: Pergamon.

Hawkins, R. C., II, & Meier, S. T. (2013). *Psychotherapeutic theories of change and measurement: An integrative model.* Unpublished manuscript, Fielding Graduate University.

Hayes, S. C., Nelson, R. O., & Jarrett, R. B. (1987). The treatment utility of assessment. *American Psychologist*, *42*, 963–974.

Hayes, S. C., Strosahl, K. D., & Wilson, K. G. (1999). *Acceptance and commitment therapy*. New York, NY: Guilford.

Hayes, S. C., Wilson, K. G., Gifford, E. V., Follette, V. M., & Strosahl, K. (1996). Experiential avoidance and behavioral disorders: A functional dimensional approach to diagnosis and treatment. *Journal of Consulting and Clinical Psychology*, *64*, 1152–1168. doi:10.1037/0022-006X.64.6.1152

Henry, G. T. (1995). *Graphing data*. Thousand Oaks, CA: Sage.

Heppner, P. P., Kivlighan, D. M., & Wampold, B. E. (1999). *Research design in counseling*. Pacific Grove, CA: Brooks/Cole.

Hess, A. K., Hess, K. D., & Hess, T H. (Eds.). (2008). *Psychotherapy supervision*. New York, NY: Wiley.

Hill, C. E. (1982). Counseling process researcher: Philosophical and methodological dilemmas. *Counseling Psychologist*, *10*, 7–20. doi:10.1177/0011000082104003

Hill, C. E. (2003). *Dream work in therapy*. Washington, DC: American Psychological Association.

Hill, C. E., & Lambert, M. J. (2004). Methodological issues in studying psychotherapy processes and outcomes. In M. J. Lambert (Ed.), *Bergin and Garfield's handbook of psychotherapy and behavior change* (5th ed., pp. 84–135). New York, NY: Wiley.

Hoffman, B., & Meier, S. T. (2001). An individualized approach to managed mental health care in colleges and universities: A case study. *Journal of College Student Psychotherapy*, *15*, 49–64. doi:10.1300/J035v15n04_06

Hoshmand, L. L. S. (1994). *Orientation to inquiry in a reflective professional psychology*. Albany, NY: SUNY Press.

Howard, K. I., Moras, K., Brill, P. C., Martinovich, Z., & Lutz, W. (1996). Evaluation of psychotherapy: Efficacy, effectiveness, and patient progress. *American Psychologist*, *51*, 1059–1064. doi:10.1037/0003-066X.51.10.1059

Izard, C. E. (2007). Basic emotions, natural kinds, emotion schemas, and a new paradigm. *Perspectives on Psychological Science*, *2*, 260–280. doi:10.1111/j.1745-6916.2007.00044.x

Jacobson, N. S., & Truax, P. (1991). Clinical significance: A statistical approach to defining meaningful change in psychotherapy research. *Journal of Consulting and Clinical Psychology*, *59*, 12–19. doi:10.1037/0022-006X.59.1.12

Jennings, T. E., Lucenko, B. A., Malow, R. M., & Devieux, J. G. (2002). Audio-CASI vs interview method of administration of an HIV/STD risk of exposure screening instrument for teenagers. *International Journal of STD & AIDS*, *13*, 781–784.

Kagan, J. (1988). The meanings of personality predicates. *American Psychologist*, *43*, 614–620. doi:10.1037/0003-066X.43.8.614

Kashdan, T. B., & Breen, W. E. (2007). Social anxiety and positive emotions: A prospective examination of a self-regulatory model with tendencies to suppress or express emotions as a moderating variable. *Behavior Therapy*, *39*, 1–12. doi:10.1016/j.beth.2007.02.003

Kazdin, A. E. (1994). Psychotherapy for children and adolescents. In A. E. Bergin & S. L. Garfield (Eds.), *Handbook of psychotherapy and behavior change* (4th ed., pp. 543–594). New York, NY: Wiley.

Kazdin, A. E. (2000). *Psychotherapy for children and adolescents: Directions for research and practice*. New York, NY: Oxford Press.

Kazdin, A. E. (2003). *Research design in clinical psychology* (4th ed.). Boston, MA: Allyn & Bacon. (ISBN-10: 0-205-33292-7)

Keating, N. (2012). *Self-care behaviors, perceived stress, burnout, and affect among master's and doctoral-level mental health trainees.* Unpublished doctoral dissertation, University at Buffalo.

Kelly, M. A. R., Roberts, J. E., & Ciesla, J. A. (2005). Sudden gains in cognitive behavioral treatment for depression: When do they occur and do they matter? *Behavior Research and Therapy, 43,* 703–714. doi:10.1016/j.brat.2004.06.002

Kendall, P. C., Hollon, S. D., Beck, A. T., Hammen, C. L., & Ingram, R. E. (1987). Issues and recommendations regarding use of the Beck Depression Inventory. *Cognitive Therapy and Research, 3,* 289–299. doi:10.1007/BF01186280

Kendall, P. C., Kipnis, D., & Otto-Salaj, L. (1992). When clients don't progress: Influences on and explanations of therapeutic progress. *Cognitive Therapy and Research, 16,* 269–281. doi:10.1007/BF01183281

Kessler, R. C., Sonnega, A., Bromet, E., Hughes, M., & Nelson, C. B. (1996). Posttraumatic stress disorder in the National Comorbidity Survey. *Archives of General Psychiatry, 52,* 1048–1060. doi:10.1001/archpsyc.1995.03950240066012

Kirshner, B., & Guyatt, G. (1985). A methodological framework for assessing health indices. *Journal of Chronic Disease, 38,* 27–36. doi:10.1016/00219681(85)90005-0

Knaup, C., Koesters, M., Schoefer, D., Becker, T., & Puschner, B. (2009). Effect of feedback of treatment outcome in specialist mental healthcare: Meta-analysis. *British Journal of Psychiatry, 195,* 15–22. doi:10.1192/bjp.bp.108.053967.

Kopta, S. M., Howard, K. I., Lowry, J. L., & Beutler, L. E. (1994). Patterns of symptomatic recovery in psychotherapy. *Journal of Consulting & Clinical Psychology, 62,* 1009–1016. doi:10.1037/0022-006X.62.5.1009

Kopta, S. M., & Lowry, J. L. (2002). Psychometric evaluation of the Behavioral Health Questionnaire-20: A brief instrument for assessing global mental health and the three phases of psychotherapy outcome. *Psychotherapy Research, 12,* 413–426. doi:10.1093/ptr/12.4.413

Lambert, M. J. (1994). Use of psychological tests for outcome assessment. In M. E. Maruish (Ed.), *The use of psychological testing for treatment planning and outcome assessment* (pp. 75–97). Hillsdale, NJ: Lawrence Erlbaum.

Lambert, M. J. (2007). Presidential address: What we have learned from a decade of research aimed at improving psychotherapy outcome in routine care. *Psychotherapy Research, 17,* 1–14. doi:10.1080/10503300601032506

Lambert, M. J. (2012). Helping clinicians to use and learn from research-based systems: The OQ-Analyst. *Psychotherapy, 49,* 109–114. doi:10.1037/a0027110

Lambert, M. J. (Ed.). (2013). *Bergin and Garfield's handbook of psychotherapy and behavior change* (6th ed.). New York, NY: Wiley.

Lambert, M. J., & Finch, A. E. (1999). The Outcome Questionnaire. In M. E. Maruish (Ed.), *The use of psychological testing for treatment planning and outcomes assessment* (2nd ed., pp. 831–869). Hillsdale, NJ: Lawrence Erlbaum.

Lambert, M. J., Harmon, C., Slade, K., Whipple, J. L., & Hawkins, E. J. (2005). Providing feedback to psychotherapists on their patients' progress: Clinical results and practice suggestions. *Journal of Clinical Psychology, 61,* 165–174. doi:10.1002/jclp.20113

Lambert, M. J., Hatch, D. R., Kingston, M. D., & Edwards, B. C. (1986). Zung, Beck, and Hamilton Rating Scales as measures of treatment outcome: A meta-analytic comparison. *Journal of Consulting and Clinical Psychology*, *54*, 54–59. doi:10.1037/0022-006X.54.1.54

Lambert, M. J., & Hawkins, E. J. (2001). Using information about patient progress in supervision: Are outcomes enhanced? *Australian Psychologist*, *36*, 131–138. doi:10.1080/00050060108259645

Lambert, M. J., Whipple, J. L., Smart, D. W., Vermeesch, D. A., Nielsen, S. L., & Hawkins, E. J. (2001). The effects of providing therapists with feedback on patient progress during psychotherapy: Are outcomes enhanced? *Psychotherapy Research*, *11*, 49–68. doi:10.1080/713663852

Last, A., Miles, R., Wills, L., Brownhill, L., & Ford, T. (2012). Innovations in practice: Reliability and sensitivity to change of the Family Life Questionnaire (FaLQ) in a clinical population. *Child and Adolescent Mental Health*, *17*, 121–125. doi:10.1111/j.1475-3588.2011.00621.x

Lazarus, R., & Folkman, S. (1984). *Stress, appraisal, and coping*. New York, NY: Springer.

Lewis, J. D., & Magoon, T. M. (1987). Survey of college counseling centers' follow-up practices with former clients. *Professional Psychology: Research and Practice*, *18*, 128–133. doi:10.1037/0735-7028.18.2.128

Licht, M. H., Paul, G. L., & Power, C. T. (1986). Standardized direct-multivariate DOC systems for service and research. In G. L. Paul (Ed.), *Assessment in residential treatment settings* (pp. 223–266). Champaign, IL: Research Press.

Linehan, M. (1993). *Cognitive behavioral treatment of borderline personality disorder*. New York, NY: Guilford.

Lipsey, M. W. (1983). A scheme for assessing measurement sensitivity in program evaluation and other applied research. *Psychological Bulletin*, *94*, 152–165. doi:10.1037/0033-2909.94.1.152

Lipsey, M. (1990). *Design sensitivity*. Newbury Park, CA: Sage.

Longwell, B. T., & Truax, P. (2005). The differential effects of weekly, monthly, and bimonthly administrations of the Beck Depression Inventory—II: Psychometric properties and clinical implications. *Behavior Therapy*, *36*, 265–275. doi:10.1016/S0005-7894(05)80075-9

Luchins, D. (2012). Two approaches to improving mental health care. *Perspectives in Biology and Medicine*, *55*, 409–434. doi:10.1353/pbm.2012.0024

Lyubomirsky, S., & Nolen-Hoeksema, S. (1995). Effects of self-focused rumination on negative thinking and interpersonal problem-solving. *Journal of Personality and Social Psychology*, *69*, 176–190. doi:10.1037/0022-3514.69.1.176

Mangold, J. (Director). (1999). *Girl, interrupted*. United States: Columbia Pictures.

Martin, L. L., & Tesser, A. (1996). Some ruminative thoughts. In R. S. Wyer (Ed.), *Ruminative thoughts: Advances in social cognition* (Vol. 9, pp. 1–47). Hillsdale, NJ: Erlbaum.

Mash, E. J., & Hunsley, J. (1993). Assessment considerations in the identification of failing psychotherapy: Bringing the negatives out of the darkroom. *Psychological Assessment*, *5*, 292–301. doi:10.1037/1040-3590.5.3.292

Mattaini, M. A. (1993). *More than a thousand words: Graphics for clinical practice*. Washington, DC: NASW Press.

McCurdy, B. L., Mannella, M. C., & Eldridge, N. (2003). Positive behavior support in urban schools: Can we prevent the escalation of antisocial behavior? *Journal of Positive Behavior Interventions*, *5*, 158–170. doi:10.1177/10983007030050030501

McDougal, J., Bardos, A., & Meier, S. (2012). *Behavioral Intervention Monitoring and Assessment System* (BIMAS). Toronto, Ontario, Canada: Multi-Health Systems.

McElroy, S. L., Hudson, J. I., Pope, H. G., & Keck, P. E. (1991). Kleptomania: Clinical characteristics and associated psychopathology. *Psychological Medicine, 21,* 93–108.

McIntosh, W. D., & Martin, L. L. (1992). The cybernetics of happiness: The relation of goal attainment, rumination, and affect. In M. S. Clark (Ed.), *Emotion and social behavior: Review of personality and social psychology* (pp. 222–246). Thousand Oaks, CA: Sage Publications.

McLaughlin, K. A., Borkovec, T. D., & Sibrava, N. J. (2007). The effects of worry and rumination on affect states and cognitive activity. *Behavior Therapy, 38,* 23–38. doi:10.1016/j.beth.2006.03.003

Meehl, P. E. (1954). *Clinical versus statistical prediction: A theoretical analysis and a review of the evidence.* Minneapolis, MN: University of Minnesota Press.

Meehl, P. E. (1957). When shall we use our heads instead of formula? *Journal of Counseling Psychology, 4,* 268–273. doi:10.1037/h0047554

Meier, S. T. (1994). *The chronic crisis in psychological measurement and assessment.* New York, NY: Academic Press.

Meier, S. T. (1997). Nomothetic item selection rules for tests of psychological interventions. *Psychotherapy Research, 7,* 419–427. doi:10.1080/10503309712331332113

Meier, S. T. (1998). Evaluating change-based item selection rules. *Measurement and Evaluation in Counseling and Development, 31,* 15–27.

Meier, S. T. (1999). Training the practitioner-scientist: Bridging case conceptualization, assessment, and intervention. *Counseling Psychologist, 27,* 846–869. doi:10.1177/0011000099276008

Meier, S. T. (2000). Treatment sensitivity of the PE Form of the Social Skills Rating Scales: Implications for test construction procedures. *Measurement and Evaluation in Counseling and Development, 33,* 144–156.

Meier, S. T. (2001). Investigating clinical trainee development through item analysis of self-reported skills: The identification of perceived credibility. *Clinical Supervisor, 20,* 25–38. doi:10.1300/J001v20n01_02

Meier, S. (2003). *Bridging case conceptualization, assessment, and intervention.* Thousand Oaks, CA: Sage.

Meier, S. T. (2004). Improving design sensitivity through intervention-sensitive measures. *American Journal of Evaluation, 25,* 321–334. doi:10.1177/109821400402500304

Meier, S. T. (2008). *Measuring change in counseling and psychotherapy.* New York, NY: Guilford Press.

Meier, S. T. (2012). Nomothetic outcome assessment in counseling and psychotherapy: Development and preliminary psychometric analyses of the Depression/Anxiety Negative Affect Scale. *Psychological Test and Assessment Modeling, 54,* 343–362.

Meier, S. T. (2014). Rediscovering the role of avoidance in psychotherapy progress and outcome. *Professional Psychology: Research and Practice, 45,* 212–217.

Meier, S., & Davis, S. (2011). *The elements of counseling* (7th ed.). Belmont, CA: Cengage.

Meier, S. T., McDougal, J., & Bardos, A. (2008). Development of a change-sensitive outcome measure for children receiving counseling. *Canadian Journal of School Psychology, 23,* 148–160. doi:10.1177/0829573507307693

Meier, S. T., & Schwartz, E. (2007). *Negative changes on new outcome assessments with adolescent clients: A social desirability effect?* Unpublished manuscript, University at Buffalo.

Mergenthaler, E. (1996). Emotion-abstraction patterns in verbatim protocols: A new way of describing psychotherapeutic processes. *Journal of Consulting and Clinical Psychology, 64,* 1306–1315. doi:10.1037/0022-006X.64.6.1306

Messick, S. (1989). Validity. In R. L. Linn (Ed.), *Educational measurement* (3rd ed., pp. 13–103). Washington, DC: American Council on Education and National Council on Measurement in Education.

Miles, M. B., & Huberman, A. M. (1994). *Qualitative data analysis* (2nd ed.). Thousand Oaks, CA: Sage.

Miller, S. D., Duncan, B. L., Brown, G. S., Sparks, J. A., & Claud, D. (2003). The Outcome Rating Scale: A preliminary study of the reliability, validity, and feasibility of a brief visual analog measure. *Journal of Brief Therapy, 2,* 91–100.

Miller, S. D., Duncan, B. L., Sorrell, R., & Brown, G. S. (2005). The Partners for Change Outcome Management System. *Journal of Clinical Psychology, 61,* 199–208. doi:10.1002/jclp.20111

Miller, S. D., Hubble, M. A., Chow, D. L., & Seidel, J. A. (2013). The outcome of psychotherapy: Yesterday, today, and tomorrow. *Psychotherapy, 50,* 88–97.

Milliken, C. S., Auchterlonie, J. L., & Hoge, C. W. (2007). Longitudinal assessment of mental health problems among active and reserve component soldiers returning from the Iraq war. *Journal of the American Medical Association, 298,* 2141–2148. doi:10.1001/jama.298.18.2141

Monroe, S. M., & Reid, M. W. (2008). Gene-environment interactions in depression research. *Psychological Science, 19,* 947–956. doi:10.1111/j.1467-9280.2008.02181.x

Moses, E. R., & Barlow, D. H. (2006). A new unified treatment approach for emotional disorders based on emotion science. *Current Directions in Psychological Science, 15,* 146–150. doi:10.1111/j.0963-7214.2006.00425.x

Murphy, K. R., & Davidshofer, C. O. (2005). *Psychological testing* (6th ed.). Englewood Cliffs, NJ: Prentice Hall.

Murphy, K. P., Rashleigh, C. M., & Timulak, L. (2012). The relationship between progress feedback and therapeutic outcome in student counselling: A randomized control trial. *Counselling Psychology Quarterly, 25,* 1–18. doi:10.1080/09515070.2012.662349

Nay, W. R. (1979). *Multimethod clinical assessment.* New York, NY: Gardner Press.

Nelson, R. O. (1977). Assessment and therapeutic functions of self-monitoring. In M. Hersen, R. M. Eisler, & P. M. Miller (Eds.), *Progress in behavior modification* (Vol. 5, pp. 263–308). New York, NY: Brunner/Mazel.

Nelson, J., Martella, R., & Marchand-Martella, N. (2002). Maximizing student learning: The effects of a comprehensive school-based program for preventing problem behaviors. *Journal of Emotional and Behavioral Disorders, 10,* 136–148. doi:10.1177/10634266020100030201

Nezu, A. M., Ronan, G. F., Meadows, E. A., & McClure, K. S. (2000). *Practitioner's guide to empirically based measures of depression.* New York, NY: Kluwer Academic/Plenum.

Nilson, L. B. (2010). *Teaching at its best* (3rd ed.). San Francisco, CA: Jossey-Bass.

Nolen-Hoeksema, S. (1991). Responses to depression and their effects on the duration of depressive episodes. *Journal of Abnormal Psychology, 100,* 569–582. doi:10.1037/0021-843X.100.4.569

Nolen-Hoeksema, S., & Morrow, J. (1993). Effects of rumination and distraction on naturally-occurring depressed mood. *Cognition and Emotion, 7,* 561–570. doi:10.1080/02699939308409206

Norcross, J. C. (2004). Tailoring the therapy relationship to the individual patient: Evidence-based practices. *Clinician's Research Digest, Suppl. Bulletin 30*, 1–2.

Norcross, J. C., & Guy, J. D. (2007). *Leaving it at the office: A guide to psychotherapist self-care*. New York, NY: Guilford.

Olfson, M., & Marcus, S. C. (2010). National trends in outpatient psychotherapy. *American Journal of Psychiatry, 167*, 1456–1463. doi:10.1176/appi.ajp.2010.10040570

Parsons, F. (1909). *Choosing a vocation*. Boston: Houghton Mifflin.

Paul, G. L. (Ed.). (1986). *Assessment in residential treatment settings*. Champaign, IL: Research Press.

Paul, G. L., Mariotto, M. J., & Redfield, J. P. (1986). Assessment purposes, domains, and utility for decision making. In G. L. Paul (Eds.), *Assessment in residential treatment settings*. Champaign, IL: Research Press.

Payne, J. D., & Kensinger, E. A. (2010). Sleep's role in the consolidation of emotional episodic memories. *Current Directions in Psychological Science, 19*, 290–295. doi:10.1177/0963721410383978

Pennebaker, J. W., Mehl, M. R., & Niederhoffer, K. G. (2003). Psychological aspects of natural language use: Our words, our selves. *Annual Review of Psychology, 54*, 547–577. doi:10.1146/annurev.psych.54.101601.145041

Perez, J. E. (1999). Clients deserve empirically supported treatments, not romanticism. *American Psychologist, 54*, 205–206. doi:10.1037/0003-066X.54.3.205

Persons, J. B. (1989). *Cognitive therapy in practice: A case formulation approach*. New York, NY: Norton.

Persons, J. B. (1991). Psychotherapy outcome studies do not accurately represent current models of psychotherapy: A proposed remedy. *American Psychologist, 46*, 99–106. doi:10.1037/0003-066X.46.2.99

Persons, J. B. (2013). Who needs a case formulation and why: Clinicians use the case formulation to guide decision-making. *Pragmatic Case Studies in Psychotherapy, 9*, 448–456.

Persons, J. B., & Fresco, D. M. (2008). Adult depression. In J. Hunsley & E. J. Mash (Eds.), *A guide to assessments that work* (pp. 96–120). New York, NY: Oxford University Press.

Persons, J. B., & Mikami, A. Y. (2002). Strategies for handling treatment failure successfully. *Psychotherapy: Theory/Research/Practice/Training, 39*, 139–151. doi:10.1037/0033-3204.39.2.139

Posavac, E. J. (2011). *Program evaluation: Methods and case studies* (8th ed.). Upper Saddle River, NJ: Prentice Hall.

Poston, J., & Hanson, W. (2010). Meta-analysis of psychological assessment as a therapeutic intervention. *Psychological Assessment, 22*, 203–121. doi:10.1037/a0018679

Prochaska, J. O. (1995). An eclectic and integrative approach: Transtheoretical therapy. In A. S. Gurman & S. B. Messer (Eds.), *Essential psychotherapies* (pp. 403–440). New York, NY: Oxford University Press.

Prochaska, J. O., & Norcross, J. (2006). *Systems of psychotherapy: A transtheoretical analysis* (6th ed.). Pacific Grove, CA: Wadsworth.

Reese, R. J., Usher, E. L., Bowman, D. C., Norsworthy, L. A., Halstead, J. L., Rowlands, S. R., & Chisholm, R. R. (2009). Using client feedback in psychotherapy training: An analysis of its influence on supervision and counselor self-efficacy. *Training and Education in Professional Psychology, 3*, 157–168. doi:10.1037/a0015673

Richter, P., Werner, J., Bastine, R., Heerlein, A., Kick, H., & Sauer, H. (1997). Measuring treatment outcome by the Beck Depression Inventory. *Psychopathology, 30,* 234–240. doi:10.1159/000285052

Richter, P., Werner, J., Heerlein, A., Kraus, A., & Sauer, H. (1998). On the validity of the Beck Depression Inventory. *Psychopathology, 31,* 160–168. doi:10.1159/000066239

Ringel, J. S., & Sturm, R. (2001). National estimates of mental health utilization and expenditures for children in 1998. *Journal of Behavioral Health Services and Research, 28*(3), 319–332. doi:10.1007/BF02287247

Ronnestad, M., & Ladany, N. (2006). The impact of psychotherapy training: Introduction to the special section. *Psychotherapy Research, 16,* 261–267. doi:10.1080/10503300600612241

Rounds, J. B., & Tinsley, H. E. (1984). Diagnosis and treatment of vocational problems. In S. D. Brown & R. W. Lent (Eds.), *Handbook of counseling psychology* (pp. 137–177). New York, NY: Wiley.

Safran, J. D., & Greenberg, L. S. (1989). The treatment of anxiety and depression: The process of affective change. In P. C. Kendall & D. Watson (Eds.), *Anxiety and depression: Distinctive and overlapping features* (pp. 455–489). San Diego, CA: Academic Press.

Sapyta, J., Riemer, M., & Bickman, L. (2005). Feedback to clinicians: Theory, research, and practice. *Journal of Clinical Psychology, 61,* 145–153.

Saylor, K., Buermeyer, C., Sutton, V., Faries, D., Khan, S., & Schuh, K. (2007). The life participation scale for attention-deficit/hyperactivity disorder-child version: Psychometric properties of an adaptive change instrument. *Journal of Child and Adolescent Psychopharmacology, 17,* 831–841. doi:10.1089 / cap.2007.0030

Schroeder, H. E., & Rakos, R. F. (1978). Effects of history on the measurement of assertion. *Behavior Therapy, 9,* 965–966. doi:10.1016/S0005-7894(78)80036-7

Segal, Z. V., Williams, J. M. G., & Teasdale, J. D. (2002). *Mindfulness-based cognitive therapy for depression.* New York, NY: Guilford.

Segerstrom, S. C., Tsao, J. C. I., Alden, L. E., & Craske, M. G. (2000). Worry and rumination: Repetitive thought as a concomitant and predictor of negative mood. *Cognitive Therapy and Research, 24,* 671–688. doi:10.1023/A:1005587311498

Shadish, W. R., Cook, T. D., & Campbell, D. T. (2001). *Experimental and quasi-experimental designs for generalized causal inference.* New York, NY: Cengage.

Sharpe, J. P., & Gilbert, D. G. (1998). Effects of repeated administration of the Beck Depression Inventory and other measures of negative mood states. *Personality and Individual Differences, 24,* 457–463. doi:10.1016/S0191-8869(97)00193-1

Shedler, J., Mayman, M., & Manis, M. (1993). The illusion of mental health. *American Psychologist, 48,* 1117–1131. doi:10.1037/0003-066X.48.11.1117

Shostrum, E. L. (Producer). (1966). *Three approaches to psychotherapy.* Santa Ana, CA: Psychological Films.

Shinn, M. (2007). Identifying students at risk, monitoring performance, and determining eligibility within response to intervention: Research on educational need and benefit from academic intervention. *School Psychology Review, 36,* 601–617.

Sloan, D. M., & Kring, A. M. (2007). Measuring changes in emotion during psychotherapy: Conceptual and methodological issues. *Clinical Psychology: Science and Practice, 14,* 307–322. doi:10.1111/j.1468-2850.2007.00092.x

Smith, M. L., & Glass, G. V. (1977). Meta-analysis of psychotherapy outcome studies. *American Psychologist, 32,* 752–760. doi:10.1037/0003-066X.32.9.752

Sommers-Flanagan, J., & Sommers-Flanagan, R. (2002). *Clinical interviewing* (3rd ed.). New York, NY: Wiley.

Sperry, L., Brill, P. L., Howard, K. I., & Grissom, G. R. (1996). *Treatment outcomes in psychotherapy and psychiatric interventions.* New York, NY: Brunner-Mazel.

Spielberger, C. D. (1991). *State-Trait Anger Expression Inventory.* Odessa, FL: Psychological Assessment Resources.

Spielberger, C. D., Gorsuch, R. L., & Lushene, R. (1970). *Manual for the State-Trait Anxiety Inventory: STAI.* Palo Alto, CA: Consulting Psychologists Press.

Stewart, R. E., & Chambless, D. L. (2008). Treatment failures in private practice: How do psychologists proceed? *Professional Psychology: Research and Practice, 39,* 176–181. doi:10.1037/0735-7028.39.2.176

Stiffman, A. R., Orme, J. G., Evans, D. A., Feldman, R. A., & Keeney, P. A. (1984). A brief measure of children's behavior problems: The Behavior Rating Index for Children. *Measurement and Evaluation in Counseling and Development, 16,* 83–90.

Stinchfield, R., Winters, K. C., Botzet, A., Jerstad, S., & Breyer, J. (2007). Development and psychometric evaluation of the Gambling Treatment Outcome Monitoring System (GAMTOMS). *Psychology of Addictive Behaviors, 21,* 174–184.

Stoltenberg, C. D., & Delworth, U. (1987). *Supervising counselors and therapists.* San Francisco, CA: Jossey-Bass.

Streiner, D. L. (1998). Thinking small: Research designs appropriate for clinical practice. *Canadian Journal of Psychiatry, 43,* 737–741.

Strong, E. K., Jr. (1943). *Vocational interests of men and women.* Stanford, CA: Stanford University Press.

Swezey, R. W. (1981). *Individual performance assessment: An approach to criterion-referenced test development.* Reston, VA: Reston Publishing.

Tang, T. Z, & DeRubeis, R. J. (1999). Sudden gains and critical sessions in cognitive-behavior therapy for depression. *Journal of Consulting and Clinical Psychology, 67,* 894–904. doi:10.1037/0022-006X.67.6.894

Teyber, E., & McClure, F. (2011). *Interpersonal process in psychotherapy* (6th ed.). Pacific Grove, CA: Brooks/Cole.

Thayer, C. E., & Fine, A. H. (2001). Evaluation and outcome measurement in the non-profit sector: Stakeholder participation. *Evaluation & Program Planning, 24,* 103–108. doi:10.1016/S0149-7189(00)00051-3

Tryon, W. W. (1991). *Activity measurement in psychology and medicine.* New York, NY: Plenum.

Tufte, E. (1983). *Visual display of quantitative information.* Cheshire, CT: Graphics Press.

Urban, H. B., & Ford, D. H. (1971). Some historical and conceptual perspectives on psychotherapy and behavior change. In A. E. Bergin & S. L. Garfield (Eds.), *Handbook of psychotherapy and behavior change: An empirical analysis* (pp. 3–35). New York, NY: Wiley.

Van Norman, E. R., Christ, T. J., & Zopluoglu, C. (2013). The effects of baseline estimation on the reliability, validity, and precision of CBM-R growth estimates. *School Psychology Quarterly, 28,* 239–255. doi:10.1037/spq0000023

Vermeersch, D. A., Lambert, M. J., & Burlingame, G. M. (2000). Outcome Questionnaire: Item sensitivity to change. *Journal of Personality Assessment, 74,* 242–261. doi:10.1207/S15327752JPA7402_6

Vermeersch, D. A., Whipple, J. L., Lambert, M. J., Hawkins, E. J., Burchfield, C. M., & Okiishi, J. C. (2004). Outcome Questionnaire: Is it sensitive to changes in counseling center clients? *Journal of Counseling Psychology, 51*, 38–49. doi:10.1037/0022-0167.51.1.38

Volker, M. A. (2006). Reporting effect size estimates in school psychology research. *Psychology in the Schools, 43*, 653–672. doi:10.1002/pits.20176

Wagner, S., Helmreich, I., Lieb, K., & Tadic, A. (2011). Standardized rater training for the Hamilton Depression Rating Scale (HAMD17) and the Inventory of Depressive Symptoms IDS C30). *Psychopathology, 44*, 68–70. doi:10.1159/000318162

Wampold, B. E. (2001). *The great psychotherapy debate: Models, methods, and findings.* Mahway, NJ: Erlbaum.

Weinstock, M., & Meier, S. T. (2003). A comparison of two item selection methodologies for measuring change in university counseling center clients. *Measurement and Evaluation in Counseling & Development, 36*, 66–75.

Weisz, J. R., Weiss, B., Han, S. S., Granger, D. A., & Morton, T. (1995). Effects of psychotherapy with children and adolescents revisited: A meta-analysis of treatment outcome studies. *Psychological Bulletin, 177*, 450–468. doi: 10.1037/0033-2909.117.3.450

Wells, K. B., Sturm, R., Sherbourne, C. D., & Meredith, L. S. (1996). *Caring for depression.* London: Harvard University Press.

Wenzlaff, R. M., & Wegner, D. M. (2000). Thought suppression. *Annual Review of Psychology, 51*, 59–91. doi:10.1146/annurev.psych.51.1.59

White, M., & Epston, D. (1990). *Narrative means to therapeutic ends.* New York, NY: W. W. Norton.

Worthen, V. E., & Lambert, M. J. (2007). Outcome oriented supervision: Advantages of adding systematic client tracking to supportive consultations. *Counselling & Psychotherapy Research, 7*, 48–53. doi:10.1080/14733140601140873

Zahra, D., & Hedge, C. (2010). The Reliable Change Index: Why isn't it more popular in academic psychology? *Psychology Postgraduate Affairs Group Quarterly, 76*, 14–19.

Zimmerman, M. (2008). An inadequate community standard of care: Lack of measurement of outcome when treating depression in clinical practice. *Primary Psychiatry, 15*, 67–75.

Ziskin, J. Z. (1995). *Coping with psychiatric and psychological testimony* (Vol. 1, 5th ed.). Los Angeles, CA: Law and Psychology Press.

Zvolensky, M. J., & Otto, M. W. (2007). Special series: Affective intolerance, sensitivity, and processing: Advances in Clinical Science Introduction. *Behavior Therapy, 39*, 228–233. doi:10.1016/j.beth.2007.01.002

Scott T. Meier is a professor in the Department of Counseling, School, and Educational Psychology, University at Buffalo. He is a licensed psychologist who received his PhD in Counseling Psychology from Southern Illinois University, Carbondale, in 1984. Meier's major research and teaching areas focus on psychological measurement (particularly progress monitoring and outcome assessment), research methods (particularly program evaluation), and counseling and psychotherapy (particularly narrative therapy as an integrative approach). He is a member of the Association for Psychological Science, the Association for Behavioral and Cognitive Therapies, and the Society for the Exploration of Psychotherapy Integration.

Meier is the author or coauthor of six books (including *Measuring Change in Counseling and Psychotherapy, Elements of Counseling*, and *Narratives and Language in Counseling and Psychotherapy*) and has published in *American Psychologist, Professional Psychology: Research and Practice, Journal of Counseling Psychology, Measurement and Evaluation in Counseling and Development*, and *American Journal of Evaluation*.